T0334455

INSIDE THATCHER'S MONETARISM EXPERIMENT

INSIDE THATCHER'S MONETARISM EXPERIMENT

The Promise, the Failure, the Legacy

Tim Lankester

First published in Great Britain in 2024 by

Policy Press, an imprint of
Bristol University Press
University of Bristol
1-9 Old Park Hill
Bristol
BS2 8BB
UK
t: +44 (0)117 374 6645
e: bup-info@bristol.ac.uk

Details of international sales and distribution partners are available at
policy.bristoluniversitypress.co.uk

British Library Cataloguing in Publication Data
A catalogue record for this book is available from the British Library

ISBN 978-1-4473-7135-9 hardcover
ISBN 978-1-4473-7137-3 ePub
ISBN 978-1-4473-7138-0 ePdf

Cover design: Mecob
Front cover image: Alamy/Liam Bailey

Bristol University Press and Policy Press use environmentally
responsible print partners.

Printed in and bound in Great Britain by CPI Group (UK) Ltd,
Croydon CR40 4YY

Contents

Acknowledgements

I owe it to my friend Jeremy Hardie, polymath and former tutorial fellow in economics at Keble College, Oxford, for encouraging me to write this book. During one of the Covid-19 lockdowns, we walked and talked about *Modern Money Theory* by the American economist L. Randall Wray.[1] This theory, while staunchly Keynesian, is different from the macroeconomics we had both learned at university because it provides a clearer account of how fiscal and monetary policy interact with the financial system. Conversations over the theory's merits and demerits led us into discussing the merits and demerits of monetarism. This led, in turn, to my wanting to retrace my experience as a close participant in the monetarist experiment of the early Thatcher years, and to the research that has gone into this book.

I am grateful to Jeremy and to a number of other individuals for their advice and for commenting on earlier drafts. These include Chris Beauman, the late Alan Budd, Terry Burns, Robin Butler, Chris Collins, John Gieve, Charles Goodhart, Anthony Hotson, Heather Joshi, William Keegan, Rachel Lomax, Kevin Mansell, Peter Middleton, Duncan Needham, Steve Nickell, David Norgrove, Gus O'Donnell, David Peretz, Stephen Powell, Andrew Turnbull and David Vines. And I am grateful to Barney Lankester for help with the charts. I would also like to thank my editor at Policy Press, Ginny Mills, and my freelance editor Dawn Rushen. Needless to say, none of them bear any responsibility for what I have written.

October 2023
Wells-next-the-Sea

Main characters

Politicians

John Biffen, Chief Secretary to HM Treasury (1979–81),
Secretary of State for Trade (1981–82), Leader of the House
of Commons (1982–87)

James Callaghan, Prime Minister (1976–79)

Ken Clarke, Chancellor of the Exchequer (1992–97)

Ian Gilmour, Deputy Foreign Minister (1979–81)

Denis Healey, Chancellor of the Exchequer (1974–79)

Michael Heseltine, Secretary of State for the Environment
(1979–83), Secretary of State for Defence (1983–86)

Quintin Hogg (Lord Hailsham), Lord Chancellor (1979–87)

Geoffrey Howe, Chancellor of the Exchequer (1979–83),
Foreign Secretary (1983–89), Deputy Prime Minister
(1989–90)

David Howell, Secretary of State for Energy (1979–81),
Secretary of State for Transport (1981–83)

Jeremy Hunt, Chancellor of the Exchequer (2022–)

Keith Joseph, Secretary of State for Industry (1979–81),
Secretary of State for Education (1981–86)

Kwasi Kwarteng, Chancellor of the Exchequer (2022)

Norman Lamont, Chancellor of the Exchequer (1990–92)

Nigel Lawson, Financial Secretary to HM Treasury (1979–81),
Secretary of State for Energy (1981–83), Chancellor of the
Exchequer (1983–89)

John Major, Chief Secretary to HM Treasury (1987–89),
Foreign Secretary (1989), Chancellor of the Exchequer
(1989–90), Prime Minister (1990–97)

George Osborne, Chancellor of the Exchequer (2010–16)

James Prior, Secretary of State for Employment (1979–81),
Secretary of State for Northern Ireland (1981–84)

Christopher Soames, Leader of the House of Lords, Minister
for the Civil Service (1979–81)
Rishi Sunak, Chancellor of the Exchequer (2020–22),
Prime Minister (2022–)
Norman Tebbit, Secretary of State for Employment (1981–83),
Secretary of State for Trade and Industry (1983–85)
Margaret Thatcher, Prime Minister (1979–90)
Liz Truss, Prime Minister (2022)
William Whitelaw, Home Secretary (1979–83), Leader of the
House of Lords (1983–88)

Civil servants

Kenneth Berrill, Head of Central Policy Review Staff (1974–80)
Alan Budd, Chief Economic Adviser, HM Treasury (1991–97)
Terry Burns, Chief Economic Adviser, HM Treasury (1980–91),
Permanent Secretary (1991–98)
Robin Ibbs, Head of Central Policy Review Staff (1980–82)
Tim Lankester, Private Secretary for Economic Affairs to the
Prime Minister (1978–81), Permanent Secretary, Overseas
Development Administration (1989–94)
Peter Middleton, Deputy Secretary, HM Treasury (1979–83),
Permanent Secretary (1983–91)
Douglas Wass, Permanent Secretary, HM Treasury (1974–83)

Special advisers

Brian Griffiths, Head of Number 10 Policy Unit (1985–90)
John Hoskyns, Head of Number 10 Policy Unit (1979–82)
Adam Ridley, Economic Adviser to the Chancellor of the
Exchequer (1979–84)
Alan Walters, Economic Adviser to Margaret Thatcher
(1981–83, 1989)

Bank of England officials

John Fforde, Executive Director, Bank of England (1970–82)
Eddie George, Governor of the Bank of England (1993–2003)
Charles Goodhart, Senior Adviser, Bank of England (1980–85)

Mervyn King, Governor of the Bank of England (2003–13)
Gordon Richardson, Governor of the Bank of England
(1973–83)

Journalists

Ben Bradlee, *The Washington Post*
Sam Brittan, *Financial Times*
Peter Jay, *The Times*
William Keegan, *The Observer*
Martin Wolf, *Financial Times*

Academic economists

Jim Ball, London Business School
Karl Brunner, Rochester University
Alan Budd, London Business School (also see entry above)
Terry Burns, London Business School (also see entry above)
Milton Friedman, University of Chicago
Brian Griffiths, City University (also see entry above)
Frank Hahn, University of Cambridge
Friedrich Hayek, University of Freiburg
Harry Johnson, University of Chicago, London School of
   Economics and Political Science
Richard Kahn, University of Cambridge
Nicholas Kaldor, University of Cambridge
John Maynard Keynes, University of Cambridge
David Laidler, University of Manchester and University of
   Western Ontario
James Meade, University of Cambridge
Alan Meltzer, Rochester University
Patrick Minford, University of Liverpool and Cardiff
   University
Robert Neild, University of Cambridge
Stephen Nickell, London School of Economics and Political
   Science and University of Oxford
Jürg Niehans, University of Bern
Joan Robinson, University of Cambridge
Paul Samuelson, Massachusetts University of Technology (MIT)

James Tobin, Yale University
Alan Walters, London School of Economics and Political
   Science and Johns Hopkins University (also see entry above)
Randall Wray, University of Missouri

Others

Olivier Blanchard, Chief Economist, International Monetary
   Fund (2008–15)
Andrew Britton, Director, National Institute of Economic
   and Social Research (NIESR) (1982–95), former Senior
   Economist at HM Treasury
Hugh Clegg, Chair of the Standing Commission on Pay
   Comparability (1979–80)
Tim Congdon, City Economist
Len Murray, General Secretary, Trades Union Congress
   (1973–84)
Gordon Pepper, City Economist
Alfred Sherman, Director, Centre for Policy Studies (1974–83)
Paul Volcker, Chair of the Federal Reserve Board (1979–87)

1

Introduction

The date was 23 July 1981, and Margaret Thatcher's[1] Cabinet had had enough; they had had enough of the experiment with monetarism. Twenty-seven months into her premiership, the economy was in serious trouble: inflation was running at a higher level than when Mrs Thatcher came to power; the country had endured the deepest recession since the 1930s; and unemployment was well over 2 million, and rising rapidly.

For the first time the Cabinet spoke out in near unison against the application of a theory for managing the economy that was untested, highly controversial and little understood. Every single member spoke, and of the 22 present besides Mrs Thatcher, 18 spoke out against the policy[2] – some in anger, some in sadness, some in sheer puzzlement. Lord Chancellor Quintin Hogg (Lord Hailsham), who had served in Winston Churchill's wartime government and had been a contender for the leadership of the Conservative Party in 1963, referred to the policies of Herbert Hoover and America's Great Depression. It was a dangerous moment for Mrs Thatcher's premiership. The day was only saved for her by her friend, Home Secretary and de facto Deputy Prime Minister Willie Whitelaw, who told his colleagues to calm down, be patient, and stick behind their Chancellor of the Exchequer Geoffrey Howe, and their leader.

This book is about the intellectual origins of monetarism; how and why it came to be adopted by Mrs Thatcher and her government; how and why it failed and after a few years had to be abandoned; and finally, its legacy.

The essence of monetarism in its purest form is that price inflation is an entirely monetary phenomenon; that increases in the money supply, however defined, are the sole cause of inflation; and that to keep inflation under control, the money supply has to be kept on a tight rein. Other factors such as supply bottlenecks or a spurt in wages may affect inflation in the short run, but such factors can only be transitory: the fundamental cause of inflation over any length of time is excessive monetary growth. In a situation where prices are rising faster than is acceptable, the only way to curb inflation is to reduce the growth of the money supply. There may be a short-term reduction in output and employment as a result of the monetary contraction, but once the inflation rate has been brought down to its desired level, output and employment will revert to where they were previously.

When Margaret Thatcher came to power in 1979, inflation was running at an annual rate of just over 10 per cent and rising. Her first priority was to bring inflation down, because inflation was bad in itself, and would stymie investment and future economic growth. Curbing the growth of the money supply, as advocated by the monetarists, was how she chose to achieve this – by curbing government borrowing, and by restraining lending by the banks to businesses and to households.

This proved to be one of the most unsatisfactory episodes of economic policy making of modern times. Restricting government borrowing and borrowing by the private sector was much more difficult than expected. Despite raising interest rates to unprecedented levels, the government was unable to achieve the reduction in money growth that it intended, and it took nearly four years to bring the inflation rate down to mid-single figures. By the time this *was* achieved, it was clearly the result not of reduced money growth, but rather of very tight monetary *conditions* – exceptionally high interest rates and a sharp rise in the value of sterling against other currencies – and a substantial fiscal tightening (reduced public spending, higher taxes). These caused a sizeable fall in national output, especially in manufacturing, and greatly increased unemployment, which did not begin to come down until 1987.

To stop inflation from spiralling ever higher, and to bring it down to an acceptable level, Mrs Thatcher and her government had no realistic option other than to deflate the economy so as to put downward pressure on wages and prices. An economic slow-down was inevitable. The Labour government's incomes policy having collapsed, if there had been no deflation at all, the consequences for the economy would have been dire – the UK would have been well on the path to hyperinflation and financial collapse. But the monetarism that guided their actions, as one of their critics later put it, 'so blinded the government that it pressed home deflation too hard and too long'.[3] Too much attention was given to high money supply figures, which wrongly suggested that monetary conditions were much looser than they actually were. The result was considerably greater unemployment and lost output than the government or the advocates of monetarism expected or would have wished.

Outline of the book

Chapter 2 provides a brief overview of how it all looked from my position at 10 Downing Street where, for the first two-and-a-half years of Mrs Thatcher's premiership, I was her private secretary for economic affairs. In Chapter 3, I explain the intellectual origins of monetarism – starting with the rejection by John Maynard Keynes in the 1930s of the classical quantity theory of money, and then its revival by the American economist Milton Friedman in the 1960s, morphing into the monetarism of the 1970s. (Readers who are familiar with Keynes's and Friedman's ideas can skip this chapter.) Chapter 4 discusses the vigorous debate that ensued between Friedman's followers and their opponents, who retained an attachment to the basic Keynesian view of the world even though, in several important ways, it had lost its relevance.

Chapter 5 explains how monetarism came to be applied in soft form by the 1970s Labour government as an adjunct to their other policies. In Chapters 6, 7 and 8, I explain how monetarism took on much greater importance and was applied in much harder form during the Thatcher government's first two years in office; and how they then reverted to applying it in softer form, before it was eventually abandoned. Chapter 9 provides an assessment of the social and economic costs that were incurred. Chapter 10 charts Mrs Thatcher's early efforts to bring in trade union reform, and how the initial slow pace of the reforms made it more difficult for the government to achieve their goals for low inflation and economic growth.

In Chapter 11, I describe how the government sought to find an alternative money or nominal 'anchor' for managing the economy, first by aligning sterling with the Deutschmark, then by joining the European Exchange Rate Mechanism (ERM), and finally by adopting inflation targeting. Chapter 12 describes the views of the monetarists and their critics looking back. Chapter 13 considers monetarism's legacy, and Chapter 14 looks at the parallels, such as they are, between the stagflation of the late 1970s and early 1980s, and the post–Covid-19 stagflation of late 2022 and 2023.

I have extended the narrative for two reasons, although in much less detail because it goes beyond the book's main theme, and because I was much less involved personally (or not involved at all). The first reason is to show that, for all the failure of the monetarist regime, there was no immediately obvious 'silver bullet' to replace it, and it took time to identify and adopt a much improved counter-inflation regime based on inflation targeting. Second, I wanted to explore the legacy of monetarism insofar as some of the ideas associated with it continued to influence the conduct of economic policy in the years after its demise, and right up to the present day.

Ideas are important for the conduct of economic policy. But so, too, are people. Besides considering the theory of monetarism and how it was applied in the UK, this book also looks at the attitudes and actions of the key individuals – and particularly those of Mrs Thatcher. In her memoirs, she says remarkably little about the theory or about her own role in attempting to apply it. This, despite the fact that she was probably more involved in economic policy decision making than any prime minister, other than Gordon Brown, in the past 100 years. She includes only a few passing references to monetarism's chief exponent, Milton Friedman, whom she greatly admired.[4] Her biographers also say relatively little on this score.

One of my subsidiary objects in writing this book has been to fill this gap in knowledge. As Mrs Thatcher's private secretary from 1979 to 1981, I had a ringside seat. I never kept a diary, but now that all the key internal documents from the period are available in the National Archives, and easily accessible through the Margaret Thatcher Foundation in Cambridge and its website, I have been able to use these to supplement, and in some cases correct, the memories I have.

The book is replete with abstract numbers, mostly pointing in a negative direction. But behind the numbers lies the loss of thousands of individual businesses and tens of thousands of jobs. By no means all of them were due to the experiment with monetarism, but many of them were. Whether it was the closure of small firms, like my wife's family-run cotton textile manufacturing business in West Yorkshire, or the closure of the largest carpet manufacturing business in Europe at the magnificent Dean Clough mills in nearby Halifax, the effect on local communities was profound and long-lasting. Although only a minor player in this sad saga, I have always found it difficult to come to terms with the part I both wittingly and unwittingly played in it. This book is, in part, my attempt to achieve some kind of personal resolution.

2

A view from Number 10

Sometime during that same month as the explosive Cabinet meeting mentioned in Chapter 1, I was at a dinner in north London hosted by the journalist and author William Shawcross. The principal guest was the editor of *The Washington Post*, Ben Bradlee, friend of President Kennedy and famous for masterminding the uncovering of the Watergate scandal and bringing down President Nixon. Shawcross had invited me so that, from my vantage point as Mrs Thatcher's private secretary, I could give Bradlee a first-hand account of her premiership so far.

A few years later, when I was posted to Washington, DC, I got to know Bradlee well – he became a friend and tennis partner. The Shawcross dinner, however, was our first meeting, and we were seated together. I had been told that he was no fan of Mrs Thatcher, and because of my position in her office, anything negative I said was likely to find its way into *The Washington Post*. So I tried to put as bright a spin as I could on her leadership and policies, which wasn't easy. The UK economy was in a terrible state, there had been rioting in several major cities, and even Mrs Thatcher's own party was wracked with dissent over the government's economic and social policies. Just a few weeks before we met, Bradlee's rival newspaper, *The New York Times*, had carried a main feature article headlined 'The Thatcher plan's failure', along with these words: 'The riots in Liverpool this week, stemming partly from the worst unemployment Britain has experienced since the Depression in the 1930s, are grim evidence of the failure of what was once regarded as a brilliant innovation in economic policy.'[1]

I presented the Downing Street line. Mrs Thatcher's policies were for the long term. First, we had to stabilise the economy by bringing down inflation, reducing the budget deficit, cutting taxes, curbing the power of the trade unions and deregulating the private sector. Once we were through the stabilisation phase, there would then be long-term recovery. It was too early to write her and her policies off.

Bradlee was sceptical and questioned whether, given the way things were going, Mrs Thatcher was likely to be in office for the long term. Sitting opposite us was a well-known *Sunday Times* journalist, Bruce Page. He had been listening to my presentation and had so far said nothing. He was glowering at me and I sensed trouble. Finally, he pointed his finger at me and shouted: 'Bradlee, don't you realize that Tim Lankester is Thatcher's Albert Speer?'

There was a stunned silence around the dinner table. Bradlee whispered in my ear: 'You either hit him or you have to leave.' I hadn't hit anyone since a failed boxing match when I was ten years old. I chose to leave.

Page's accusation was as absurd as it was offensive. And yet, as I walked back to my home, I wondered whether there wasn't a grain of truth in Page's charge. Was I not complicit in Mrs Thatcher's economic policies, the effects of which had so far been quite dismal? Had I done as much as I could have to soften the edges of these policies? I thought of Henry Neuberger, the brilliant left-wing economist at the Treasury, who had recently resigned from the Civil Service to become economic adviser to Michael Foot, leader of the Labour Opposition.[2]

As a non-political civil servant, it was my job to do all I could to assist Mrs Thatcher in the implementation of her economic strategy, and I would not have lasted a week in my post had I tried to seriously question it. Yet I did feel compromised through having worked perhaps too diligently in support of a strategy in which I didn't really believe. Page would have said I was obviously someone who preferred position to 'telling truth to power'. In later years I felt I could have done more, had I been more robust, and also better qualified.

For a bird's eye view of what actually happened, see Tables 1 and 2, and Figures A1–A4 in the Appendix.

Table 1: Key economic data, 1979–84

	1979	1980	1981	1982	1983	1984
Real GDP (% increase)	3.6	–2.2	–0.9	1.7	3.9	1.9
Manufacturing output (% increase)	–0.2	–8.6	–6.2	–0.2	2.2	3.7
Unemployment rate (%)	5.4	6.8	9.6	10.7	11.5	11.8
Unemployment (millions)	1.4	1.8	2.6	2.9	3.1	3.2
Inflation (% increase)[a]	13.4	18.0	11.9	8.6	4.6	5.0
Average earnings (% increase)	15.2	19.4	12.8	8.9	8.5	5.8
Dollar/sterling exchange rate (end June)	2.17	2.36	1.94	1.74	1.53	1.36
Base Rate (end June)	14.0	17.0	12.0	12.6	9.6	8.9

Note: [a] Inflation figures relate to the Retail Price Index (RPI), which, until the 1990s, was the most commonly quoted price index. The RPI includes housing costs. Over time, it was succeeded by the Consumer Price Index (CPI), which covers a slightly different basket of goods and services and, notably, excludes housing costs.

Sources: For the first five items, data is from ONS websites. Data for average earnings is from Britton, A. (1991), *Macroeconomic Policy in Britain 1974-87*, NIESR, Table 16.3. Data for dollar/ sterling exchange rate and for Base Rate is taken from relevant Bank of England websites.

Table 2: Medium-term financial strategy (MTFS), 1979/80–1983/84

	1979/80	1980/81	1981/82	1982/83	1983/84
Sterling M3					
Target[a]	7–11	7–11	6–10	5–9	4–8
Actual[b]	16.2	18.4	12.8	11.1	9.5
PSBR/GDP[c]					
Projection	4.5	3.75	3.0	2.25	1.5
Actual	4.8	5.7	3.5	3.25	3.25

Notes: [a] Source: Hotson, A. (2017) *Respectable Banking: The Search for Stability in London's Money and Credit Market Since 1695*, Cambridge: Cambridge University Press, p 144. The target range for 1979/80 was announced in the June 1979 budget statement. The MTFS, with target ranges for later years, took effect from April 1980. The target ranges for 1982/83 and 1983/84 were each adjusted upwards by three percentage points in the March 1982 budget statement, and these new targets were to apply to M1 and PSL2, as well as to £M3.

[b] Source: Lawson, N. (1992) *The View from No 11: Memoirs of a Tory Radical*, London: Bantam Press, p 1079.

[c] Source: Walters, A. (1986) *Britain's Economic Renaissance: Margaret Thatcher's Reforms 1979–84*, Oxford: Oxford University Press, Table 5.1. Projections for 1980/81 onwards are from the MTFS. Projections for 1979/80 were in the June 1979 budget statement.

In the Thatcher government's first three years in power, from the second quarter of 1979 to the second quarter of 1982, retail prices increased by 48 per cent. The year-on-year rate of inflation, which stood at just over 10 per cent when the government took office, had doubled by the second quarter of 1980. It then started to decline, but by the second quarter of 1982 it was still at 9.4 per cent – almost as high as when the government was elected. Wage and salary earnings accelerated into the early part of 1980, thus feeding into higher costs and higher prices. Although the government had never indicated how quickly they expected inflation to come down, this was a poor outcome by any stretch of the imagination.

At the same time, there was a sharp drop in output and employment. Over the 21 months starting in the third quarter of 1979, gross domestic product (GDP) on a quarterly basis fell by 5.7 per cent. This was approximately the same as the drop in output during the 2008–09 recession that accompanied the Global Financial Crisis (GFC) (5.9 per cent), and much less than in the 2020 recession due to the Covid-19 pandemic (23 per cent). But the 1979–81 recession was considerably longer-lasting than either, and it was much more heavily concentrated – in the North and in the Midlands, and in Wales and Scotland, and in manufacturing industry in particular.

Over the same 21-month period, manufacturing output fell by 17 per cent, with textiles and motor vehicles (and motor vehicle parts) among the hardest-hit industries. For the full years 1980 and 1981, their output fell by 24 per cent and 28 per cent respectively. During this period, there was a slow-down in economic activity in all the major advanced countries, mainly due to higher commodity prices and higher interest rates, but the UK's performance was markedly worse than that of any other.

Over the three years, 1979 to 1982, unemployment in the UK more than doubled, from 1.4 million to 2.9 million. From the second half of 1981, although there was a slow recovery in output, unemployment numbers continued at around 3 million, with the rate of unemployment remaining at over 11 per cent until early 1987.

In April 1982, the monetarist economist Tim Congdon, whose writings had been influential with Mrs Thatcher in the run-up to the 1979 General Election, wrote: 'Too small a reduction in inflation seems to have been gained at too great a cost in terms of lost employment.'[3] For the modest improvement in inflation that was achieved over the three years, the cost was indeed extraordinarily high.

Later that year, the inflation situation would look considerably better. By December 1982, the annual rate of inflation had dropped to 5.4 per cent. By then, unemployment would be even higher, at just over 3 million. Seen on its own without reference to the rising unemployment, this was quite an achievement, considering the inflation rate had reached over 20 per cent in 1980. But in no way could it be attributed to the application of monetarist doctrine. The annual percentage growth rate of 'broad money' (£M3)[4] had been 19 per cent in the fourth quarter of 1980, and it had continued at around this level well into 1981. On the monetarists' assumption of a one-and-a-half to two-year lag between money supply growth and inflation, inflation should still have been running in the high teens. It clearly wasn't. The explanation for the large drop in inflation can only have been the tight monetary policy that was pursued from late 1979, the accompanying high exchange rate, and then the very tight 1981 budget.

Fundamentally, the path of monetary growth proved a very poor predictor of inflation and gave an entirely false idea of the tightness or laxity of monetary policy. The focus on an unstable monetary aggregate, £M3, led to a tightening of policy that was more than intended and would not have happened if the government had focused on a broader range of indicators.

Apologists for the early Thatcher years argue that, while the targeting of the money supply proved a chimera, the broad 'thrust' of policy was correct, and lower price inflation was achieved. They ignore the exorbitant cost in terms of lost output and jobs, and lost industrial capacity. The government, by its own actions, made the inflation problem worse, and monetary and fiscal policies were too restrictive. A better mix of policies could have achieved a similar outcome for inflation, although possibly over a longer period, without such heavy costs. Even against a seemingly unelectable Labour leader in Michael Foot, it seems all too likely that the Conservatives would have lost the 1983 General Election had it not been for victory over Argentina in the Falklands campaign.

Mrs Thatcher was intimately involved in all the key decisions on monetary and fiscal policy in her early years in office: she took pride in her formal title 'First Lord of the Treasury' and, unlike most prime ministers, she acted the part. And these were the days when decisions on interest rates were taken not by the Bank of England but by the chancellor of the exchequer in consultation with the prime minister. In practical as well as formal terms, she very much shared the responsibility for what happened with her chancellor, Geoffrey Howe. Some would argue that, since she was more ideologically committed to monetarism than he was, her responsibility was the greater.

None of this is to suggest that there was an easy or ready solution to the problem of rising inflation or the other economic challenges when Mrs Thatcher came to office; on the contrary. She inherited an economy in which productivity had been near stagnant for several years, and in which inflation and unemployment were on the rise. Labour's non-statutory prices and incomes policy, reasonably successful for its first three years starting in 1975, had collapsed, with multiple strikes and inflationary pay settlements in its fourth year. Keynesian orthodoxy – the regulation of aggregate demand through taxation and public spending – had proved incapable of dealing with the duo of rising inflation and rising unemployment. There had to be another way, and monetarism appeared to offer that way. Yet the assumptions according to which monetarism was supposed to work turned out to be wrong, and while the general thrust of policy did eventually bring down inflation and lay the basis for economic recovery by the mid-1980s, the attempt to control the money supply in the way the monetarists advocated proved extremely costly.

Before Mrs Thatcher was elected, I had been private secretary for seven months to the outgoing Labour prime minister, James (Jim) Callaghan. It might seem incomprehensible to some that, having been involved in the very different policies and eventual failure of the Callaghan government, Mrs Thatcher would have taken me on. But I was a civil servant in the Administrative Service, and our role was to serve the government of the day on a non-political basis. I was on secondment from the Treasury, where I had worked since 1973. It was the normal convention for civil servants in private secretary roles to continue with a new government. The fact that I got on well with her from the start certainly helped.[5]

My job as private secretary was to act as an intermediary between Mrs Thatcher and her economic ministers, especially Geoffrey Howe – presenting and commenting on their submissions, recording her comments and decisions, chasing them up, and preparing records of their meetings. It also involved a similar role in relation to the governor of the Bank of England and many other individuals and external bodies on economic and financial matters. Until the arrival of Professor Alan Walters in January 1981 as her economic adviser, I was the only official at 10 Downing Street with a formal training in economics – there wasn't even an economist in the prime minister's Policy Unit.[6] As a member of the Administrative Service, I wasn't expected to be up to date on macroeconomic theory in general, or monetarism in particular, in the same way as I would have been had I been a member of the government's Economic Service; but in view of my training as an economist, and in the absence of any other trained economist on her staff, I felt bound to offer Mrs Thatcher economic advice as best I could.

From the start I had reservations about the monetarist approach, but it was central to the government's economic strategy. As a civil servant and as Thatcher's private secretary, it was my job to do all I could to assist her in helping to make monetarism work. It did not cross my mind as a middle-ranking civil servant that I could seriously question it.

Mrs Thatcher had a schizophrenic attitude to the Civil Service. On the one hand, it was one of instinctive distrust – for her, the Civil Service en masse was synonymous with inefficient service delivery and a bloated public sector. As for the Senior Civil Service, it had, in her view, spent the past two decades just managing the UK's decline rather than finding ways to reverse it. There was more than a grain of truth in these charges, and over the 1980s there were many useful changes in the way government departments operated and in the way services were delivered as a result of the work undertaken by an Efficiency Unit set up in the Cabinet Office immediately after the 1979 General Election under the leadership of a former Marks & Spencer chair, Derek Rayner. But the hostility of Mrs Thatcher's rhetoric against the Civil Service, exemplified at a famously unsatisfactory dinner she gave for all permanent secretaries in May 1980, was enough to persuade many talented officials to leave the Civil Service for more lucrative careers outside.

On the other hand, she greatly valued those of us who worked most closely with her (often, it seemed, more than her non-Civil Service special advisers), as well as the great majority of individual officials in other departments of government with whom she came into contact. As she wrote in her memoirs, what mattered for her were 'ability, drive and enthusiasm ... political allegiance was not something I took into account'.[7] She welcomed and encouraged vigorous debate with officials on most policy matters.

The monetarist strategy was the one policy matter on which Mrs Thatcher, in her early years at least, did *not* welcome debate. She was happy to discuss the detail with Treasury and Bank of England officials, and with me, which she did on numerous occasions; it was the job of the Civil Service, and of the Bank of England, to make the monetarist strategy work, and not to question it.

Within the Treasury, there was greater openness. Geoffrey Howe wanted to hear and understand the arguments on both sides. One civil servant who made plain his reservations about monetarism was Permanent Secretary Douglas Wass. But once adopted and his reservations overruled, he never held back from trying to make the strategy work as best he could. Howe valued Wass's experience and his expertise, and never sought to unseat him. Mrs Thatcher would have preferred it if he had taken early retirement, but she never sought his resignation either. In contrast to Liz Truss, short-lived Tory leader and prime minister four decades later, she understood that forcing out a highly respected and talented Treasury permanent secretary would do more harm than good.[8] For his part, Wass had to endure several years of behind-the-scenes sniping from Mrs Thatcher's political advisers and associates.

The majority of those Mrs Thatcher appointed to her first Cabinet were sceptical of the monetarist approach, but except at that Cabinet meeting in July 1981, when the damage had been mostly done, they chose not to challenge it openly. Those few who did were demoted, dismissed or ignored.

In the following chapters, I trace the rise of monetarism, from its small beginnings in the early 1960s, when I was an economics student and Keynesianism was the dominant school of economic thought. By the time I found myself in 1976 in a junior role in the Treasury dealing with macroeconomic policy, there had been a swing towards monetarism that few in my period as a student would have thought conceivable. Well before 1976, a small band of academic economists, in tandem with several influential economic journalists and economists working in the City of London, aided and abetted by Milton Friedman in the USA, had begun to argue that monetarism was the answer to the UK's economic woes. By 1979, for reasons that I will describe, they had won over the hearts and minds of the Conservative Party's leadership.

3

Keynes and Friedman

I chose to study economics at Cambridge after hearing an inspirational lecture by one of the leading development economists of the day, Princeton University's W. Arthur Lewis, while I was working as an 18-year-old volunteer teacher in Belize. He had been adviser to Ghana's first prime minister, Kwame Nkrumah, and would later win a Nobel Prize.[1] I knew nothing about economics at the time – at school, my GCE A Levels had been in Latin, Greek and Ancient History. Lewis's lecture was a seminal moment for me. I wanted a career in which I could 'do some good' in the world. Lewis said enough to convince me that learning economics, and then working as an economist for government or for an international agency, could be a great avenue for trying to achieve that goal.

In the early 1960s, the ideas of John Maynard Keynes were at their zenith in terms of popularity and influence. Cambridge, which had been his home for most of his illustrious career, was the citadel of Keynesianism. It was only 15 years since Keynes's death, and many of his students and collaborators were still active there. These included Richard Kahn, Joan Robinson, James Meade, Richard Stone, Dennis Robertson, Brian Reddaway and Austin Robinson; and there were brilliant younger faculty members such as Nicholas Kaldor, Frank Hahn and Amartya Sen. I attended lectures by most of these, and for one term the wildly eccentric and brilliant Joan Robinson was my supervisor.

Kahn and Robinson had been Keynes's most important confidants and helpers in the 1930s. Kahn had contributed one of the most important ideas in Keynes's economic model – the concept of the 'multiplier'. Robinson was instrumental in encouraging Keynes to develop his key idea, first outlined in an earlier book published in 1930, that disharmony between planned saving and planned investment was a principal cause of unemployment.[2] Meade and Stone (who both went on to win a Nobel Prize) had created the first set of national accounts for the UK. Meade thought up the guiding principles behind the post-war General Agreement on Tariffs and Trade (the GATT). Robertson, the inventor of a concept made famous by Keynes, the 'liquidity trap', had been an illustrious collaborator and later critic. Kaldor and Hahn were preeminent in promoting and extending Keynes's ideas, and were later to be among the most vigorous critics of monetarism. Sen, although not involved in the macroeconomic debates, would win a Nobel Prize for his work in development economics.

After Cambridge, I studied for a Master's degree at Yale. The faculty included James Tobin, one of the USA's most illustrious macroeconomists and a leading Keynesian, who had recently been a member of President Kennedy's Council of Economic Advisers – which, unlike today, was a key policy organ in the US government. I attended his class. He was critical of my lack of mathematics, which had not been a requirement for the Cambridge degree.

It is hard now to recapture the excitement of my introduction to Keynes's ideas. I had grown up in the long shadow of the Great Depression. My doctor grandfather had been forced to close his general medical practice in 1930, and there wasn't enough money for my father to complete his secondary education or to attend university. I knew, from reading George Orwell's *Road to Wigan Pier* and John Steinbeck's *The Grapes of Wrath*, about the miseries of the mass unemployed. It struck me as I was growing up that there was nothing to guarantee this not happening again. So for me, Keynes's ideas were a revelation and a blessing. As the American economist Robert Lekachman put it: 'Keynes informed the world that fatalism towards economic depression, mass unemployment and idle factories was wrong. He demonstrated that intelligent action, deploying known tools of analysis in unconfined ways, was perfectly capable of marrying once again human needs and human resources.'[3]

Keynes and the Classics

Keynes made many important contributions as an economic theorist and as a policy maker, but his most important and greatest work was concerned with the biggest economic problem of his time – the problem of mass unemployment. Classical economists believed that economic downturns were things that naturally happened, and that there wasn't much that governments could do to prevent them from happening. Natural forces would bring about recovery, and more quickly if wages and prices were flexible. Keynes's view, by contrast, was that there was no mechanism in a market economy, which, unaided by government, would automatically bring about recovery.[4]

His crucial discovery was to show that the supply of goods and services did not automatically create the demand for those goods and services, and that there could be a deficiency of aggregate demand caused by society planning to save too much and spend too little on investment in capital equipment, buildings and infrastructure. If left to its own devices, the economy was capable of operating at below its full potential, not just temporarily, but semi-permanently. To prevent this from happening requires increased government spending or tax cuts, and this, in turn, may mean the government having to run a budget deficit and borrowing from the public, or even from the banking system, thus expanding the money supply.

But for Keynes, budget deficits and government borrowing did not matter provided there was genuine spare capacity and unemployed resources in the economy. Unless the government had to borrow from abroad, the budget deficit could always be financed, since the government – if thought of as the community of taxpayers – was effectively borrowing from itself.

Contrary to the view of the classical economists, in his view changes in interest rates could not on their own be relied on to bring savings and investment into balance at a high level of employment. They could help, but were unlikely to be sufficient on their own. It was the government's job to manage aggregate demand so that it neither fell short of what was necessary to ensure full employment nor caused inflation by running at too high a level. This was to be achieved by adjustments in fiscal policy (changes in public spending and taxes), supported by monetary policy (changes in interest rates). Fiscal policy was made the more powerful by the operation of the 'multiplier', whereby a pound of extra government spending (or reduced taxes) has a multiple effect on aggregate spending and output in the economy.[5]

It was on the basis of the Keynesian model that the Treasury, just like the finance ministries of most other Western countries, sought to manage the economy at macro level from the 1950s through into the 1970s. The Treasury would prepare a forecast of total spending on goods and services – that is to say, consumer spending, investment, stock building and net exports (exports minus imports), all at constant prices – and then decide whether this forecast of total spending matched total potential output, with the latter defined as the level of output that was consistent with a 'target' rate of unemployment, normally assumed to be 2 per cent.[6] If the forecast showed a deficiency of demand, this would be made good by lower taxes or higher public spending or a mix of the two, and vice versa if the forecast showed excess demand. The amount of fiscal stimulus or contraction considered necessary at constant prices would then be adjusted to reflect the forecast rate of inflation. In practice, any fiscal stimulus that was deemed necessary on the grounds of prospective unemployment was often constrained by the need to maintain a satisfactory balance of payments with the rest of the world. Under the prevailing fixed exchange rate system that existed until 1972, interest rates would be used mainly to ensure that the parity of sterling was maintained against the dollar rather than as a regulator of domestic demand.

In retrospect, my teachers at Cambridge and Yale made it all sound too simple. Even if the Keynesian model was correct, which I assumed it was, they didn't adequately explain the difficulties of making it work in practice – which required the correct estimation of coefficients in respect of the relationships between the economy's many moving parts and accurate forecasting. The economy was not a well-oiled machine that could be seamlessly and accurately manipulated by the pulling of one lever or another. This was a problem enough in applying the Keynesian model; it would be an even greater problem when it came to applying the monetarist model.

The problem of inflation

Because he advocated budget deficits to combat unemployment, Keynes's critics would later accuse him of being an 'inflationist'. Yet he well understood the evils of inflation. He once wrote: 'Lenin was certainly right. There is no subtler, no surer means of overturning the existing basis of society than to debauch the currency.'[7] He also wrote: 'We must make it a prime object of deliberate state policy that the standard of value should be kept stable.'[8]

Comparing the evils of price inflation and deflation with its attendant unemployment, he did say that 'deflation is, if we rule out exaggerated inflations such as that of Germany, the worse; because it is worse, in an impoverished world, to provoke unemployment than to disappoint the rentier'.[9] Yet his aim was to avoid both unemployment *and* inflation.

Inflation in the UK averaged around 4 per cent per annum in the 1950s. It wasn't a really serious problem, yet it was still worryingly high by pre-war standards. Unemployment was low, with a rate of under 2 per cent on average, and many economists thought that, at such a low rate, and with little or no spare capacity, prices were being driven up by excessive demand for products and for labour. This was the 'demand-pull' effect. Others thought there were 'cost-push' factors at work too. Higher import prices, especially after the Korean War (1950–53), was one such factor. There were two others: the ability of trade unions to extract higher wages for their members even when there was a degree of slack in the labour market, and the ability of monopolistic firms to push up prices.

Based on the experience of the 1950s and early 1960s, it seemed that governments had a choice between, on the one hand, full employment and some inflation, and on the other hand, next to zero inflation and some unemployment. This was encapsulated in the famous Phillips curve, which purported to show a predictable relationship between inflation and unemployment. Governments couldn't have zero inflation and full employment at the same time. The problem for policy makers was captured by one of Keynes's leading followers in the USA, Abba Lerner, when he wrote in 1964: 'The Keynesian policy seemed to be calling for expansionary and restrictionary [sic] monetary and fiscal policies at the same time to deal with the unemployment and inflation side by side.'[10]

Subsequent experience in the 1960s suggested that the problem for policy makers was even more difficult. It seemed that the trade-off wasn't between a particular rate of inflation and a particular rate of unemployment; it was actually between the rate of unemployment and the *acceleration* or *deceleration* of the rate of inflation. In other words, there was a rate of unemployment below which inflation tended to *accelerate* and above which it tended to *decelerate*. This rate was christened rather inelegantly by Milton Friedman as the 'natural rate of unemployment'.

The reason why the simple Phillips curve trade-off no longer seemed to be working was that trade union wage bargainers were focused on securing not just an increase in *money* wages, but also an increase in *real* wages (that is, an increase in excess of the current rate of inflation). When the labour market was relatively tight, they were able to achieve such an increase, and if the wage increase exceeded the growth in labour productivity, it was all too likely to lead to accelerating inflation until unemployment rose to its 'equilibrium' level – at which point the rate of inflation would stabilise.

The natural rate of unemployment for any particular country would depend principally on the wage-bargaining arrangements in place, and especially the bargaining strength of its trade unions. In the UK, the natural rate seemed to be steadily increasing in the 1960s and then into the 1970s. Retrospectively, leading labour economist Stephen Nickell estimated that the natural rate had risen from 3.8 per cent in the period 1969–73 to 7.5 per cent in 1974–81, and to a peak of 9.5 per cent through the 1980s.[11] This trend had disappointing implications for demand management as advocated by Keynes. It meant that lower unemployment could not automatically be 'bought' by reflating the economy and accepting a higher but steady rate of inflation. It meant that, if *accelerating* inflation was to be avoided or unless the natural rate of unemployment could somehow be brought down, the economy might have to operate at a level well below its full potential.

It also meant that, in the face of an exogenous price shock such as an oil price increase from abroad or a price shock initiated by government, for inflation to be returned to its previous level there would have to be downward pressure on wages and prices, and this would require creating and accepting greater slack in the economy and unemployment above its natural rate, at least for a while. With more unemployment, employees would be in a weaker position to ask for higher wages; with reduced aggregate demand, companies would find it harder to increase their product prices.

This was well explained by Franco Modigliani, an economist whom as a student I greatly admired, in his address to the American Economic Association in 1976. He said: 'Once a price shock hits, there is no way of returning to the initial equilibrium except after a period of both above equilibrium unemployment and inflation.'[12] This is the situation that prevailed in 1979 following the near-doubling of VAT and the increase in oil prices that year; and it also applied to the price shocks decades later caused by Brexit, Covid-19 and the war in Ukraine.

Prices and incomes policy

For most Keynesians in the 1960s and 1970s, there was a better alternative to deflating the economy in order to curb inflation: voluntary, or if necessary, statutory restraints on wages and salaries. The object would be to keep wages growing more or less in line with productivity increases, so avoiding the trade-off between low unemployment and higher or accelerating inflation. To make wage restraint acceptable to trade unions, and to make sure that firms didn't simply take advantage of lower wages to boost their profit margins, there would also need to be voluntary agreement or statutory controls on prices.

As early as 1961, President Kennedy's Council of Economic Advisers had concluded that full employment without inflation would prove intractable unless there was a policy to restrain prices and incomes. They wrote that 'continuing efforts should be made to enlist the cooperation of labor and management in a voluntary program of price and wage restraint'. They also argued that economic expansion and productivity improvements would be a useful antidote to upward cost pressures, and that effective labour market policies (skills training, greater mobility and other measures to improve labour market flexibility) were needed to reduce the level of unemployment before inflationary wage pressures kicked in.[13] Few economists at that time realised how very difficult prices and incomes policies would be to implement politically and without incurring significant economic costs.

The quantity theory of money

At Cambridge and Yale it was generally accepted that inflation was due to some combination of 'demand-pull' and 'cost–push' factors, and that, consequently, some combination of monetary and fiscal restrictions on the one hand, and prices and incomes policy on the other, was the best approach if inflation was to be kept under control.

But there was another theory of inflation that we studied more as an historical curiosity than a theory to be taken seriously. This was the theory of inflation based on the quantity theory of money that held sway in the late 19th and early 20th centuries, and still had a wide following when Keynes was writing his *General Theory*.

The quantity theory comprised four concepts or variables. The *first* is the money supply (M), defined as cash with the public and the banks, or on a broader basis, to include bank deposits. The *second* concept is the volume of goods and services produced in the economy, weighted by their value (T). The *third* is the average level of prices (P). The volume of goods and services and the average level of prices in combination equate to the value of national output at current prices, or money GDP (PT). The *fourth* concept is the ratio of money GDP to money supply, known as velocity of circulation (V).

The quantity theory in its crude form starts from a simple and indisputable axiom – that the money supply times its velocity of circulation must equal money GDP.[14] The theory then makes three large assumptions. The first is that there is a causal relationship from money supply to money GDP rather than from money GDP to money supply. Second, it assumes that the velocity of circulation is stable. Third, bearing in mind that money GDP comprises a split between output volume and prices, it assumes that the effect of any change in money supply is on prices and not on volume. It follows from these three assumptions that any change in the money supply will cause a proportionate change in prices.

Keynes took issue with all three assumptions, especially the second and third: the alleged stable velocity of circulation, and the alleged unchanged output in response to a change in the money supply. He considered both of these implausible in theory and not backed up by historical evidence. Changes in the money supply, in his view, affected both prices *and* output, and their effect was all the more uncertain because of variability in the velocity of circulation. Regarding the latter, he argued that it could go up or down for several reasons. Lower interest rates would increase the desire on the part of the public to hold money balances, and this would therefore reduce velocity, and vice versa with higher interest rates. Velocity was also unstable because the public might want to hold more or less money for precautionary or speculative purposes. Keynes noted that in the 1930s people were holding a considerably higher proportion of their wealth in cash than they had in earlier decades because of worries about the banking system. If velocity of circulation was going down, as it did then, this would wholly or partially offset the impact of an increase in the money supply on money GDP.

The quantity theory and its conclusions were well rehearsed in the 1958 report of an official inquiry into the working of the monetary system chaired by Lord (Cyril) Radcliffe. Their report, widely read and studied at the time, concluded that controlling the money supply was not a suitable policy objective. They accepted that the 'whole liquidity position' of the economy did influence aggregate spending, and therefore the authorities needed to take this into account in the setting of interest rates. But the money supply was only one part of 'whole liquidity', and the existence of 'near-money' substitutes made the money supply much too unstable in relation to money GDP to make it suitable for control purposes. They also came out firmly in support of the Keynesian view that interest rate adjustments had a relatively weak effect on spending, and that fiscal policy should be the main instrument for regulating overall demand in the economy with respect to both output and inflation.[15]

At Cambridge, *Economics: An Introductory Analysis* by the American economist Paul Samuelson was the most popular introductory economics textbook.[16] In its 1961 edition, the edition I would have read, Samuelson wrote that the quantity theory might be of interest in explaining episodes of hyperinflation, and long upswings in price levels such as the large inflations following the Spanish discovery of gold and the California gold rush, but in other respects, the theory was a 'blind alley or possibly a red herring'. In the 1964 edition he wrote that 'few people still alive subscribe to the crude quantity theory'.

Friedman and monetarism

One of the few prominent economists who still subscribed to the quantity theory was Chicago's Milton Friedman. He, and co-researcher Anna Schwartz, had spent years researching the history of money and inflation in the USA, and published their results in 1963.[17] (For this and other contributions, he would win the Nobel Prize in 1976.) Their conclusion was that over the period 1867 to 1960, despite year-to-year fluctuations and an increase in velocity in the 1950s, there had been a long-term, stable trend relationship between the money supply, defined in broad terms, and inflation. Having established, so they said, a long-term correlation between money supply and prices, they drew the sweeping conclusion that changes in the money supply, and changes in the money supply alone, had been the cause of US inflation historically. Hence, Friedman's famous statement in a talk he gave in India in 1963: 'Inflation is always and everywhere a monetary phenomenon.'

In fact, Friedman and Schwartz's data, when looked at closely, did not support their optimistic conclusion that, historically, there had been a close relationship between monetary growth and inflation. In a series of publications over the years, the UK's leading econometrician, David Hendry, and his co-researchers, would show that their work suffered from serious empirical and statistical shortcomings.[18]

Friedman swept such criticisms aside. He said that his theory and his empirical evidence were 'scientific', and that his findings showed that, when the money supply increased significantly faster than output over any extended period, the result was inflation. He explained this by saying that if people found themselves holding money in excess of their immediate needs, they would soon spend the excess, and this would, in due course, lead to higher inflation.

He claimed that it took about six months for an increase in the money supply to produce an increase in spending. Initially, the accelerated spending would be reflected primarily in higher output and employment. It would take another 18 months for accelerated spending to be translated into higher inflation. Output and employment would then revert to their former level, and eventually, because inflation is bad for investment and savings, to *lower* output and employment. With a curbing of monetary growth, these effects would work in reverse: a slow-down in spending is followed first by a temporary slow-down in output and then by a permanent reduction in inflation, and ultimately in *higher* output.

Friedman believed that budget deficits could do little, if anything, to influence output and employment. Just as the classical economists had opined, higher government borrowing would cause interest rates to rise, and would thereby crowd out private spending. The higher interest rates would come about through the government having to offer higher rates in order to sell additional bonds. If, on the other hand, the budget deficit was monetised (that is, financed by the banks or by the central bank), it would simply lead to an increase in the money supply and, after a lag, to higher inflation. He argued strongly against public deficits on any scale because governments were all too likely to be tempted into monetisation. The smaller the public sector, the less danger there was of this happening.[19]

In his view, neither governments (through fiscal policy) nor central banks (through monetary policy) should attempt to fine-tune the economy. Either their actions would have little or no effect, or they would make things worse. He wrote:

> We simply do not know enough to be able to recognize minor disturbances when they occur or be able to predict either what their effects will be with any precision or what monetary policy is required to offset the effects. We do not know enough to be able to achieve stated

objectives by delicate, or even fairly coarse, changes in the mix of monetary and fiscal policy.[20]

He accepted that monetary policy 'can contribute to offsetting major disturbances in the economic system' such as the effects of war or an explosive budget deficit.[21] But for normal times, he favoured a simple 'rule' whereby money supply should be set to grow at the same rate as typical GDP growth based on past averages, and kept at this rate irrespective of any divergence in GDP from trend.[22] With such a rule, policy mistakes would be avoided, and long-term stability would be achieved. Like the classical economists, and in contrast to Keynes, Friedman believed that interest rates would respond of their own accord to any cyclical disturbances so as to stabilise aggregate demand and, consequently, stabilise output and employment.[23]

The best government could do for output and employment was to limit inflation by controlling the money supply; make labour and product markets more flexible and competitive; ensure a positive environment for private enterprise to flourish; provide adequate public goods (defence of the realm, infrastructure, the rule of law, public health and public education, and so on); and allow the exchange rate to fluctuate so as to maintain international competitiveness.

Sometime in the late 1960s Friedman's revived version of the quantity theory of money and his rejection of Keynesian demand theory would be christened 'monetarism'.

At the two universities I attended, none of my teachers took Friedman's views on money seriously. I left those two citadels of Keynesian economics believing that, as Samuelson had said about the classical quantity theory, his views were no more than a 'blind alley'. This proved far too sanguine a view as, over the next 10 to 15 years, Friedman's ideas gradually gained ground and Keynesianism went into retreat. Starting in 1976, I would find myself in the Treasury and then in the prime minister's office helping to implement an increasingly monetarist economic strategy.

4

The monetarists' challenge

After I graduated from Yale in 1965, it would be 11 years before I returned to macroeconomics. During those years, I worked as an economist with the World Bank, evaluating development projects and programmes in Africa and in India, and then, for three years starting in 1973, I worked as an administrator in one of the Treasury's public spending divisions.[1] My responsibility there was to monitor and attempt to control public spending, and provide advice to Treasury ministers, on a rag-bag of activities: subsidies to our declining shipyards, subsidies for the building of oil rigs, spending on lighthouses and the coastguard, policy on shipping and the Law of the Sea, the UK's contribution to the European Space Agency, and funding of the Science Budget.

I had nothing to do with macroeconomic management. The Treasury was so secretive and so divided into separate silos in those days that it was hardly more possible to know what was going on in regard to macroeconomic policy than if I had been a member of the public. The closest I came to macroeconomic policy was the debate as to whether we should be planning and monitoring public spending in constant or current price terms.

Since the 1960s, public spending had been planned, monitored and controlled on a constant price or volume basis. This made sense when inflation was in low single figures. But when, in the early 1970s, inflation was running at a much higher level, it was madness. Since spending departments were able to secure additional funding from the Treasury to cover any cost (as opposed to volume) increases in their programmes, the system validated and even encouraged cost inflation across wide swathes of the economy. This way of doing things only came to an end in 1976 when programme spending was made subject to 'cash limits'.

Stagflation and the declining relevance of Keynes

In July 1976 I moved to the small policy unit supporting Permanent Secretary Douglas Wass, and in so doing became engaged with macroeconomics once again. I was surprised and shocked by how much thinking on macroeconomics had changed since my student days, and in particular how Keynesian ideas had been relegated and how Milton Friedman's monetarism had moved up and was becoming even half respectable.

This had happened for two reasons. First, just as classical economics had lost its relevance in the face of seemingly intractable unemployment in the 1930s, so Keynesian ideas seemed to have lost much of their relevance in the 1970s due to the emergence of 'stagflation' – the combination of rising unemployment and rising inflation. In a situation of high inflation, it seemed that governments could no longer look to extra spending or lower taxes to stimulate output and employment; the extra spending and lower taxes would too easily seep into higher inflation.

The standard Keynesian approach to forecasting and managing the economy was no longer working. In a speech to his party's annual conference in 1976, Jim Callaghan, who had succeeded as Labour's prime minister in April of that year, expressed this as follows:

> We used to think you could spend your way out of a recession and increase employment by cutting taxes and boosting government spending. I tell you in all candour that that option no longer exists, and that insofar as it ever did exist, it only worked on each occasion since the war by injecting a bigger dose of inflation into the economy, followed by a higher level of unemployment as the next step.[2]

This was pure Friedman.

The previous Conservative government had attempted to control inflation, first through a voluntary prices and incomes policy; and when that failed to work, from late 1972, through a prices policy and incomes policy backed by law. But this had broken down in the face of trade union opposition and damaging strikes, most notably in the coal industry. It had been followed by the Conservatives losing office and by a wages and salaries free-for-all – which resulted in inflation rising to over 25 per cent in 1975.

Then, at the start of the 1975/76 wage-bargaining round, the Labour government reached an understanding with the trade unions – known as the Social Contract – to limit their wage demands on a voluntary basis in return for certain pledges on taxes and spending. No one knew how durable the Social Contract would be or for how long it would last. Many believed it would not survive for long. It actually survived for three years, and then broke down disastrously in the winter of 1978/79.

Monetarist ideas to the fore

The second reason why monetarism was on the up was that it now seemed to offer a plausible framework for controlling inflation. If curbing the growth of the money supply could really be shown to be a solution to bringing down inflation without impacting adversely – except possibly in the very short term – on output and employment, then it was surely the answer. It also had the appeal of common sense: more money in the economy surely had to mean higher prices, and vice versa.

Friedman was prolific with his writings and lectures, and managed to convince an increasing body of academic economists and economic journalists. An important moment was his address to the American Economic Association in 1967.[3] For people who were not expert in monetary theory, Friedman was a persuasive communicator, both on television and in his writings. One critic described him as 'artful'.[4] Paul Samuelson disliked debating with him in public because, he said, with uninformed audiences Friedman always seemed to be the winner.

Because he wrote and spoke so extensively and not always consistently, Friedman's critics found him hard to pin down. For example, he chopped and changed about which of the several definitions of money should be considered as the most important for monetary policy and for controlling inflation. Should it be the narrowest aggregate M0 (cash in the hands of the public and cash in the banks' vaults plus their reserves with the central bank), the narrow aggregate M1 (currency in circulation plus current account deposits), the broad aggregate M3 (M1 plus savings deposits) or a still broader aggregate to include certain types of financial securities?

Some monetarists considered M1 to be the appropriate aggregate since it most closely represented spending power. Friedman tended to prefer M3 because savings deposits could be relatively easily mobilised for spending. He called savings deposits a 'temporary abode of purchasing power'. But he didn't feel strongly about this. In his view, it mattered much less *which* particular aggregate was chosen for targeting and for control purposes than that one *was* chosen.

In his more extreme moments, he would repeat the classical quantity theory that changes in the money stock would directly and proportionately impact on prices, with no impact on output and employment. At other times, and increasingly so over the years, he would accept that the impact would be on money GDP – that is, a combination of prices and output – and that the impact on *prices* of a slow-down in monetary growth would be greater when the economy was operating at nearly full capacity, and the impact on *output* would be greater when it was operating at well below full capacity.[5]

Furthermore, for all the stability in the velocity of circulation that he claimed to have found in his studies of US financial history, he would sometimes accept, as Keynes had argued all along, that such stability could not be counted on, and therefore – particularly in the short run – money GDP and prices would not necessarily increase or decrease proportionately to the percentage increase or decrease in the money supply. This was a critical admission since it meant that controlling the money supply would be a much less reliable tool for controlling inflation, and the money supply figures a less reliable indicator of inflationary pressures.

Equally striking, in one essay he agreed that the causation was not necessarily always from money supply to money GDP, but could also be from money GDP to money supply.[6] To the extent that the latter was true, as the critics of monetarism repeatedly argued, trying to control the money supply in order to control inflation was a pointless exercise.

In contrast to his famous statement that 'inflation is always a monetary phenomenon', he wrote in another essay that there were other factors besides excessive monetary growth – for example, excessive wage increases, profiteering and supply interruptions – which could be a cause of inflation.[7]

For all these qualifications, Friedman stuck to his basic belief that there was a stable relationship between monetary growth and inflation, and that governments and central banks should target and control the expansion of the money supply if they wanted to curb inflation. While M3 was his preferred monetary aggregate, the latter could only be controlled indirectly and unreliably through adjustments to interest rates. He suggested instead that central banks should target and control M0, which was the one monetary aggregate they *could* directly control.[8] Although M0 constituted only a small fraction of M3, he argued that in normal times the banks could be relied on to maintain a fairly stable relationship between their reserves and their customers' deposits, and therefore controlling M0 would have the effect, albeit indirectly, of also controlling M3.

Friedman favoured the publication of monetary targets, provided governments and central banks were firm in sticking to them. This should help to persuade trade unions in their pay bargaining, and businesses in their setting of prices, of the government's firm intention to bring inflation down. Lower inflation would thereby be achieved more quickly and at lower cost in terms of unemployment. A further benefit of publishing monetary targets was that they would reassure the financial markets that the government accepted the need for financial discipline. This, in turn, would hopefully persuade the markets to behave in a manner that would reinforce, rather than impede, the quest for stability.

Friedman's critics in the USA

Friedman's most prominent critics in the USA were Paul Samuelson and James Tobin. Samuelson was a persistent critic, and as Friedman's flame brightened, he sharpened his criticisms.

In a 1970 essay, he maintained that 'a crude monetarism is now stalking the land'. He praised Friedman for forcing economists to pay more attention to money, but he disagreed fundamentally with Friedman's interpretation of US monetary history, and argued, in Keynesian fashion, that it was spending – not changes in the money supply – that affected prices and output.[9] Speaking of Friedman and his monetarism some years after his death, he said: 'It is a tragedy when somebody really takes the wrong train in life.'[10]

Tobin argued, in true Keynesian fashion, that demand restriction was only justified when aggregate demand threatened to exceed the economy's output potential. If there was inflation at below full employment, this couldn't be for demand reasons. It must be due to monopoly pricing, or to cost pressures due to wages rising faster than productivity. If the former, there needed to be improved anti-monopoly policies; if the latter, which in his view was the bigger problem, there needed to be an effective incomes policy. Any extra labour market rigidities arising from incomes policies were a small price to pay against the huge loss of output and incomes consequent on trying to tackle inflation solely via demand management. If the cost pressures came from higher import prices, they would have to be accepted in higher domestic prices, but prevented from creating an inflation spiral – again, through holding down wages via incomes policy, even though this would have to mean a drop in real incomes.

Tobin had a number of particular issues with Friedman:

- He questioned whether increases or reductions in monetary growth would necessarily feed through into additional or less spending. He argued that the velocity of money would tend to speed up with a tightening of monetary policy (since, with higher interest rates, people would tend to economise on their holding of money), and this would counteract the depressive force of a reduced money supply. And vice versa for velocity and spending in the case of a monetary expansion.
- He questioned Friedman and Schwartz's claim of stability of velocity over time. In a review of their *Monetary History of the United States*, Tobin noted that it was hardly reassuring that velocity fell within 90–110 per cent of trend in only 53 years out of the 93 years of their study.[11]

- He argued that Friedman was wrong in claiming that the effect of a monetary expansion or reduction, after a two-year lag, was entirely on prices. In Tobin's view, when the economy was running at below full employment, roughly 90 per cent of the effect was on output and only 10 per cent on prices.
- At a more fundamental level, Tobin viewed monetarism as providing a justification for governments to shrug off their rightful responsibilities for managing the economy. In evidence to the House of Commons Treasury Select Committee in 1980, he described the UK's 'risky experiment' with monetarism as implying that 'the government has no responsibility for the real outcomes of the economy, all it does is provide money and let the economy decide what its real outcomes are'.[12]

Two economists 'across the water' who positioned themselves between the Friedmanites and the antis were the Canadian Harry Johnson, who taught at Chicago and the London School of Economics and Political Science (LSE), and Paul Volcker, chair of the Federal Reserve Board from 1979.

Samuelson would say of Johnson that he 'leads the campaign to export monetarism to the British Isles'.[13] This was unfair. In his 1970 address to the American Economic Association, Johnson said that monetarism deserved a serious hearing because it attempted to deal with a problem – stagflation – for which the prevailing orthodoxy, Keynesianism, had no solution. Friedman had done a service by forcing economists to be 'more conscious of monetary influences on the economy and more careful in our assessment of their importance'.[14] But Johnson also said that 'monetarism is seriously inadequate as an approach to monetary policy, judged by the prevailing standards of academic economics', because it failed to explain exactly why a change in the money stock could be expected to impact prices. Like Tobin, he was also critical of monetarism's 'abnegation of responsibility for explaining the division of the effects of monetary change between price and quantity movements'.[15] However, unlike Tobin and other Keynesians, Johnson had little faith in the feasibility or effectiveness of incomes policies. Instead, if governments wanted to curb inflation, they had no option but to keep a damper on aggregate demand, while at the same time working to improve the functioning of the labour market.

Volcker was a determined anti-inflationist. Addressing the American Economic and Finance Associations in 1976, he said that over the long run there was a clear parallel between excessive monetary growth and inflation. He favoured the publication of monetary targets as a means of 'communicating our intentions both to the political authorities and to the market place', and providing 'discipline for our own debate within the Federal Reserve'. He called this an 'experiment ... [in] practical monetarism'. He went on to note, however, the considerable instability in the relationship between money and money GDP over the short run (that is to say, velocity), which made the actual setting of monetary targets far from easy, and also made it important not to overreact to deviations from the targets; and he pointed to the technical difficulties of actually achieving a given monetary target – even controlling M0, the simplest aggregate to control, was not the easy panacea monetarists tended to think it was.[16]

In 1978, Volcker wrote that publishing monetary targets 'can and has had some value in calming and stabilizing inflationary expectations'.[17] Yet his support for monetary targets, he said, 'does not start from a "monetarist" perspective'.[18] In saying this, he was distancing himself from the more radical monetarist view that all, or nearly all, of inflation could be attributed to excessive money supply expansion. He wrote:

> I believe there are in fact a variety of non-monetary cost and supply factors that can affect the rate of inflation in the short – and not so short – run. To say that the price impact of such developments can always be offset with suitable monetary adjustments seems to me to display an enormous faith in the flexibility of prices and wages over meaningful periods and/or a magisterial indifference to the potential implications of cost and supply developments for real output in the face of restricted monetary growth. ... I see no need to accept as complete, or even adequate, a simple causal explanation running from monetary behavior to price behavior.[19]

Volcker cautioned against an 'immediate jump' to a monetary growth rate designed to achieve much lower inflation in case it had a 'sharp effect on real economic activity'.[20]

And yet this is exactly what he and the Federal Reserve Board attempted to do in 1979 when US inflation had begun to climb dangerously. This involved a sharp rise in interest rates. The latter failed to have the hoped-for effect of reining in the growth of M1. It did, however, have the effect of bringing inflation down, while at the same time causing a sharp, although short-lived, recession. Not being a genuine believer in monetarism, Volcker arguably used the language of monetarism as a veil to explain and justify what he regarded as a necessary tightening of monetary policy.

The 'Volcker shock' caused much controversy at the time, but was later lauded as a necessary adjustment in monetary policy to bring inflation down. But the latter was not achieved in the way monetarists would have expected – that is, through successful restriction of the money supply. Money supply turned out both less easy to control and less closely related to prices and incomes than had been assumed. As Volcker told an American writer: 'There didn't seem to be the relationship between money growth and the economic numbers you would have expected.'[21]

The UK's experience a year or two later was not dissimilar, and in both countries the experience led to a disillusionment with monetary targeting.

Volcker pulled the plug on his quasi-monetarism in 1982 by cutting the Federal Reserve Bank's discount rate when the money supply figures would have suggested it should be increased. Mrs Thatcher and her chancellor were in the process of abandoning their hard version of monetarism at around this time, moving to a more flexible, more pragmatic version. Volcker felt able to cut his ties with monetarism more quickly because he lacked their ideological commitment to the monetarist cause.

Friedman's British critics

In the UK, Friedman's most prominent critic was Nicholas Kaldor at Cambridge. A determined Keynesian, he had been an influential witness to the Radcliffe Committee in 1958. In his evidence to that Committee, he had focused on the instability and lack of predictability in the velocity of circulation. In 1970, he took up the cudgels against Friedman on a different issue.[22] His main point of attack was Friedman's assumption in most of his writings that money growth is determined exogenously – that is to say, by the central banks – whereas for years in both the UK and the USA, in his view, it had been mainly determined endogenously – by changes in income and wealth. Consequently, it could not be the case that changes in the money supply were the cause of inflation.

He also challenged Friedman's contention that central banks are able to influence the growth of broad money by increasing or reducing the monetary base (M0): he pointed out that the money supply on a broad definition in the USA in the 1930s had contracted by one third while M0 actually increased. This was because currency held by the public increased substantially as a ratio to bank deposits because of worries about bank failures.

Kaldor's Cambridge colleague Joan Robinson was scathing about the 'unearthly, mystical element in Friedman's thought', and his view that 'the mere existence of a stock of money somehow promotes expenditure'.[23]

Telling though their criticisms might be, economists like Kaldor and Robinson in the UK and Tobin and Samuelson in the USA failed to acknowledge that orthodox Keynesian policies were no longer working. They had little to say about the difficulties caused by governments trying to manage their economies without a robust nominal anchor following the demise of fixed exchange rates, or about the costs incurred by the implementation and then the breakdown of incomes policies. They offered no credible alternative policy solution to the combined problem of rising inflation with rising unemployment. They could only offer prices and incomes policy, which by 1979 in the UK and the USA no longer seemed politically feasible, and a more careful deflation of demand than could be possible by attempting to control the money supply.

The British monetarists

Despite the criticisms of monetarism from these 'big guns' on both sides of the Atlantic, by the mid-1970s in Britain there was a small cadre of Friedmanite economists in the universities and in the City who signed up to the idea of monetary targets and controlling the money supply as the means of controlling inflation. None of them, except possibly Alan Walters, were considered by their academic peers to be economists of the first rank. There was only one big-name economist working in Britain who showed any sympathy for Friedman's ideas. This was the Nobel laureate James Meade at Cambridge, but, as explained below, he was opposed to monetary targets and trying to control the money supply.

The leading advocates of monetarism in Britain were Alan Walters at LSE and Johns Hopkins University; Brian Griffiths at City University; Patrick Minford at Liverpool; Michael Parkin and David Laidler at Manchester and the University of Western Ontario; Terry Burns, Alan Budd and Jim Ball at the London Business School; and two economists working for firms in the City – Gordon Pepper and Tim Congdon.

Walters would later be Mrs Thatcher's economic adviser – from January 1981 to October 1983, and again from May to October 1989. Griffiths was an active participant from 1976 in the work of the Conservatives' Economic Reconstruction Group (see Chapter 6), and would become head of the Number 10 Policy Unit from 1985 to 1990. He wrote a book in 1976, *Inflation: The Price of Prosperity*, in which he argued in fairly apocalyptic terms that inflation had to be conquered and that Friedman's monetarism was the answer.[24] In 1980, Burns would become chief economic adviser at the Treasury and then permanent secretary in 1991. Budd would succeed him as chief economic adviser. Together, they would prove an exceptionally effective duo in helping to introduce inflation targeting and achieve low inflation and renewed economic growth after the UK's exit from the European Exchange Rate Mechanism (ERM) in 1992.

Pepper was the publisher of the stockbroker Greenwell's regular Monetary Bulletin. He and Congdon were highly influential with asset managers and traders in the City. They played a major role in converting the City for a few years into a bastion of monetarism, which, in turn, affected the way the markets behaved. They also had personal contact with Mrs Thatcher, especially before the 1979 General Election, and occasionally afterwards.

Two of Britain's most influential economic journalists, Sam Brittan and Peter Jay, also became converts and spread the word through the *Financial Times* and *The Times* respectively, as did Jay's editor at *The Times*, William Rees-Mogg.[25] Jay was Jim Callaghan's son-in-law and was credited with the anti-Keynesian quote in Callaghan's speech mentioned earlier. Other key organs for spreading monetarist ideas were the Conservative-leaning think tanks – the Institute of Economic Affairs (established in the 1950s) and the Centre for Policy Studies (CPS) (co-founded in 1974 by Keith Joseph, Mrs Thatcher and Alfred Sherman). Sherman, the CPS's first director, was a brilliant intellectual, a former communist turned neoliberal economist and ideologue – to whom Mrs Thatcher was greatly attached, although she regarded him as a loose canon politically.

UK monetary developments in the early 1970s played a significant part in convincing the British monetarists that they were on the right path. In the two years to September 1973, M3 grew at an average annual rate of 26 per cent, and this was followed two years later by a surge in inflation (15 per cent in 1974 and 25 per cent in 1975).

The view of the majority of economists at the time – including those at the Treasury – was that the inflation surge actually had little to do with excessive monetary growth and instead was due mainly to the quadrupling of oil prices in 1973, fiscal expansion in the 1972 budget (resulting in the so-called 'Barber boom'), and 'cost-push' due to much higher wage settlements following the breakdown of the Conservatives' statutory incomes policy. The money supply figures, which the monetarists blamed for the inflation, were grossly distorted by the dash for growth among the London clearing banks after the freeing up in 1971 of controls on their borrowing and lending.[26] The monetary expansion, as recorded, was, in their view, only a minor contributing factor behind the inflation spiral.

This was definitely not the view of the British monetarists. For them, the surge in inflation following the explosive monetary growth two years earlier confirmed the Friedmanite proposition that the basic cause of inflation was excessive monetary growth, and that a first task for government and for the Bank of England was to bring monetary growth under control. They were agreed that prudent fiscal policy (that is to say, limiting government deficits and borrowing) was an essential ingredient in helping to limit monetary growth; otherwise, there would have to be too much reliance on higher interest rates. They were agreed on the need to publish medium-term monetary targets and to achieve these through appropriate monetary and fiscal policies. They were agreed that there was enough stability and predictability in the relationship between the money supply and money GDP and prices over time to make the money supply an appropriate tool for controlling inflation, although variations in the relationship over the short term could make it problematic.[27] They agreed that monetary targets would serve as a useful nominal anchor and fill the void that had been left by the abandonment of a fixed exchange rate in 1972, and, if properly understood, have a beneficial influence on wage bargaining and on price setting.

The British monetarists, however, were not at all a uniform group in terms of their precise thinking – either regarding the theory or how it might be applied in Britain. There was no single view on how monetarism was supposed to work, or could be made to work, in the British context.

In the first place, for Burns and Budd, there was a significant distinction between, on the one hand, what they saw as a reasonably close relationship between the money supply and inflation over the long term, and on the other hand, trying to control the money supply in a precise manner over the very short term. They favoured monetary targets covering the medium term in order to influence inflationary expectations and to provide a nominal anchor to the system, not as a short-term control system.

Walters was of the same view. He wrote that, while the long-term relation between money supply and inflation was stable, it was 'impossible to adduce any such stability for the short run, month by month, or quarter by quarter periods'.[28] This was why he would warn Mrs Thatcher not to be too concerned about month-to-month variations in monetary growth. But it went against her instincts to ignore such variations. She would rightly question how monetary targets could really act as an anchor and influence expectations in a helpful manner unless they were closely adhered to from month to month, or at least quarter to quarter. The financial markets were certainly unforgiving of short-term deviations from the targets. In fact, the velocity of money in the 1970s and 1980s turned out to be more like a switchback than a stable function (see Figure A6 in the Appendix), and this was one of the reasons why monetarism turned out to be so unsatisfactory.

Second, there was division on which was the best monetary aggregate to target and control. For Walters, M1 had the attraction of being more responsive to interest rate changes, as well as representing money that people were able to immediately spend. Congdon, on the other hand, followed Friedman in preferring M3 because it was relatively easy for depositors to mobilise money from their savings accounts for spending. M3 also had the advantage of being controllable through the banks' 'credit counterparts', since changes in bank lending to the private sector and to government, broadly speaking, are equal to changes in the banks' liabilities and therefore to changes in M3.[29]

Third, they had different views on the mechanism whereby a change in the money supply translated into a change in money GDP. Burns and Ball emphasised how, once the UK had abandoned a fixed exchange rate, as it did in 1972, monetary expansion made itself felt through a declining exchange rate – which then impacted on inflation.[30] Others followed Friedman in believing that the amount of money that people want to hold is relatively stable compared to their incomes and wealth, and when their holdings of money exceed their desired holdings, they will spend the excess sooner rather than later, causing prices to rise. For one or two, it seemed, the exact mechanism didn't really matter: all that mattered was the evident link, as they saw it, between monetary expansion and inflation.

Fourth, they disagreed on how the amount of money in the economy was to be controlled. The majority, with Pepper the leading advocate, were attracted by monetary base control (MBC) – controlling the banks' cash holdings and reserves with a view to influencing, by this means, the level of their deposits and thus M1 and M3. This was the control system also advocated by Friedman. They were unconcerned that this would be a radical departure from the way monetary policy had been executed over many decades and would involve significant institutional changes, and it would mean the government and the Bank of England no longer having control over short-term interest rates. For the minority, however, continued reliance on interest rates to influence the demand for borrowing and for holding money was the better way of ensuring that the money supply grew at an appropriate rate.

Fifth, they were divided on how quickly, when inflation was running at a high level, the government and the Bank of England should try to reduce the growth of the money supply. This hinged partly on how much of the impact was likely to be felt in the first instance on output and employment as opposed to prices. Burns favoured the setting of monetary targets based on a gradual adjustment of inflation targets, and bearing in mind the lags in the system, waiting patiently for inflation to decline. Griffiths argued that too sharp a reduction would cause an unacceptably large fall in output and employment; he also favoured a gradual reduction in monetary growth.

Minford, on the other hand, argued that it was important to hit inflationary expectations hard, and that only a sharp reduction in monetary growth could achieve this; and moreover, that if more unemployment was accepted early on, less unemployment would be needed later.[31] Brittan suggested that it would be politically difficult to have unemployment at a high level over several years, and he, too, therefore favoured an early sharp reduction in monetary growth.[32]

Finally, most of the British monetarists were agreed that causation was mainly from money supply to inflation and money GDP, and not the reverse, as argued by Kaldor and others. Thus, Griffiths wrote: 'If an increase in money supply growth today leads to an increase in real output growth in approximately nine months' time and an acceleration of prices eighteen months later, it is difficult to see how current money supply growth is determined by current income.'[33]

For monetarism to work, the causation really had to be in this direction. And yet, in a surprisingly critical review of Friedman and Schwartz's 1982 book on British monetary growth and inflation,[34] Congdon complained that the authors had falsely assumed that monetary growth in the UK was exogenous, whereas it was, in fact, largely endogenous – 'the result of an economic process which is complicated and intricate'.[35] This was an odd complaint coming from one of the monetarists who believed most strongly in causation from the money supply to prices.

In view of all these differences, it is not surprising that there would be differences of view on how the monetarist strategy should be implemented, and how it would be judged with hindsight.

Keynesian monetarist

There was one leading British economist who saw the merits of the monetarist approach, but also its perils. This was the Nobel laureate James Meade, who called himself a 'Keynesian monetarist'.

In 1977 Meade won the Nobel Prize for his work on international trade and payments in the 1950s. However, his Nobel Lecture in Stockholm was devoted not to that subject, but rather to the current problem of stagflation, and how to reconcile the twin objectives of price stability and low unemployment.[36]

Meade was a paid-up member of the Keynesian establishment. He had spent the academic year 1930/31 in Cambridge (on assignment from his new fellowship in economics at Oxford to, as he put it, 'learn [his] subject'). He became a member of Keynes's famous 'circus', contributing to and imbibing Keynes's ideas. Then, during the Second World War, he was a colleague of Keynes in the Cabinet Office, helping to create the first set of national accounts for the UK for the purpose of actively managing the economy on Keynesian lines.

Yet now, at the age of 70, he turned his back on the idea of using demand management to influence the *real* level of output and employment, and instead argued that, in the current inflationary situation, aggregate demand should be managed so as to restrain inflation. In contrast to what was to be the policy regime that followed in the 1990s, he did not advocate a specific target for inflation. His preference was to set a target for money expenditure and money GDP because, in some circumstances with an inflation target, too much of the necessary adjustment would fall on output and employment.

In suggesting that demand management should be aimed at money GDP rather than real GDP, Meade had quite a lot in common with Friedman and other monetarists. For example, in

1981, in an address in Washington, DC, Burns said: 'Government policy is based on the view that the control of inflation requires some control over the growth of total nominal incomes in the medium and long term.'[37]

Unlike Burns and other monetarists, however, Meade could not accept that the pursuit of money supply targets was an effective way of controlling the growth of money GDP. This was for two reasons: first, the impossibility, as he saw it, of defining exactly what *is* money; and second, the unstable and unpredictable velocity of circulation. Consequently, his strong preference was to use interest rates, as well as fiscal policy, to target money GDP and money expenditure directly. Targeting money GDP did have one significant disadvantage, namely that there is normally a two- to three-month time lag before estimates for actual money GDP are available. But Meade still thought it a better variable to target than the money supply.[38]

Meade remained deeply concerned about the problem of rising unemployment, but unlike a few of the anti-monetarists, he didn't think – given the inflationary environment that existed then – that it could be addressed by a more expansionary fiscal policy. His solution was the reform of wage-fixing arrangements so as to match supply and demand in the labour market. This was not to be a replica of the incomes policies of the 1970s. He recommended, instead, the setting up of arbitration boards for different industries, which, if pay negotiations reached an impasse, would determine an appropriate settlement. The boards' guiding principle would be the promotion of employment. He argued that, without reform on these lines, the only alternative was to compress the growth of money GDP and tolerate very high levels of unemployment until inflation came down. He thought this was a wasteful and unjust arrangement, and deeply unfair on those workers who had been made redundant. He admitted that his proposals might be seen as an 'optimist's utopian fantasy', but given what was at stake, that shouldn't stop them from being seriously considered.[39] When Meade first mooted the idea of arbitration boards in his 1977 Stockholm Lecture, with the Labour government and the trade unions working well together under the Social Contract, it might have been a possible runner. Two years later, with a Conservative government and the trade unions regarding each other more like enemies than partners, it was a non-starter.

Meade defended himself against the charge that his assignment of demand management to the tackling of inflation rather than unemployment was contrary to what Keynes would have recommended. He said that Keynes

> would have been appalled at the current rates of price inflation. It is a complete misrepresentation of the views of a great and wise man to suggest that in present conditions he would have been concerned only with the maintenance of full employment, and not at all with the avoidance of price and wage inflation.[40]

I didn't read Meade's Stockholm Lecture at the time; I don't remember it being referred to by colleagues or in the media, and the idea of a target for money GDP does not appear to have featured in the strategy discussions prior to the Conservatives coming to power.[41] It was discussed within the Treasury as a possible alternative to targeting the money supply, but it was never adopted.

I wish I had been familiar at the time with Meade's work. If I had been, I feel sure I would have felt comfortable with his view that it would be better to set targets for money GDP rather than the money supply. I would happily have called myself a 'Keynesian monetarist'. I suspect many of my colleagues at the Treasury and the Bank of England would have felt the same. Instead, we found ourselves juggling backwards and forwards between outmoded Keynesianism and the monetarism of Friedman and his British disciples. As one former Treasury colleague told me, 'We were like beached whales.'

Peter Middleton, the senior Treasury official who took the lead in developing and attempting to apply monetarism on behalf of the Conservative government, and who would succeed Wass as permanent secretary, in a lecture several years after monetarism's demise, distinguished between 'dedicated monetarists', 'reluctant monetarists' and 'disbelieving monetarists' (those who went along with monetarism because the markets believed in it, although they themselves did not).[42] I would have placed myself within the category of 'disbeliever'. I had serious reservations about the theory, but I went along with it because the markets believed in it, because the anti-monetarists didn't seem to have a credible alternative policy, and because it was my job as the servant of a prime minister who *was* a dedicated monetarist to do my best to make the policy work. I was a member of what Ian Gilmour called 'the baggage train for the Thatcher crusaders'.[43] Many years later, the economic journalist William Keegan, who was one of the first to publish a book-length critique of the monetarism experiment,[44] recalled an unnamed Treasury official as having told him at the height of monetarism: 'Ministers do crazy things: my job is to see that they do crazy things properly.'[45]

Meade was the greatest British economist after Alfred Marshall and John Maynard Keynes of the 20th century, and yet, on the most pressing economic issue of the time, Mrs Thatcher's government largely ignored him. Burns did have several discussions with him in the early 1980s, and wrote a paper in September 1981 that considered the case for a switch to a money GDP target. It was decided, nonetheless, to carry on with targeting the money supply, albeit by then on a much less strict basis. More's the pity, in my view, since Meade's idea of setting a target for money GDP and using monetary and fiscal policy to achieve it would almost certainly have been superior to the setting of targets for the money supply. If the idea was to influence wage bargaining and inflation expectations generally, it would have been better understood, and policy wouldn't have suffered from the uncertain vagaries of the money supply and the actual difficulties of controlling it.

For Conservative politicians and some of their monetarist acolytes, Meade's lack of interest in the money supply as an instrument of policy no doubt seemed to them counter-intuitive; he may have seemed still too much of a Keynesian at heart, and they were probably suspicious that his interest in the reform of wage-fixing arrangements would involve some form of government intervention or a return to discredited incomes policy. His long-time support for the Labour Party may not have helped either.

This, then, was roughly how the debate about macroeconomics and counter-inflation policy stood in the mid to late 1970s. The anti-monetarists' critique was scathing, but they had little or nothing new to offer themselves. The monetarists, on the other hand, *were* offering a new approach, but one that was based on flimsy theoretical and empirical foundations. On the British side, there was one senior figure, James Meade, who was offering a plausible 'middle way', but the monetarists' obsession with the money supply and with monetary targets made most of them unwilling to take his views seriously.

In 1970s Britain, there was no serious appetite for monetarist ideas in the governing Labour Party, even though at the bidding of the International Monetary Fund (IMF) they felt obliged to start applying them. There was only a minority interest within the Conservative Party. What was to shift the balance in monetarism's favour was the disastrous collapse of Labour's Social Contract in 1978/79, and monetarism's growing appeal to Mrs Thatcher and a few of her close political colleagues.

5

Labour and soft monetarism

The 1970s was a bad decade for the British economy and for British economic policy. Ted Heath's Conservative government (1970–74) and the Labour government, headed first by Harold Wilson (1974–76) and then by Jim Callaghan (1976–79), found themselves having to grapple with high inflation, high unemployment, slow economic growth and a weak balance of payments posing risks to the value of the pound. Their problems were made all the more difficult by a deterioration in the international economy caused by the breakdown in 1972 of the Bretton Woods system of semi-fixed exchange rates and the quadrupling of oil prices in 1973.

The ending of the Bretton Woods system of semi-fixed exchange rates was initially seen as giving governments greater freedom to boost output and employment through exchange rate depreciation, and thereby put an end to the stop–go cycles of previous years. But exchange rate depreciation meant higher import prices, and if wage increases followed, the immediate gain in competitiveness was lost and inflation could take off. The Bretton Woods system had acted as a powerful counter-inflation financial discipline and anchor for prices. Without the need to maintain the exchange rate at a fixed level, it became too easy and too tempting for governments to try to spend their way to lower unemployment and faster economic growth at the expense of higher inflation. The experiment with monetarism was, in a way, an attempt to find an alternative counter-inflationary discipline and price anchor.

When unemployment was rising and prices were going up at the same time, the central prescription of Keynesian economics

– a budget deficit to avert recession – was no longer a solution. In one year, 1972, the Conservative government experimented with reflating demand in the belief that expanding output would increase productivity and make higher pay more affordable *without* igniting inflation. The resultant so-called 'Barber boom' did lead to improved output and reduced unemployment, but it also set off a new inflationary spiral. (The short-lived Truss government's Growth Plan and announcement of tax cuts in 2022 seems to have been based on a similar false rationale.)

That experiment having failed, the solution attempted by both Conservative and Labour governments was to rein back wage and salary increases through statutory or voluntary means – with a view to curbing inflation and finding space, within a given level of aggregate demand, for increased employment. The Conservatives attempted the statutory route. In the face of trade union opposition and strikes, the legislation had to be withdrawn. There followed the election of a new Labour government and a wages free-for-all: average earnings between August 1974 and July 1975 rose by 28 per cent, and prices increased by 26 per cent for the 12 months up to October of that year. The wage explosion was exacerbated by the Conservative government having agreed, under their prices and incomes policy, that earnings would be increased automatically to compensate fully for any increase in the rate of inflation above 7 per cent.

Faced with this inflation crisis, under a new Social Contract with the trade unions, the Labour government and unions agreed a voluntary arrangement whereby the unions would limit their pay demands over the coming pay round (1975/76) to just £6 per week per worker, or half the average increase for the previous year – whichever was higher. Although it entailed the government offering various budgetary concessions in return, which boosted the government's borrowing needs, it proved remarkably successful for wages and prices: average earnings growth in 1975/76 was cut in half, and by the summer of 1976, price inflation was down to around 15 per cent.

But this inflation rate was still roughly double the average of that of the UK's main competitors. We were spending substantially more abroad than we were earning from abroad (that is, the balance of payments on current account was in substantial deficit), and this was being funded to a large extent by the Bank of England drawing down its foreign exchange reserves. The value of sterling had earlier been bolstered by the fact that many oil producers remained within the sterling system, and had added to their sterling balances after oil prices quadrupled in 1973. By the spring of 1976, the value of sterling was under severe downward pressure – partly because of the current account deficit, and partly because several of the oil producers (Nigeria in particular) started cashing in their sterling balances for dollars.

When it became known that some in the Treasury favoured a lower exchange rate in order to boost exports and deter imports, the Bank of England feared an imminent sterling collapse, which it would be unable to prevent owing to its declining foreign exchange reserves. The only short-term solution was large-scale borrowing from overseas. Yet the Bank's and the government's access to overseas borrowing was severely limited. The only likely source was the International Monetary Fund (IMF). But this would involve bowing to the IMF's requirements, which, for political reasons, the government was desperate to avoid.

IMF to the rescue

This was the situation when I joined Permanent Secretary Douglas Wass's small Central Policy Unit in July 1976. Within weeks of my arrival, Chancellor of the Exchequer Denis Healey introduced a mini-budget consisting of spending cuts and tax increases for the following fiscal year (1977/78) amounting to £1.5 billion in total, the equivalent of 1 per cent of GDP. It was hoped that this would be sufficient to restore confidence, but it did not. Interest rates were raised, but this provided only temporary relief. Finally, after fraught exchanges within the Cabinet, where a minority led by Tony Benn[1] tried to insist that recourse to the IMF must be avoided at all costs, the government agreed to seek an IMF loan. In December, the IMF agreed a loan of US$3.9 billion, the largest loan ever made to one of its members up until that date.

In return, Healey had to agree a further £1 billion of spending cuts for 1977/78; and in line with the IMF's normal methodology, he also had to agree limits on domestic credit expansion (DCE) for 1977/78 and 1978/79 – that is to say, lending by the banks to the private sector and to the government.

It had been a dangerous few months, and even at my level, which was quite distant from the actual decision making, I shared the palpable relief at the Treasury that the loan had been secured. It was not just the extra foreign currency that was now available to bolster the reserves; it was also the further £1 billion fiscal adjustment that was necessary to improve the external balance, but which almost certainly could not have been achieved without the IMF's insistence, as well as the confidence-boosting effect of the IMF's imprimatur.

In economic terms, the IMF package was a success. Helped by the arrival of North Sea oil, the period up until the autumn of 1978 was a time of relative stability for sterling, with lower inflation and improving economic growth. Only half of the IMF loan was actually drawn. Along with actions to improve control over public spending (the introduction of cash limits mentioned in Chapter 4) and public borrowing, the IMF's insistence on targets for DCE helped to restore confidence in the financial markets.

The other key contributory factor was the initial success of the Social Contract, which – until the autumn of 1978 – saw the trade unions' continued cooperation on pay. In his formal letter applying for the IMF loan, Healey called the Social Contract one of the two 'pillars' on which his strategy was based. He was surely right to imply that, without it, his strategy would have had far less chance of success. James Tobin and all the other eminent economists, who believed that some kind of incomes policy was needed in a world of powerful trade unions, would have agreed. (The other 'pillar' was the government's so-called Industrial Strategy, which, in practice, amounted to rather little, and would be dropped by the Thatcher government.[2])

From a political standpoint, the IMF loan was widely seen as a humiliation for the government. It became such a familiar and long-standing trope among Labour's critics that it was arguably one factor that made Gordon Brown especially cautious two decades later, in his early years as chancellor.

Monetarist ideas and monetary targets

In what respect, if any, did monetarist ideas feature in the Labour government's economic policies in the mid to late 1970s, or indeed earlier, with the Heath government?

We would not be asking such a question about a government today, because it is the Bank of England that decides on the conduct of monetary policy, and not the government. Until the Bank became operationally independent in 1997, all important decisions on the conduct of monetary policy were taken by the chancellor of the exchequer, and usually only after they had sought and obtained the approval of the prime minister. (This is why monetary policy would take up such a significant portion of Mrs Thatcher's time.) Such decisions included those pertaining to the setting of interest rates, the sale of government debt, the setting of monetary targets and control mechanisms for achieving them, and any quantitative controls over bank lending. It was the Bank of England's job to execute the policy. But the Bank also played a key role in advising the chancellor on all these matters, and did so normally through the Treasury's monetary policy group, of which, between 1983 and 1985, I was the head. The Treasury permanent secretary was also heavily involved in advising on monetary policy matters.

One of the main criticisms from the monetarists, including Mrs Thatcher herself, was that the Heath government of the early 1970s, and the Labour predecessor of the late 1960s, had taken little or no interest in the money supply and in monetary growth. As they saw it, the policy had been to keep interest rates as low as possible for the sake of investment, subject to maintaining the value of the pound, and hang the consequences for the growth of the money supply.

This was, in fact, not entirely true.[3] In 1967, when the Labour government borrowed US$1.4 billion from the IMF, the then chancellor of the exchequer, Jim Callaghan, stated publicly that he expected 'domestic credit expansion (DCE) to be sufficiently limited that the present growth of the money supply will be less in 1968 than the present estimate for 1967'.[4] In 1969, at the time of further IMF borrowing, the Treasury published a numerical ceiling for DCE. This, together with a quantified target for the balance of payments, implied a target for M3 growth.

Admittedly, these objectives for monetary growth were at the behest of the IMF. Nonetheless, they went hand in hand with a growing interest, within the Treasury and the Bank of England, in the money supply as a potential instrument for combating inflation. This interest was stimulated by new research from Bank of England economists, which concluded that in the 1950s and 1960s velocity of circulation had been quite stable, and that there was some weak evidence of causation from money supply to money GDP.[5] Greater emphasis started to be placed on the money supply in determining the level of interest rates, and in 1972 the Treasury and the Bank decided – this time without any pushing from the IMF – to adopt a quantitative, but unpublished, monetary target. They did the same again in 1973.

These targets, however, proved to be of little worth as monetary growth in those two years ran amok owing to the decontrol of bank lending under the new Competition and Credit Control policy (see Chapter 4). This unexpected surge in lending had not been factored into the targets that had been set. And while Prime Minister Heath had signed up to the targets, he resisted calls from his chancellor for interest hikes to curb the monetary expansion.

This experience, and the accompanying evidence that velocity was far less stable than the Bank's economists had suggested, made both the Bank and the Treasury more cautious about the usefulness of monetary targets. And yet, in both institutions, there was an acceptance that monetary growth could not be ignored in quite the same way it had been in the Keynesian heyday.

In 1974, after he became chancellor of the exchequer, Denis Healey was persuaded that excessive monetary expansion had to be avoided. From his first budget speech in March 1974 to his last in April 1978, we always find the money supply mentioned and the need for it to be kept under control, and year by year, there is a hardening of the language.

In his 1975 budget speech, he said: 'I have aimed to keep the rate of monetary expansion firmly under control and avoid a repetition of the experience of 1972 and 1973 when excessive monetary growth contributed substantially to inflationary pressures.'[6]

Announcing his mini-budget in July 1976, Healey announced a *projection* for the money supply of 12 per cent for the financial year. This was quickly interpreted in the markets as a *target*. City economist Tim Congdon described the announcement as a 'major innovation of policy'.[7]

In his 1977 budget speech, Healey announced an explicit target for the money supply of 11–13 per cent for the coming financial year, and in his 1978 budget speech a target of 10–12 per cent for 1978/79. Having a range for the target rather than a single percentage point was intended to allow for the known uncertainties regarding velocity of circulation and ability to control the money supply.

Healey's actions and words from that period certainly imply that he attached at least some importance to controlling the money supply. Quite how important in reality is debatable. In his memoirs he wrote: 'I never accepted Friedman's theories. ... I decided to publish monetary targets largely to placate the financial markets.'[8]

Whatever Healey might have thought about monetarist theory, he certainly recognised the growing importance that the financial markets attached to movements in the money supply. The publication of monetary targets, backed by action to stay within them, was almost certainly a factor in helping to make a success of the IMF loan. But, unlike his Conservative successor Geoffrey Howe, Healey never accepted that there was a close causal connection between monetary expansion and inflation. For him the key factor behind price inflation was wage increases not matched by productivity improvements, for which the only solution – short of allowing unemployment to increase to an unacceptably high level – was an effective incomes policy. His words and actions to restrain money expansion were really to satisfy the IMF and the increasingly monetarist-leaning financial markets.[9]

On the whole, Treasury officials went along with Healey's scepticism, although not quite to the same degree. By contrast, the Bank of England – although with some notable individual exceptions[10] – was somewhat more inclined in the direction of monetarist thinking. The Bank's views on monetary targets, and on monetary policy more generally at around this time, are well set out in Governor Gordon Richardson's 1978 Mais Lecture.[11]

The Bank was far from endorsing the neat and exclusive link between money and prices propounded by Friedman and his followers in the UK, but accepted that a link existed, that 'monetary targets have an important place to play in the relevant armoury' in combating inflation, and that 'they ... provide the framework of stability within which other policy objectives can be more easily achieved'.[12] Richardson, in effect, aligned himself with the 'practical monetarism' of Paul Volcker.

The category of money supply chosen for the published 'projection' in July 1976 and for the targets thereafter was a broad definition, namely M3 – consisting of notes and coins in circulation plus current and savings accounts with banks. (It was later changed to a slightly narrower category called sterling M3 [£M3], which excluded deposits of overseas holders of sterling in UK banks.) M3 seemed the most sensible category for targeting because:

- It meant continuity with the definition the Bank of England had used for its internal targets
- The acceleration of inflation in the early 1970s had been matched more closely by M3 than by M1
- M3 was a better indicator than M1 or M0 of society's capacity to spend
- There was a practical linkage between M3 and bank lending to the private sector and to the government (the so-called 'credit counterparts'), which the government needed to monitor and keep under control if the monetary targets were to be met.[13]

These considerations in favour of M3 were regarded as outweighing the one disadvantage compared with the narrower aggregate M1 – namely that it was less responsive to interest rate changes. Thus, whereas an increase in interest rates tends to make people economise in their holdings of cash and non-interest-bearing bank deposits, thereby having the effect of reducing M1 and M0, the effect is more muted in respect of M3 because the latter is composed partly of interest-bearing deposits. This makes M3 harder to control using interest rates, as we would find out with a vengeance in 1979 and 1980.

The decision to publish a monetary target, rather than have a target purely for internal purposes within the Bank of England and the Treasury, was not without controversy. Prior to 1976, the Bank had been opposed to published targets. But now it had come round to publication. The Bank felt this would bolster market confidence at a time when it was sorely needed, and it would put pressure on the Treasury to limit public sector borrowing.[14]

The Treasury was less sure about the merits of publication. At first, Douglas Wass was strongly opposed. The crux of the problem for him was that, if the target was made public, the financial markets would expect the government to take whatever action was needed to meet it. He worried that the figure chosen for the target might be wrong. In July 1976, the annual inflation rate was still in the high teens, whereas M3 had been growing relatively slowly, at an annual rate of well under 12 per cent. This meant that velocity of circulation, after falling in the early 1970s, had been rising rather fast (see Figure A6 in the Appendix). But would velocity now stabilise or continue to rise? It was all too uncertain. A monetary target for the coming year of 12 per cent − if it was going to be adhered to − might turn out to be too restrictive and push the economy once more into recession.

Second, if there turned out to be significant deviation from the target number, how should the Treasury and the Bank respond? The tools for bringing the money supply back on track in the short term were limited to interest rate changes and sales of public debt, plus the scheme that had been in place since 1973 to control bank lending, called the 'corset'.[15] These, taken together, could not be relied on to bring about swift adjustments to the money supply unless the change in interest rates was substantial.

Third, would the Treasury and the Bank necessarily *wish* to bring the money expansion back to the target? This would depend on one's interpretation of the deviation from target and what was happening to other economic variables such as the rate of inflation and the exchange rate. A published target would limit the government's discretion.

In short, Wass accepted that monetary targets were probably useful if they were purely internal, but they were potentially disruptive and dangerous if made public.

The views of the monetarists outside government were precisely the opposite of this. They discounted concerns about the instability of velocity and that the target might be 'wrong'. They favoured publication of a target precisely because it *would* reduce the Treasury and the Bank's ability to ignore it. They also felt – and this view was shared to some extent more widely – that published targets for the money supply could be a useful tool for influencing inflationary expectations in wage negotiations.

In the end, Wass persuaded himself, despite his misgivings, that publication was the right thing to do. In an internal memo shortly before the July 1976 announcement, he wrote of the confidence-raising value of a published target that 'could make all the difference between success and failure. Since we cannot afford failure, we must have a target'.[16]

The announcement of monetary targets under Labour marked a distinct up-tick in the shift in the direction of monetarism. But we were still a long way from the harder, more explicit monetarism that characterised the first years of Mrs Thatcher's premiership. Monetary policy, including a target for the money supply, was not yet the main instrument for combating inflation: under Labour, the main instrument remained incomes policy.

Monetary developments between 1976/77 and 1978/79 turned out to be relatively benign, with £M3 expanding within or very close to its target range in each of the three years. This was helped by the effective containment of government borrowing and strong sales of public debt outside the banking system.

One notable action to restrain monetary growth was the decision in October 1977, following upward pressure on the pound, for the Bank of England *not* to intervene in the foreign exchange market to prevent the pound from rising further. If the Bank had bought foreign exchange from the market in return for sterling, this would have added to £M3. This was controversial because – although it helped to keep monetary growth on track – it meant an unwelcome further worsening of the UK's export competitiveness. Thus, the containment of monetary growth was given clear precedence over other considerations. The same issue would arise, and with greater consequence, in 1980 when, in the name of sticking to the monetary target, action was again not taken to limit the rise of sterling.

In summary, in the decade or so prior to Mrs Thatcher's government, the money supply as an indicator and possible cause of inflation was by no means ignored. Controlling its expansion started to become one of the weapons for keeping inflation under control, especially after the IMF loan in 1976. The publication of monetary targets and more or less success in achieving them played a modest part in the improved performance of the economy in 1977 and 1978. But for both Labour and the Conservatives in the earlier part of the decade, monetary policy and monetary targets were very much subsidiary to incomes policy in their fight to control inflation. They did not believe that curbing monetary growth alone would be enough to keep inflation under control. Both governments relied heavily on incomes policy in their fight against inflation. When the Conservative incomes policy had broken down, inflation took off. If Labour's Social Contract with the trade unions was to break down, it seemed all too likely that inflation would also accelerate once more.

And this is exactly what happened. During the winter of 1978/79 the Social Contract broke down, and despite monetary growth having stayed more or less in line with the targets set, wage inflation, and then price inflation, took off.

The Winter of Discontent

I was appointed private secretary to Jim Callaghan in October 1978, and my seven months working for him were dominated by the breakdown of the Social Contract.

After three years of accepting wage restraint, trade union leaders had been led to understand that for the 1978/79 pay round there would be a return to free collective bargaining. By this means, they hoped to achieve rising real wages again. Callaghan, however, had other ideas. He was determined that inflation should come down to low single figures before the next general election, and this, in his view, required a further phase of pay restraint. He and Healey proposed a figure of 5 per cent, even though the 12-monthly inflation rate was still running at over 7 per cent, with allowance for higher settlements if productivity improvements could be demonstrated.

This was too much for the unions. In July 1978 the Trades Union Congress (TUC) voted for a return to free collective bargaining. It said that a further year of incomes policy, especially with a percentage norm as low as 5 per cent, was undeliverable. In early September the TUC annual conference voted to reject the 5 per cent policy. The government, nonetheless, decided to proceed as if the trade unions would fall into line. In the public sector, the 5 per cent would be imposed as a maximum. In the private sector, the government would impose financial sanctions on companies that agreed pay settlements in excess of the 5 per cent, with a let-out for any productivity improvements they could demonstrate.

Callaghan further upset the trade unions, which were the Labour Party's main source of finance, by deciding to postpone the general election until 1979, October 1978 having been the month he had been expected to call one. With a non-existent majority in the House of Commons – the government at this point was relying informally on the votes of the minor parties – many, and not just the trade unions, felt the postponement was asking for trouble.

Trouble was not long in coming. In my first few weeks in post, I was the note-taker at a late evening meeting in the Cabinet Room between Callaghan and half of his Cabinet with a dozen trade union leaders. The proverbial beer and sandwiches were served, although I remember the trade minister, Peter Shore, asking for whisky, which I had to tell him wasn't available in Callaghan's puritanical set-up. There was an impasse. The union leaders said that if the government tried to impose the 5 per cent, their members would be likely to take matters into their own hands and take industrial action whether or not they (the leaders) recommended it.

On 17 November 1978, workers at Ford plants across the country went on strike demanding a 40 per cent pay increase. An increase of 17 per cent was eventually agreed after a vote in the House of Commons forced the government to withdraw the threat of sanctions against Ford. The Social Contract and the 5 per cent norm were in tatters. After the Ford settlement, there was no way other companies in the private sector or workers in the public sector would accept anything close to 5 per cent.

Shortly before Christmas, David Basnett, the leader of the largest public service union and the union leader whom Callaghan respected more than any other, asked to see Callaghan on his own. Basnett warned him in the starkest terms that he had to change the policy immediately or else there would be industrial strife on the scale of 1973/74, and Labour would suffer the same fate in the upcoming general election as the Conservatives had in 1974.

Callaghan was adamant that he wouldn't change course. In this, he was encouraged by Healey. Healey was determined not to throw away what he had achieved for the economy since the 1976 IMF loan. An intellectual heavyweight, he saw the matter perhaps too much in intellectual terms: he believed that the unions would, in the end, accept the rationality of continued pay restraint, for the sake of their members and for the country. He was also a political bruiser and not averse to a fight with the unions. Callaghan, who knew the unions much better, was less optimistic. But he considered that, electorally, he had no alternative but to stick with the 5 per cent figure. If he allowed inflation to take off again, he would lose the upcoming general election.

Over Christmas and into the New Year there were increasing outbreaks of unofficial industrial action across the country, just as the union leaders had warned. Strikes or go-slows by ambulance drivers, cemetery workers, refuse collectors and lorry drivers, and secondary picketing at oil refineries, all made daily headlines. My job was to report to Callaghan each day on the deteriorating situation – about which little could be done short of changing the policy. The Department of Prices and Consumer Protection was tasked with reviewing pay settlements in the private sector as they came along, to check whether they could be said to conform to the policy on the basis of purported productivity improvements. The claimed-for productivity improvements were either insufficient or were more imagined than real, and in any case, the government didn't have the political will to penalise companies that contravened the policy.

The situation was made worse by two things. First, January 1979 turned out to be the third coldest month in the 20th century, and this led to widespread disruption in the transport sector, especially when local authority drivers refused to grit the roads. Callaghan came close to requesting Emergency Powers from Parliament so that he could order in the Army to clear the roads, bury the bodies and move oil from the refineries. He was dissuaded from going down this route on the grounds that it might provoke even more widespread industrial action, and there was a real question, too, as to whether – with no majority to count on – he would get Parliament's approval. Transport Secretary Bill Rodgers, who later defected to the Social Democratic Party (SDP), was incandescent at what he saw as Callaghan's weakness.

Second, Callaghan – who, over a lengthy political career, had built a reputation for shrewdness – lost his political touch. In the second week of January 1979, when the industrial and political situation had reached a dangerous point, and it would have been wiser if he had stayed in the UK, Callaghan left for a conference of the G4 leaders[17] in Guadeloupe. I sent him daily reports but he did not engage and it seemed he was clearly enjoying the sun, and – cossetted with his Foreign & Commonwealth Office (FCO) advisers – discussing issues far away from home. On arrival back at Heathrow, he ignored the advice of his press secretary and gave a disastrous press conference in which he effectively told the media to stop exaggerating the seriousness of the domestic situation. The next day, *The Sun* newspaper had as its headline, 'Crisis. What crisis?'

Reality quickly set in. Callaghan told me to call in the trade union leaders once again. This time he saw them on his own, with me as the only civil servant present, and without the presence of other ministers. The union leaders were unmovable. I have a vivid memory of Moss Evans, leader of the Transport and General Workers Union, banging his fist on the Cabinet Room table and saying: 'It's your job, Jim, to get inflation down to 2 per cent; it's my job to get 18 per cent for my members.' Callaghan turned to me as if to say: 'It's all over in that case.'

After the Road Haulage Association (RHA), with the government's acquiescence, agreed a settlement of 20 per cent in mid-January, the big question was, at what level would workers in the public sector be prepared to settle? The government's spending plans were predicated on wages and salaries rising by 5 per cent, but this was clearly now unrealistic. To drive home the point, on 22 January 1979 the public service unions called for a national

'Day of Action', and one-and-a-half million workers stayed at home. Rolling unofficial action continued through February – another exceptionally cold month – until early March, when the government established, under the chairmanship of Professor Hugh Clegg, the Standing Commission on Pay Comparability. The implicit understanding was that the Commission would recommend pay increases for public sector workers comparable to those in the private sector, and that the government would underwrite them.

Those first three months of 1979 were a sombre and scary time. The appalling weather, loss of essential services, conflict at the workplace, widespread lay-offs, patchy supplies of fuel and food – all these taken together spelt serious distress for millions of people. And on top of these, the government seemed no longer able to govern.

Callaghan had played a leading role ten years earlier, as a member of Harold Wilson's Cabinet, in blocking proposed legislation to reduce the power of the trade unions.[18] The legislation would have included compulsory balloting by unions before calling a strike, and an end to the 'closed shop', both of which would have made a significant difference. Having supported the unions in their opposition to these reforms, their withdrawal from the Social Contract, and the chaos that followed, were, for Callaghan, an especially bitter blow. Callaghan's critics said he got his just deserts because he had opposed the trade union reforms in 1969 in order to bolster union support for his own advancement in the Labour Party.

I remember only one light moment in those grim months. Early in the morning on New Year's Day, with several feet of snow and blocked roads across the country, the telephone switchboard at Chequers patched me into a call between Callaghan and Denis Howell, who, besides being Minister for Sport, also had the Alice in Wonderland title of 'Minister for Snow'. The call went like this:

Callaghan: Good morning, Denis. I invite you to open
                  your curtains, see what is outside, and advise
                  me what is to be done.

[After a long minute's silence and the swishing of curtains]

| Howell: | Prime Minister, I will ask my civil servants to let you have a report by lunchtime. |
| Callaghan: | I thought that is what you would say. Good day to you. |

It came as no surprise when, on 28 March 1979, on a motion of no-confidence brought by the Conservatives, Callaghan was defeated in the House of Commons. He was forced to call a general election. This took place on 3 May, and the Labour Party lost with the largest swing between the two major parties in any general election since 1945.

Callaghan was a decent man (and a decent, if unsparing, boss) and in many respects an effective political leader – whose ten years in the four highest offices in the land, a record in itself, had been more successful than those of many of his predecessors. With Healey, he had brought the economy back from the brink in 1976 and achieved two years of relative economic stability – only to be brought down by over-ambition on pay restraint and by over-powerful trade unions, their excessive power partly the result of his own actions back in 1969.

I felt far from sure what would happen if the Conservatives won the election. I felt they would need the cooperation of the trade unions if, short of allowing unemployment to rise to extraordinary heights, they were to successfully tackle inflation. Yet, with Mrs Thatcher's uncompromising talk about curbing their power, the unions' cooperation seemed unlikely. As I sat in the Civil Service box next to the Speaker's Chair, and heard the result of the voting on 28 March, I was unimpressed by the whooping cheers of the Conservative back-benchers. They would soon find out just how difficult getting inflation down and keeping the economy on an even keel was going to be.

6

Mrs Thatcher and hard monetarism

Preparing for power

It is sometimes argued that the monetarism adopted by Mrs Thatcher when she came to power was no more than a continuum of the monetarist-leaning policies of the previous Labour government. However, this interpretation seriously understates what was, in fact, a step-change in the conduct of policy. It was a step-change because, under Labour, controlling the money supply had been conceived as merely supportive of the principal counter-inflation tool – namely prices and incomes policy – and the Labour chancellor, Denis Healey, didn't really believe in it anyway, and didn't take it particularly seriously. Under Mrs Thatcher, by contrast, at least for her first two years in power, controlling the money supply became virtually the single tool for curbing inflation and regulating the economy at macro level – almost entirely to the exclusion of other considerations or measures. Furthermore, she and her chancellor, Geoffrey Howe, were strong believers. This is why it is fair to characterise her early years in power as a period of hard monetarism before this gradually gave ground to a less doctrinaire, more pragmatic, monetarism, and by the mid-1980s was effectively abandoned.

How did this espousal of hard monetarism by Mrs Thatcher and others in her inner circle come about?

The first British politician of any note to espouse monetarism was the Conservative Enoch Powell. From the time he resigned in 1958 as financial secretary at the Treasury, along with his chancellor Peter Thorneycroft, over a relatively minor dispute about public spending, he began to advocate Milton Friedman's ideas on monetarism and the free market. Mrs Thatcher, elected to Parliament in 1959, was an open admirer – until in 1968 Powell made an incendiary speech on race (his infamous and racist 'rivers of blood' speech). She was then a silent admirer until, extraordinarily, prior to the February 1974 General Election, Powell recommended that voters should turn against his party and support Labour's Harold Wilson.

With Powell's reputation on the decline, the standard-bearer for Friedman's views within the Conservative Party became Keith Joseph. A serious intellectual like Powell, but without his oratorical flare, as an unhappy member of Ted Heath's Cabinet he became disillusioned with the then Keynesian approach to policy making. Joseph bought into Friedman's theories, and became convinced that monetarism, the free market and rolling back the public sector were the answer to the UK's rising inflation and sluggish economic growth. He was a great admirer of the libertarian philosopher and economist Friedrich Hayek. Joseph had a major influence on Mrs Thatcher's thinking, and especially after the Heath government fell in 1974. She considered Joseph her intellectual and policy mentor. On the face of it, he would have been a natural shadow chancellor of the exchequer, but she doubted his political skills, and went on to appoint the 'safer' Geoffrey Howe instead.

After becoming party leader in 1975, Mrs Thatcher asked Joseph to undertake a wide-ranging review of economic policy aimed at planning for the next Conservative government. Joseph delegated much of this work to an Economic Reconstruction Group (ERG) chaired by Geoffrey Howe, its members representing a wide range of views on economic policy.[1]

Howe was a cerebral lawyer – with a deceptive steeliness of character that would serve him well through the ups and downs of the Thatcher premiership, and that would surprise her when they eventually fell out over Europe. As chancellor of the exchequer, he was more comfortable dealing with fiscal policy (taxation and spending) than with monetary policy. Yet the latter was to become the biggest area of contention during his chancellorship, and in those days before the Bank of England became operationally independent, there was no ducking his responsibility for it.

The most technically proficient member of the ERG was Nigel Lawson, an Oxford-trained economist and former financial journalist, who succeeded Howe as chancellor of the exchequer in 1983. Like James Meade, he was a strong advocate of the view that government should stop trying to regulate the real economy so as to achieve certain objectives for output and employment, and should instead define their objectives in money terms. He was insistent that there must be a counter-inflation anchor for the economy. His first preference was a return to a fixed exchange rate, but if that wasn't feasible, his second best was monetary targets and control of the money supply, as advocated by the monetarists.[2]

Lawson, however, didn't get his way, and the ERG opted for monetarism instead. In 1977 it published the results of its work in a document entitled 'The right approach to the economy'. It advocated 'monetary targets, openly proclaimed and explained', and strict control and a gradual reduction in the rate of growth of the money supply.[3] It saw this as vital for enabling a return to 'realistic' collective wage bargaining. Monetary targets were to be the 'anchor' for influencing and managing inflationary expectations, and against which to monitor and control the growth of the money supply, and thereby to control inflation.

At the same time, the ERG document sounded a cautious note: 'This is not to say that one only has to follow the right money supply path and everything in the economy will become right. That would be to oversimplify a vastly complicated area of the financial and political system.'[4] It also said that, for wage bargaining to be realistic and non-inflationary, there would need to be 'patient explanation and patient efforts to foster the right climate for responsibility' and to explain how the 'monetary targets have been fixed and their implications for output and inflation'.[5] The long-standing National Economic Development Council (NEDC) could be used as the forum for this.

In proposing the latter, the ERG was influenced by Concerted Action, as practised in Germany, whereby each year the government, trade unions and employers agreed a general framework for responsible wage bargaining over the coming year. The Germans regarded Concerted Action as a necessary adjunct to strict monetary control.

Despite this apparent hankering for some kind of voluntary incomes policy, the general drift was clearly in a monetarist direction. The document contained no mention of the possible option of a return to a fixed exchange rate. However, a year later, in October 1978, this option was suddenly very much on the table as the Labour government had to decide whether or not to join the plan devised by Germany and France to establish a new system of managed exchange rates within the European Community, the European Exchange Rate Mechanism (ERM). If the UK was to join, this would involve sterling being linked to a basket of European currencies, with a commitment to keep the exchange rate within a band of up to 6 per cent on either side of an agreed central rate – and the possibility, if absolutely necessary, of changing this rate with the agreement of the ERM partners. There would be a short-term financing facility, in practical terms a German-financed fund, to help countries if their currencies reached the margin of their band.[6]

The Shadow Cabinet had to decide what its position should be. At a meeting on 27 October 1978 chaired by Howe, Lawson argued the case for the UK joining the ERM. This was on the grounds, first, that the UK would benefit from the greater exchange rate stability within Europe, and also in relation to the US dollar, which the Germans and the French hoped the ERM would deliver; and second, because the UK would essentially be operating to the tune of German domestic policy, which had been so successful in delivering low inflation in Germany. In other words, joining the ERM would provide the anti-inflationary anchor that had been missing since the demise of the Bretton Woods system in 1972. If the Labour government would decide to join ahead of the forthcoming general election, Lawson argued, this would be all for the better, since the UK's membership would then be a fait accompli and the inevitable controversy around joining would be Labour's problem. The Conservatives should try to nudge Labour in that direction.[7]

Lawson followed up with a personal letter to Mrs Thatcher along the same lines, and so did Howe – although in rather more guarded terms. One thing neither of them mentioned was that joining the ERM would not sit comfortably with a commitment to monetary targets. The ERM would be a system of managed rather than fixed rates, with a degree of flexibility because of the 6 per cent band. Yet any intervention by the Bank of England to stabilise sterling and keep it within its agreed band would increase or decrease the money supply – unless the intervention could in some way be neutralised while still making the intervention effective.

Judging from her marginal comments on Howe's supportive letter, Mrs Thatcher was not impressed.[8] From her discussions with her monetarist contacts, she knew that there was an inconsistency between having a managed exchange rate and having monetary targets. They had persuaded her that monetary targets and a floating exchange rate were better than a renewed attempt at a fixed or managed rate. Nor did the alleged advantages of being connected to German policy appeal. She decided that the Conservative Party should not take a public position on the ERM, one way or the other.

Time would tell as to how firmly she would stick to monetary targets in preference to managing the exchange rate, especially when it was under downward pressure. At heart, monetary targets and a floating exchange rate would undoubtedly remain her strong preference over a managed exchange rate right through her premiership; she devotes a whole chapter to this in her memoirs.[9] Yet, perhaps unsurprisingly, there proved to be inconsistencies in her thinking and in her actions. Thus, in 1985, when sterling was in danger of dropping to one pound against the dollar, she would order the Bank of England to intervene to prevent it from doing so, and would eventually, in her last year in office, agree to the UK joining the ERM. Although she favoured control of the money supply (and in particular, control of the monetary base) as the means above all else of controlling inflation, she would never be willing to give up political control of short-term interest rates. Nor would she be prepared altogether to let the exchange rate find its own level.

Returning to the ERM question in October 1978, the Labour government had, in fact, already decided earlier in that month that the UK would *not* be joining the ERM (it was due to start from 1 January 1979). Although personally in favour of joining, Prime Minister Callaghan feared the turmoil it would unleash in the Labour Party. When he announced the decision in early December in the House of Commons, Mrs Thatcher in her reply merely castigated him for presiding over an economy too weak to make it sensible to join.

After this flurry over possible ERM membership, Mrs Thatcher and the Conservative leadership were now on course to embrace the monetarist approach favoured by the ERG. Their manifesto in the run-up to the May 1979 General Election contained the following:

> To master inflation, proper monetary discipline is essential, with publicly stated targets for the rate of growth of the money supply. At the same time, a gradual reduction in the size of the Government's borrowing requirement is also vital. This Government's price controls have done nothing to prevent inflation, as is proved by the doubling of prices since they came to power. All the controls have achieved is a loss of jobs and a reduction in consumer choice.

Mrs Thatcher had not been directly involved in any of the ERG's discussions. However, she had been seeing a number of economists of a monetarist and free market persuasion on a fairly regular basis, which included some of the British monetarists mentioned in Chapter 4. She also had meetings with the extreme free-marketeer Friedrich Hayek. On a visit to the USA in December 1978, she met with Milton Friedman, and she also met the Swiss monetarist Karl Brunner and the American Alan Meltzer.[10]

As I would soon learn from my near daily interactions with her, she was very interested in ideas – especially when it came to the natural sciences, political theory, history and economics – and to a degree relatively unusual among her political colleagues. Although interested in economics, she nonetheless found it disappointing as a discipline. It wasn't the science many in the profession claimed it to be.[11] There seemed to be precious few economic 'truths', so that, when economists did address actual issues, their recommendations were too often bounded by qualifications. As a scientist, she should have regarded such caution as a strength and not as a weakness. Instead, she found it frustrating that economic theory, and economists' prescriptions, seemed subject to so much uncertainty. Too much of the debate among economists, in her view, was like 'angels dancing on a pin' and irrelevant to actual economic conditions. Too much in economics, whether in macro- or microeconomics, seemed to point to a larger state, to state interventions supposedly to correct market failure but which, in her opinion, more often made markets less efficient, and to less freedom and autonomy for the individual. All of these were antithetical to her political philosophy. She wasn't much interested in engaging with economists – whether in person or in their writings – if she believed they shared these state-interventionist tendencies.

One of the few economic truths, which for her did seem to exist, was the theory of monetarism and its approach to combating inflation.

Mrs Thatcher had a passion for sound money that was deeply felt and entirely authentic. It grew, first of all, from her knowledge, growing up as a teenager in the 1930s, of the catastrophic Weimar Republic hyperinflation and its role in Hitler's rise to power. It arose from the damage she believed inflation was doing in the UK – for individuals and families, for investor confidence, and for trust in government. She thought it was morally wrong for people to have the real value of their savings eroded by inflation, and likewise for people on fixed incomes; morally wrong that clever bankers could benefit from it (although she didn't seem to mind home owners doing so); and morally wrong for governments to gain from inflation through the erosion of the real value of the national debt, to the disadvantage of the holders of that debt. Maintaining a stable currency was one of the first and foremost duties of government, and that is what the vast majority of people expected of government.

She didn't mind *how* inflation was going to be brought down and vanquished. The key thing was that it *should* be, and in an efficient and relatively costless manner. Although a loyal member of Heath's Cabinet, she had had serious reservations about the prices and incomes policies that he had tried to operate, and these reservations, in her mind, were fully borne out by the collapse of these policies and then again by the breakdown of the Callaghan/Healey incomes policy in 1978/79. Monetarism seemed to offer a real alternative, and it appealed to her because it did not require the cooperation of the trade unions or incomes policy in any form.

Monetarism came naturally to her. Its key nostrum – the link between money supply and prices – seemed obvious. Its simplicity appealed to her; it appeared to be relatively painless in its application (although, of course, it wouldn't prove to be); and as a scientist, she liked it because of its allegedly scientific basis. Friedman called it a 'scientific doctrine', like the law of gravity.[12] In a speech to the Press Association, she repeated the analogy. But ultimately, it was not its alleged scientific basis that appealed to her. She was really a monetarist by conviction: monetarism just had to be true.

There was one idea closely associated with monetarism that Mrs Thatcher never accepted, or at least said she didn't. This was the concept of the natural rate of unemployment (see Chapter 3 and also the Glossary). She went on the record several times saying she didn't believe in it. This was odd, given its Friedmanite provenance, when one of the main points of her trade union reforms was to reduce the natural rate of unemployment, and thereby allow the economy to run at a higher level without igniting inflation. Saying she didn't believe in it may have been because she felt that saying she *did* believe in it would be represented by her opponents as indifference to unemployment.[13]

In most respects, however, monetarism came perhaps *too* naturally to her because it made her less open to considering and understanding its possible theoretical and empirical shortcomings: that is to say, the issues around the best definition of money, variability of velocity, the responsiveness of the money supply to interest rate changes, the exact causation between the money supply and inflation, the effect of money supply changes on output, and so on. It also has to be said that the monetarists she met, in their enthusiasm to impress her with their views, too often skated over these questions or failed to mention them at all, and were unduly optimistic about monetarism's efficacy. If she had been exposed to a wider range of views, she would have perhaps appreciated that the application of monetarism was going to be more complicated and riskier than she imagined.

Because she was so convinced of the rightness of monetarism, it was the detail rather than these more fundamental questions that she usually preferred to discuss.[14]

The monetarist economist with the clearest and most agile mind with whom she was in contact was Alan Walters. He was spiritedly optimistic that if the strategy was properly pursued, all would eventually be well. She also liked and admired him personally for his working-class background and his lack of respect for rank. In Opposition, she would see him on his occasional visits from the USA, where he worked at the World Bank and at Johns Hopkins University. In January 1981 he became her official economic adviser at 10 Downing Street.

Until the general election, the only regular contact that she had with any professional economist was with Adam Ridley. Ridley had worked in the Treasury and the Department of Economic Affairs under Labour in the 1960s, and then for Heath's Central Policy Review Staff, after which he became the top economist in the Conservative Research Department. He supported the turn towards monetarism, but his support was by no means unqualified, and his views on economic policy more generally were too centrist and nuanced for Mrs Thatcher. Denis Thatcher told John Hoskyns that he would get the job of head of the Downing Street Policy Unit because Ridley 'cannot see the wood for the trees'.[15]

In public, on monetarism and on economic strategy in general, Mrs Thatcher kept her cards close to her chest. She preferred to criticise Labour's failures and its humiliation before the International Monetary Fund (IMF) and in dealing with the trade unions, rather than say what she would do if elected prime minister.

It was clear that the incoming Conservative government would adopt a monetarist approach. What was less clear was the form it would take, and the extent to which Mrs Thatcher would be personally involved.

First days in power and core beliefs

After her decisive election victory on 3 May 1979, and after entering 10 Downing Street the following day, Mrs Thatcher immediately got to work reading the voluminous briefing books that had been prepared for her. At my first session with her, she took out three books from a little brown suitcase and said she'd like me to read them.

She thought, not unreasonably, that, after working at the heart of the Labour administration, if I was to work for her, I needed some re-education. The first book was Friedrich Hayek's wide-ranging polemic against socialism, *The Road to Serfdom*;[16] the second was a book by the City economist Tim Congdon;[17] and the third was *The Revolt of the Masses* by the Spanish political philosopher José Ortega y Gasset.[18] She also told me to read up on the American economist Arthur Laffer.

I was hazy on her economic and political beliefs, and her reading suggestions gave me an early introduction to some of her thinking. She admired Hayek as a political theorist and philosopher, and would see him on several occasions for one-to-one meetings when she was prime minister. His thinking helped drive her passion for freedom and individualism, for free enterprise and a smaller state. But his views on macroeconomic policy were too extreme, even for her: he was opposed to both Keynes's *and* Friedman's macroeconomics because he believed governments should leave the economy at macro level to look after itself. Even attempting to regulate the money supply was too much for him. In an interview in 1984, he said: 'Has monetary policy ever done any good? I don't think it has. I think it has done only harm'; and, echoing the 1958 Radcliffe Committee (see Chapter 3), he said: 'To believe there is a measurable magnitude [of the money supply] that you can keep constant with beneficial effects is completely wrong.'[19]

Laffer had the dubious reputation of being Ronald Reagan's favourite economist. His famous Laffer curve purported to demonstrate how raising the tax rate, when tax rates were already high, would reduce rather than increase government revenue. Whether this was of any relevance to the UK, except quite possibly in respect of the highest income tax band (which had a top rate of 83 per cent), was questionable to say the least. Congdon's book was a simplified introduction to monetarism on which she correctly judged I needed some training.

Ortega y Gasset's book, an account of how the power of the masses in a democratic state, for good or bad, cannot be ignored, was a curiosity. Perhaps it was a reminder to herself and for me that, having been elected partly on a populist platform, she had to avoid giving way to populist policies at the expense of long-term growth and stability. Or was it to remind herself that she would need to offer populist giveaways if she was to remain in power – for example, the sale of local authority-owned homes?

An early surprise – for me at least – was my discovering a few days after the election that she was not going to have an economic adviser on her staff. Adam Ridley had been widely expected to take on this role, but it was not to be. He did spend a couple of days at 10 Downing Street, but then, without any explanation, he disappeared to the Treasury, where he was to serve with distinction for the next five years as economic adviser to Geoffrey Howe and to Howe's successor, Nigel Lawson. It seemed Mrs Thatcher didn't want an economic adviser who wasn't a fully paid-up monetarist. She would have liked to have brought in Alan Walters as her adviser, but he wasn't available. She made no effort to bring in any other economist onto her staff – which says something about her confidence in her own economic beliefs and in being able to handle economic issues on her own.

As a consequence, I was going to be her only staff member with formal training in economics. Yet my job was not, strictly speaking, to provide her with economic advice. I was classed as an administrator with the task of acting as her go-between with the Treasury, the other economic departments of government and the Bank of England. That, indeed, is how she saw my role. If anyone had told her that I had been trained at the two citadels of Keynesian economics, Cambridge and Yale, she might have had second thoughts about keeping me on. To the extent that I was familiar with monetarist theory, I was not impressed. I was at best a 'disbelieving monetarist', as Peter Middleton would have categorised me – someone who believed in monetarism only because the markets believed in it (see Chapter 4).

Mrs Thatcher brought in John Hoskyns to head her Policy Unit with Norman Strauss as his assistant, and also the businessman David Wolfson as senior adviser. But none of them had a background in economics. Hoskyns was a former soldier and successful businessman; Strauss was a marketing expert; Wolfson came in from his family's retail business.

Hoskyns and Strauss had worked on a project for Keith Joseph called 'Stepping Stones'.[20] This laid out a strategy for a Conservative government over ten years. Its main features consisted of stabilising the economy (oddly, they talked about the need for a stable currency, but made no mention of the money supply); shifting the burden of tax from income to spending; deregulation to help the private sector; curbing public spending; reforming the public sector; using the revenue from North Sea oil to reduce the public sector borrowing requirement (PSBR) so as to keep interest rates low; and above all, curbing the power of the trade unions and taking them on as and when necessary. They wrote: 'Avoiding confrontation with the unions is not an available option.' Their views and advice on the trade unions and on public sector reform were what interested and influenced Mrs Thatcher most. But once in office she disliked Hoskyns's soldierly style and what she saw as his lack of political awareness. He thought she didn't understand the concept of strategy and that she was a poor manager of people – by which he meant her Cabinet colleagues, and probably himself. He left in frustration after three years.[21]

Working with Mrs Thatcher

Mrs Thatcher and I got on well from day one. I was competent at doing all the basic things that private secretaries were expected to do, and I was good at anticipating and interpreting her views, but there was also a strong chemistry between us, which made working for her both easy and enjoyable. I was her committed, hard-working servant. I knew instinctively how far I could go in expressing my views without making her feel I was overstepping the mark as a civil servant. She was a kind and generous boss, regularly inviting me to share supper or a drink with her and Denis in her flat, and after I left Downing Street, inviting me and my family to Chequers. In two-and-a-half years, she never once spoke out in irritation or anger against me.

The closeness of our relationship surprised me then and it surprises me to this day. In many ways our attitudes were different. I believed in the power of government to do good – something I had grown up to believe in – and it had been enhanced by my study of economics. She believed in strong government, but she also believed that governments were easily capable of doing harm.

She attached supreme importance to the individual and the family. She once told an interviewer that there was no such thing as society. I certainly didn't agree with the latter; having lived and worked abroad in some very poor countries, I perhaps had a greater sense of our common humanity and interconnectedness than she did.

She was deeply patriotic, and not greatly interested in the world outside the UK except insofar as it affected British interests for better or for worse. I was intrigued by and proud of my hybrid ancestry – English, Anglo-Irish, Canadian, German and Huguenot French – and my birthplace in Egypt. Theresa May would have called me a 'citizen from nowhere'.[22] I was intensely interested in world affairs and in the problems of the developing countries, and in the making of a better world for all. Yet I, too, was patriotic, especially in my support for England's cricket and rugby teams. I was committed as a public servant to doing my very best for the UK.

Mrs Thatcher gave higher priority to bringing inflation down than to holding down unemployment (although to be fair, she didn't believe there was really a choice between the two). I believed that, over the short run at least, there was a choice, and that unemployment was the greater social evil. I found it hard to accept her strong adherence to monetarist doctrine. As the 'good' civil servant, however, I did my best to suppress my differences.

I would soon come to admire her extraordinary self-belief; her relentless drive and effort; her physical and mental resilience; her firmness of purpose in the face of criticism; her courage in transcending expedience in favour of principle and what she believed was right; her personal integrity and commitment to high standards in public life; her demonstration, for the first time in the UK, that almost anything was possible for a woman in elective public life. She was quintessentially a politician, as the former Labour Prime Minister Clement Attlee would have described her, who lived *for* public service, as opposed to one who lived *off* politics. She understood that big changes were needed in the UK if the country's relative decline was to be arrested, and she was determined to make these changes. While my economics training had tended to focus on market imperfections and failures, after witnessing the failure of state planning and anti-market interventions in India, and on a lesser scale in the UK, I had a sneaking admiration for her almost messianic belief in the virtues of free markets and private enterprise.

It was these qualities and beliefs that would, in due course, make possible, with the outstanding and indispensable support of Geoffrey Howe and then, even more so, of Nigel Lawson, the many important economic policy achievements of her premiership, which, by the 1990s and early 2000s, would put an end to the UK's relative economic decline vis-à-vis our main competitors. Most notably:

- For all the adverse consequences of the monetarist strategy, putting an end to the idea that the government – through accommodative monetary and fiscal policies – could and should enable wage-driven cost increases to be translated into rising prices.
- The curbing of trade union power so that the economy could operate closer to its full supply capacity without reigniting inflation; so that managers could achieve improved working practices and efficiency; and so that, in the words of economic historian Nicholas Crafts, the unions would no longer have a 'veto on economic-policy reform',[23] or have the ability to bring down the government as they had done twice in the 1970s.
- The retreat from industrial subsidies and foreign exchange controls.
- Lower personal taxes and tax reform to incentivise investment, and personal effort and initiative, while at the same time stabilising the public finances.
- The liberalisation of services, especially in the financial sector.
- The championing of, and having the UK join, the European Single Market, alongside achieving a substantial rebate on the UK's contribution to the European Community budget.
- Closing down inefficient publicly owned businesses, and the privatisation of many others (although some of the privatisations were a good deal more successful than others).

But these achievements would mostly come later in Mrs Thatcher's premiership, and the same qualities and beliefs did not prevent her from making her biggest economic policy mistake at the start, namely the attempt to adopt unalloyed monetarism. Indeed, they arguably contributed to it – particularly her uncritical conviction that she was doing the right thing – and her firmness of purpose, which, in the case of monetarism, to her critics and most of her Cabinet colleagues, looked more like obduracy. Her belief in free markets was another contributing factor insofar as Friedman and other monetarists were mostly free-marketeers, and she assumed that there must be some logical connection, even though there wasn't.

Of course, there were other economic policy mistakes that bore Mrs Thatcher's imprint. One was the introduction of a new system of local authority taxation (the 'Poll Tax') from 1989. Another was her agreement, against her better judgement, and shortly before she resigned in 1990, that the UK should join the ERM. But the economic consequences of neither of these mistakes was on a par with the consequences of her attempt to implement monetarism – even though the political consequences for her personally in the case of the 'Poll Tax', and for the Conservative Party in the case of the ERM, may have been greater.

Mrs Thatcher made it clear early on that she would not be looking for advice from me except on points of interpretation and detail. The broad economic strategy was laid out in her party's election manifesto and, in contrast to foreign policy, on which she knew she was more accepting that she was a novice, she felt she knew what needed to be done and roughly how to do it. My job was to present her with the relevant information and help her to work with her chancellor, Geoffrey Howe, and her other economic ministers to make it all happen.

With hindsight, my admiration for her at a personal level, and my wish for her to succeed, made me work almost *too* hard on her behalf. I put to one side my reservations about monetarism and made myself see the world through her monetarist lens. Since monetarism was so central to her strategy, I really had no other option. But in retrospect, I have long felt that, within the confines of my role as a civil servant, I might have done more to push back on what Lawson would later call her 'primitivist monetarist' thinking.

For she really did believe that reducing the growth of the money supply would reduce the inflation rate more or less proportionately and would do so quickly; that any negative impact on output and employment would be small and short-lived; that a target range for the money supply, once chosen and announced, had to be adhered to irrespective of what was happening in the real economy; and that the government and the Bank of England together had the ability to control the growth of money within a few percentage points. She was attracted by monetarism because it seemed to offer not just a prescription for dealing with inflation, but also a new rationale for curbing public spending, curbing the role of the state, promoting the free market, and curbing the power of the trade unions. I should have done more to impress on her that monetarist theory had to be interpreted with great care and that, even in the minds of the more committed monetarist economists, the prescriptions it offered were neither simple nor likely to be painless.

It became evident early on that she would personally be taking a very hands-on approach to economic policy making. However, unlike the majority of 20th-century prime ministers, she had reached the top without ever having served in the Treasury or in any other ministerial (or shadow ministerial) post with substantial economic policy responsibilities. Her one Cabinet role had been in education and science.[24] It seemed doubly odd therefore that she had decided not to have an economic adviser on her staff. I would try to fill in the gap, although I did not have the up-to-date knowledge or expertise, or the time – given my administrative role – to provide the level of advice she really needed.[25] This would only change with the arrival of Alan Walters in 1981.

Ridley's non-appointment was an early sign that Mrs Thatcher wasn't much interested in views on the economy that might not be aligned with those of her monetarist devotees and with what she had picked up from them. This became even clearer later in the summer when she turned down a proposal from Ridley, supported by Howe, that she should appoint an Economic Advisers' Council modelled on the Council of Economic Advisers in the USA. She said she didn't want another quango, and that the focus should be on improving the quality of economic analysis within Whitehall.[26] What she really didn't want were discordant voices at close hand that might try to push her off her chosen course.

Key questions and early steps

There were very few, inside or outside government, who shared Mrs Thatcher's 'primitivist monetarist' views. Even for her monetarist devotees in the City and elsewhere, her views would probably seem a little over the top. Yet the fact that she held them, and held them so strongly, the fact that counter-inflation was at the top of her political agenda, and that she was so involved in the making of economic policy, meant that her views on monetarism would be of the greatest significance.

No one else in her Cabinet except Joseph – and not even her chancellor Howe – had the same strong belief in monetarism. In fact, only a minority really believed in it at all. The majority were prepared – in fact, they had no option – to let her and her chancellor try it out to see whether it worked. A small minority were very unhappy but found it difficult to speak out. The two leading critics were Deputy Foreign Secretary Ian Gilmour and Employment Secretary Jim Prior. Gilmour had less opportunity than Prior to argue his case within government. He was less than silent behind the scenes, and Mrs Thatcher would sack him in September 1981.

In the summer of 1980, Mrs Thatcher required all members of the Cabinet to attend a presentation by Terry Burns, appointed earlier that year as the Treasury's chief economic adviser, on the recently announced medium-term financial strategy (MTFS). Clearing up after the meeting, I found a slip of paper written by Gilmour and addressed to his ministerial boss, Foreign Secretary Lord Carrington, which read as follows: 'This is all mad, isn't it?'

Lawson later said it was regrettable that Howe's ERG hadn't given more attention to monetary policy in their work prior to the election.[27] Given the central role that monetary policy and monetarism were to play in the new government's economic strategy, he was right. In fact, the new ministerial team at the Treasury, and Mrs Thatcher herself, were alarmingly ill prepared. They had failed to give any serious thought to such key questions as:

- Which monetary aggregate should they target?
- What would be an appropriate single figure or range for the target, and over what time period?
- What mechanisms would they use to control the money supply and achieve the monetary targets?

On the first point, as the former Bank of England economist Anthony Hotson wrote, 'It was surprising that the incoming government professed to take Friedmanite monetarism seriously, but stuck with the previous government's leaky £M3 framework, using a monetary aggregate that palpably failed to exhibit a stable demand for money function'.[28] The other main contender, the narrow aggregate M1, hadn't exhibited a stable demand for money function either, but, as discussed in Chapter 4, it was easier to control through changes in interest rates. The narrower aggregate still, cash plus the banks' reserves with the Bank of England (M0), did seem to exhibit a reasonably stable relationship with money GDP, but intuitively the causal connection from M0 to money GDP was murky, to say the least. Given the way that cash was available to the banks on demand from the Bank of England, the causation was much more likely to be in the reverse.

As for the target numbers, the ERG had talked about a gradual reduction in the growth of the money supply, and this is what most of the British monetarists envisaged. But what did 'gradualism' mean when inflation was bound to be on the rise following the large pay settlements over the previous winter? How hard and how fast should the government attempt to clamp down on monetary growth and on inflation?

The ERG also hadn't given serious thought as to how the money supply was to be controlled. Mrs Thatcher, of course, wanted it to be controlled as efficiently and painlessly as possible. By this she meant keeping money growth within the chosen target range, and at the lowest interest rate possible. For obvious political reasons, she hated high interest rates because of their impact on mortgage holders. Most of her monetarist contacts – notably Pepper, Griffiths, Walters and Brunner – were in favour of monetary base control (MBC). It was hardly surprising therefore that she was also inclined to favour it.

No one doubted that the current arrangements for controlling £M3 were less than satisfactory. They involved a mixture of: controlling the level of government borrowing; funding the latter as much as possible by borrowing (selling government debt) from the public and from non-bank financial institutions; influencing the level of bank lending to the private sector; and influencing the demand for holding money. The tools for achieving these were essentially taxes and public spending for control of government borrowing, and interest rates for the selling of government debt, and for influencing bank lending and the demand for holding money, supplemented at least for the time being by the 'corset', the penalisation of the banks if their deposits were to grow at too fast a pace.

There were a number of problems with these arrangements. First of all, attempting to control lending by the banks to the private sector through the 'corset' was becoming increasingly ineffectual as other financial institutions simply took over the business: the £M3 figures might look better, but with little or no impact on underlying monetary conditions. Second, the government's borrowing requirement was hard to predict and bring under control in the short run because it was the difference between two very large numbers (total revenue and total expenditure). Third, while an increase in interest rates was supposed to reduce bank lending and the demand for money, and make government debt more attractive, the actual effect on each of these was also relatively unpredictable. In summary, with existing arrangements, as monetary growth in the early years of the Thatcher government would amply show, control of the money supply over the short term was extremely difficult.

Under a system of MBC, by contrast, the Bank of England would directly control M0 (also known as 'high-powered money') by reducing or increasing the amount of cash available on loan to them at the Bank's Base Rate, or through its open market operations.[29] In this way, they would be indirectly controlling not just the demand for credit and the *demand* for holding money, but also the *supply* of money. With less high-powered money, the banks would feel able to lend less and take in fewer deposits, and vice versa with more high-powered money. Crucially, the Bank would no longer automatically supply a bank with cash if it ran short; instead, the bank would either have to bid for cash in the money market, or quickly adjust its lending. There could be a mandatory requirement for the banks to hold a certain ratio of high-powered money to their deposits (a fixed 'money multiplier'). Alternatively, in a non-mandatory scheme, it could be left to each bank to decide on what was the right ratio for itself, and provided their chosen ratios remained constant, bank lending and deposit taking would likewise be indirectly controlled by the Bank of England.

MBC in either mandatory or non-mandatory form had the appearance of simplicity, but in fact it wasn't as simple or advantageous as it looked. Advocates of MBC such as Pepper claimed that interest rates on average would be lower because there would be greater confidence in the markets that the money supply and inflation were under proper control. On the other hand, there would be more interest rate volatility, and because the Bank of England would no longer be providing cash to the banks on demand, there would be greater risks for depositors and for the banking system if a bank ran into liquidity difficulties. Furthermore, in a mandatory scheme there was likely to be disintermediation (that is, credit creation moving outside the banking system), and in a non-mandatory scheme there was no certainty that banks would maintain a constant ratio of high-powered money to deposits.

The Bank of England was firmly opposed to MBC for these reasons. It also disliked the prospect of the institutional changes that it would involve. This would mean the demise of the Discount Houses, which, for the past 150 years, had acted as an intermediary between themselves and the banks. (In fact, for reasons unconnected to MBC, the Discount Houses disappeared during the 1990s, and the Bank of England from then on dealt directly with the banks – just as central banks already did in most countries.)[30]

In the Treasury, the only minister who fully understood the issues was Lawson. For similar reasons, he, too, was not in favour of MBC. He doubted Pepper's assertion that MBC would bring about lower interest rates on average. Switching to MBC would be a leap in the dark, both for the banks and for the Bank of England, and not worth the risk. Lawson convinced Howe that MBC was a bad idea and not worth pursuing. Some Treasury officials, however, not least because the existing system of monetary control could hardly be said to be working well, were prepared to look at MBC more positively. The most forward in this regard was Peter Middleton, the senior official in charge of monetary policy, who would succeed Douglas Wass as permanent secretary in 1983. He correctly felt that, given Mrs Thatcher's inclination in favour of MBC, to oppose it *tout court* would likely cast a pall over the Treasury's relations with her. He cleverly played a long game by overseeing the production of a mildly discouraging Green Paper on MBC, organising various consultations on it with economists and bankers outside government, and in due course proposing minor changes in the way the Bank of England operated, which could be said to be in preparation for a move to MBC if the government finally decided adopt it, but were, in fact, largely cosmetic.

Mrs Thatcher was to spend a startling amount of time on monetary policy.[31] She had numerous meetings on the subject with Howe and the Bank of England governor, Gordon Richardson, and on several occasions with Richardson on his own. The archives show that she nearly always read the many detailed papers on monetary policy and on MBC with great care.

In the end, a key point that held her back from insisting on moving to MBC was the fact that she and the Treasury would no longer decide on the level of interest rates: instead, interest rates would be market-driven, depending on the monetary target and the Bank of England's supply of cash to the system to make sure the target was met.

She also reluctantly realised that she didn't have the expertise or the experience to force her views on MBC on the Bank and the Treasury. I didn't have the expertise to help her much on the MBC question either, and until Walters's arrival in 1981, there was no one else at 10 Downing Street capable of helping her on this issue. Once there, Walters complained about the Bank's intransigence, but held back from pressing Mrs Thatcher to impose a decision in favour of MBC. For her part, as her preoccupation with the money supply figures began to wane, she gradually lost interest in the subject.

There was also the fundamental question, unresolved among academic economists, as to whether money supply growth was the main cause of inflation, or whether inflation caused the money supply to grow. The former, Friedmanite view was, of course, the reason for targeting the money supply. It seemed to be supported by the experience of the mid-1970s, when inflation had surged two years after a strong expansion of 'broad money' (M3). It was enough to persuade Treasury economists to add a monetarist-type equation, alongside their more orthodox Keynesian-type equations, to their forecasting model for the economy. Critics such as Nicholas Kaldor and Robert Neild argued that the apparent evidence of causal linkage from monetary growth to inflation in the early 1970s was merely coincidence, and that, in any case, the period in question was far too short on which to base a whole policy.

This was not a subject for polite conversation with Mrs Thatcher. Indeed, I never remember it being discussed in her presence. The causation from monetary growth to inflation was one of her core beliefs, and she expected everyone involved in the making of monetary policy to share it, whether or not they actually believed it. Many officials at the Treasury and the Bank of England did not, but had no option but to go along with it. I was in that position too.

In considering these issues, Mrs Thatcher and her monetarist colleagues would have done well to have looked at the experience of other countries with monetary targets. It was a very mixed picture. Even in Switzerland and Germany, which were held up as paragons of monetary discipline, the monetary authorities had shown considerable flexibility in the way they operated – in the case of Switzerland, actually moving at one stage from targeting the money supply to targeting the exchange rate.[32]

Once in office, there was no time for a root-and-branch discussion of these questions because, within a month, there would have to be a budget, and Howe would have to announce his plans for the money supply. Officials in the Treasury needed to win the confidence of the new ministers, and had to bury their doubts. For the sake of continuity, Howe decided to carry on with £M3 as the target variable. Having inherited from Labour a monetary target range of 8–12 per cent for the year up to October 1979, he decided to opt for a target range of 7–11 per cent (at an annual rate) for the nine months to March 1980. With £M3 by now growing at an annual rate of around 14 per cent and inflation on the rise on account of the previous winter's pay settlements, rising oil prices and a near doubling of the VAT rate (see below), the only possible economic rationale for this lowering of the target range was that he wanted to hit inflationary expectations hard and fast, even if it meant a sharp squeeze on the real economy and increased unemployment. In reality, the choice of a lower target range was mainly political and to satisfy the markets. To show that it was serious about getting inflation down, the government had to have a target that was lower than Labour's.

This was a critical decision, the import of which neither Howe nor Mrs Thatcher fully appreciated. If they had, they would have discussed it, and they did not. The one minister who did understand it was Lawson, who had been appointed financial secretary at the Treasury (a non-Cabinet role). He understood that the target would be very tough to meet, but he went along with it because, as he put in his memoirs, he believed that 'some degree of shock treatment was essential if inflationary expectations were to be wrenched down ... [though I] wasn't quite sure how far Geoffrey recognized this [shock treatment]'.[33]

While the chosen target range might suggest gradualism, the implied impact – if the target was adhered to – was going to be very far from the gradualism recommended by the ERG. What no one knew, although we should have been more aware of the possibility, was that velocity was going to peak in early 1980 and then steadily decline – making the monetary target even harder to achieve, and requiring even tighter monetary conditions in any serious attempt to stay within the target.

1979 budget

Howe unveiled his first budget on 6 June. He discussed it in considerable detail with Mrs Thatcher. The two most important issues for her were the planned level of government borrowing, and his proposal to increase the basic rate of VAT from 8 per cent to 15 per cent. Despite mounting pressures owing to higher pay bills in the public services and higher losses in the nationalised industries, they were both determined to prevent any increase in government borrowing. They agreed a number for the PSBR, which Treasury forecasters optimistically said would be consistent with reduced monetary growth.

In the Conservative Party's manifesto, they had committed to reducing income tax at all levels. But if government borrowing was to be held down, a near doubling of VAT would be necessary to pay for the income tax cuts. The Conservatives had been planning on a switch from direct to indirect taxes, which would include a rise in VAT – but nothing on such a scale. Mrs Thatcher was at first strongly opposed to this. I had advised her that the VAT increase would lead to a one-off increase of 3.5 per cent in consumer prices – thus giving an immediate spurt to the rate of inflation. In discussing the matter with Howe, she cautioned that it would be better to delay the income tax reduction: she cited Howe's predecessor from the early 1950s, R.A. (Rab) Butler, who had waited three years into his chancellorship before lowering the basic rate of income.

At their next meeting, Howe was accompanied by his colleague John Biffen, his deputy at the Treasury. Biffen now took the lead, arguing that to postpone the income tax reduction would be to resile from their election promises, and if there was to be unpopularity due to the proposed VAT increase, it was better to endure it early on rather than later. On this basis, Mrs Thatcher was persuaded. She told me that 'we will prevent the VAT increase from adding to inflation by holding down the supply of money', which, of course, was sheer fantasy – and in more measured terms I told her so.

By this one act, they were immediately making the monetary target exceptionally difficult to achieve, barring drastic action on interest rates to rein in credit. Howe realised this, and decided he would need to announce a 2 per cent increase in the Bank of England's Base Rate on budget day, from 12 per cent to 14 per cent. He would also announce that the 'corset' would continue. This, despite the fact that the Conservative Party had hoped to abolish it on the grounds of fairer competition between financial institutions.[34]

Mrs Thatcher hated it whenever interest rates had to rise because of the feed-through to the mortgage rate for home owners. Right until the last moment before budget day, she tried to persuade Howe to limit the Base Rate increase to 1.5 per cent. Only when he and the governor of the Bank of England, Richardson, both lined up to tell her that, without at least a 2 per cent rise, they would be taking a serious risk with market confidence, did she relent.

She went along with this very reluctantly. But then, on 25 June, she went ballistic about mortgage rates. Since the Base Rate increase was bound to lead to an increase in the banks' lending and deposit account rates, it was inevitable that the building societies would need to follow suit if they weren't to see a large-scale withdrawal of funds. Nonetheless, in a personal note to Howe, she wrote:

> I am very worried about the report in today's press that mortgage rates may have to go up within a few days. This must *not* [double underling] happen. If necessary, there must be a temporary subsidy (as in 1973) from the contingency reserve to keep the rate where it is.[35]

Howe replied that he saw 'grave objections' to an interest subsidy because it would be costly and would damage the government's credibility in the markets. Mrs Thatcher wasn't to be put off. At a meeting on 4 July with Howe and other ministers, it was agreed that pressure should be put on the building societies to postpone any increase in their mortgage rates, and that the government should be prepared, on a contingency basis, to offer them loans to offset any significant withdrawal of funds.

The result of the meeting was that the building societies (which in those days operated effectively as a cartel) did agree to defer their planned mortgage rate increase until the following January and to limit the increase to just three quarters of 1 per cent. By January, Base Rate had risen by a further three percentage points, and the building societies raised their mortgage rates by 3.25 per cent. The loan scheme was quietly dropped for being far too expensive if it was to have any noticeable impact, and Mrs Thatcher made no further attempt to stop the rise. She had reluctantly learned the lesson that home owners couldn't be protected from the pain of tighter money.

In spite of the 2 per cent Base Rate increase alongside the budget, monetary expansion accelerated over the summer and into the autumn. Higher bank lending and higher government borrowing, made worse by the faltering of gilt sales, was the main cause. The situation was made worse still by the decision in October to abolish all remaining controls on foreign exchange transactions. This had been a long-held wish on the part of the Conservatives, and the strength of sterling led Howe to decide that this was an opportune moment to do it.

I remember Mrs Thatcher's shock when Howe told her of his intention, and she took some persuading. Howe wasn't much concerned whether the abolition of exchange controls would lead to an inflow or outflow of funds; he just wanted to do it as part of his wish to free up the economy. He thought that, if anything, it would lead to a flow of funds out of, and not into, sterling. Mrs Thatcher thought the opposite.

Her caution on this occasion proved correct, and the abolition of controls increased the upward pressure on sterling, which manufacturing industry could well have done without; and because of intervention by the Bank of England to moderate sterling's rise, there were consequential increases in the money supply. The abolition of foreign exchange controls would also make the 'corset', which Howe had only four months earlier said would continue in place, ineffectual – since companies would, from now on, be able to borrow offshore. Such, unfortunately, was the lack of joined-up thinking.

However bad the situation, Howe nearly always managed to put on a calm air, but by October 1979 he was getting seriously worried about the money supply figures. Bank lending was rising rapidly in spite of the 14 per cent Base Rate, reflecting the distressed financial state of the corporate sector. There was an unexpected increase in the personal savings rate (people saving more for precautionary reasons in risky times and because of the higher interest rates), and this, too, was fuelling bank deposits and therefore the money supply. In addition, government borrowing was running ahead of forecast. And because the markets were expecting a further increase in interest rates, there was a temporary halt to the buying of government debt (the financial press called it a 'gilts strike'), which was also putting upward pressure on the money supply.

Mrs Thatcher was far from calm. She was furious that her flagship monetarist plan seemed to be falling apart so soon. I wrote in a memo to the Treasury that she was 'profoundly unhappy with monetary developments', which, in Civil Service speak, was as strong a ticking off from the prime minister as you could get. She complained to Richardson that he had misled her on how fast bank lending was rising. She was deaf to the point that velocity might be slowing. Fearing that interest rates would have to go even higher, she told Howe and Richardson that she didn't think higher interest rates would restrain the thirst for borrowing, and suggested various other options – reintroducing direct controls on bank lending, a tax on bank profits, reintroducing hire purchase controls, or the early introduction of MBC. At one meeting she complained that Treasury officials were 'showing excessive zeal in their effort to demonstrate that they were pursuing a policy of monetary discipline'. Some probably were because they didn't want to be seen as backsliders on the monetarist project. Mrs Thatcher was at her wits' end. The absence of an expert adviser on monetary policy at her side was becoming a serious disadvantage.

Howe ignored her suggestions and came back with a proposal to increase Base Rate by three percentage points to a record level of 17 per cent, aimed at restricting bank lending and encouraging the purchase of gilts. For her, this was a shocking development, but with gilts sales at a standstill, and the markets now expecting a large interest hike, she had no option but to acquiesce if there was to be any semblance of trying to get the money supply back on track. On a forward-looking basis (that is, taking account of borrowers' inflation expectations), real interest rates were now distinctly positive. The only crumb Mrs Thatcher obtained from Howe was a commitment that he would consult widely and publish a Green Paper on MBC.

As we headed for Christmas 1979, the economic situation seemed increasingly dire. Anti-monetarists had long warned that the money supply figures were capable of giving false signals about the state of the economy, and this is exactly what was happening. Money supply was growing well outside its target range, and the government was seeking to rein it back through extraordinary measures. On the other hand, by all other indicators, particularly interest rates and the strong exchange rate, monetary policy was now extremely tight, and was beginning to cause serious distress in industry and for mortgage holders. Both unemployment and inflation were rising; strike action was brewing in the steel, automobile and coal industries as well as in the public services; and most forecasters were expecting the economy to go into recession very shortly. The employers' organisations were unhappy, and the TUC was up in arms.

7

Monetarism's high noon

The Conservative government's first eight months with monetarism clearly hadn't gone well. Mrs Thatcher and Geoffrey Howe's response to the various setbacks was not to ask for a reassessment of the policy; rather, it was to double down on the monetarist plan. The inflation rate and the monetary aggregates were both going in the wrong direction. For them, the answer was to strengthen and extend – not weaken – the plan. It was to be high noon for the monetarism experiment in the UK.

The arrival of Terry Burns as chief economic adviser at the Treasury in January 1980 gave it renewed impetus. With his colleague Alan Budd at the London Business School, Burns had argued the case for multi-year monetary targets.[1] The idea was that, by announcing monetary targets several years ahead, this could have an important influence on inflationary expectations. If wage bargainers, companies in their price setting and the financial markets could be persuaded that inflation was genuinely on a downward path, this could greatly facilitate its achievement. And multi-year targets would provide a useful framework against which to take decisions on monetary and fiscal policy over the shorter term.

These ideas underpinned the medium-term financial strategy (MTFS) that Treasury officials, with substantial input from Nigel Lawson, produced in the early months of 1980. (In 1979, Lawson had been appointed financial secretary at the Treasury, a rank just below Cabinet level.) It was announced and came into effect alongside the 1980 budget in March.

Medium-term financial strategy

The key innovation with the MTFS was the publication of targets for the money supply and projections for government borrowing going forward several years. Published targets for the money supply had, of course, been in place since 1976. Publishing multi-year targets was a much more significant step. There would be targets for the growth of £M3 and projections for government borrowing (more precisely, the PSBR) covering the four years 1980/81 to 1983/84. For £M3, the MTFS proposed a target range of 7–11 per cent for 1980/81, and a gradually declining trend for the subsequent three years. For the PSBR, expressed as a ratio of GDP, it proposed a reduction of two thirds over the same period.

Geoffrey Howe and Nigel Lawson believed there were great advantages in publishing a medium-term plan:

- It would show that the government's policies were consistent and technically sound.
- It would show how determined and ambitious the government were in tackling inflation.
- It would serve as a warning to employers and trade unions that inflationary pay settlements would not be accommodated by faster monetary growth.
- The projected downward path for the PSBR would demonstrate consistency with the monetary targets, and would indicate the possibility of tax cuts eventually.
- It would bring cheer to the markets and provide hope to the public that there was light at the end of the tunnel.

They were supported by the monetarists outside the government. Writing in the *Financial Times*, Sam Brittan urged Mrs Thatcher to publish 'a medium term framework this instant ... if anti-inflationary policy is to carry any conviction'.[2]

In testimony to the House of Commons Treasury Select Committee in June 1980, Milton Friedman would express his strong support for the medium-term framework and for the monetary targets, which, he said, 'were the right order of magnitude, and were set to decline at about the right rate'.[3] But he criticised the inclusion of the projections for the PSBR – on the grounds, he argued, that fiscal deficits and monetary growth had no necessary relationship. He misunderstood that – at least in the UK context – a declining level of government borrowing was necessary so as to be consistent with lower monetary growth if exorbitantly high interest rates were to be avoided.[4] Moreover, some monetarists argued that, even if a high PSBR was fully funded, it would in itself be inflationary because the high interest rates that would be required would result in people economising on their holdings of money, and therefore there would be an increase in money velocity.[5]

So much for the arguments in favour of publishing a medium-term financial plan. But there were some serious arguments against. The money supply was just too unstable and unpredictable in relation to money GDP to justify publishing targets four years ahead. It was too hard to control with any degree of accuracy; and yet, once the targets were published, the Bank and the Treasury would be expected by the markets to adhere to them, whether or not underlying monetary conditions or conditions in the real economy (that is, output and employment) suggested they should do so.

And as regards the particular numbers proposed, the targets for monetary growth looked extremely tight. The previous year's target had already been missed by a wide margin, and there was little reason to think it would be any easier in the coming few years – in fact, more likely the reverse.

There were two main problems. First, the velocity of circulation, which had been rising since 1975, had peaked and was likely to start falling because of Howe's intention, which he planned to announce in his budget statement, to abolish the 'corset'. Abolishing the 'corset' was bound to increase deposits with the banks and therefore expand the money supply in relation to money GDP – meaning a likely fall in velocity.[6] And this is exactly what happened (see Figure A6 in the Appendix).

Second, the monetary targets assumed a highly ambitious downward path for the PSBR. It was ambitious because there could well be a shortfall in revenue owing to the likely depth of the recession, and because of known difficulties in holding public spending to plan. The MTFS would state that the PSBR might be allowed to deviate from the projections if the deviation was purely for cyclical reasons – that is, if output and incomes in real terms turned out worse than expected. (For this reason, the PSBR figures in the MTFS were called 'projections' rather than 'targets', although the financial markets quickly assumed they *were* targets.) Nonetheless, whether the deviation was for cyclical or non-cyclical reasons, higher government borrowing would mean the government having to sell more gilts to the public and to the non-bank financial institutions, and therefore higher interest rates. Or else the government would have to rely on more borrowing from the banks, which, in turn, would increase the money supply.

When I told Mrs Thatcher how challenging I thought the proposed targets were likely to be, she said I was being defeatist. In her view, the tougher the targets, the better. She thought that by having really tough targets, this would force the Bank of England to take control of the money supply more seriously, and likewise the Treasury with public spending. Talk of velocity slowing down was just an excuse, in her view, for allowing the money supply to carry on expanding at too fast a pace. She didn't accept the risks to the real economy if monetary growth was forced down to stay within its target range. Nor did she set much store by the fact that, if the money supply target was overrun, as it had been for 1979/80, this would damage market confidence and make inflationary expectations worse.

At official level in the Treasury, Permanent Secretary Douglas Wass argued against publication. For him, this was a rerun of the argument over having a published target for the money supply in 1976, but this time his reservations were all the greater. He didn't think the publication of one-year targets had actually served any particularly useful purpose, and he couldn't see how the publication of multi-year targets would do any better.

Another senior official who was opposed was Ken Berrill, head of the Central Policy Review Staff (CPRS) in the Cabinet Office. He had been chief economic adviser at the Treasury at the end of Heath's premiership, and then head of the CPRS during the Labour government. He was therefore somewhat suspect in Mrs Thatcher's eyes, although she respected his deep knowledge and experience. He sent Mrs Thatcher a careful note setting out the pros and cons, with an emphasis on the cons – but concluding rather lamely that the decision 'is in the end more a matter of political than economic judgement'.[7]

The Bank of England was equally opposed to multi-year targets. It had supported one-year targets, but multi-year targets were another matter. Charles Goodhart was especially scathing in his opposition, advising Bank of England Governor Gordon Richardson that the draft of a paper Budd had sent him, which purported to justify multi-year targets, was 'not up to proper academic standards, even less providing a guidance for responsible policy-making'.[8] Goodhart and Richardson both felt that what mattered in order to convince the markets the government was serious about bringing inflation down was deeds, not the publication of spurious money targets.

While Howe and Lawson were strongly in favour of publication, Howe's ministerial deputy at the Treasury, Chief Secretary John Biffen, was against. He sent Mrs Thatcher a memorandum in which he wrote: 'Our monetary policy is still at the stage of apprenticeship. The Financial Strategy, on the other hand, will suggest a certainty of pace and direction that we do not possess, either technically or politically.'[9] Biffen had been an early supporter of the monetarist approach, and Mrs Thatcher admired him for his intellect and political views, but she felt he had been ineffective in his principal role at the Treasury, which was to control public spending. (Bernard Ingham, Mrs Thatcher's press secretary, famously called him 'semi-detached'.) His dissent regarding the MTFS surprised and shocked her. From then on, she felt she would no longer consider him as one of her 'inner circle'. In January 1981, she moved him from the Treasury to the Department of Trade.

Before a final decision was taken, Mrs Thatcher held a meeting with Howe, Richardson and Wass. Richardson told Mrs Thatcher that he was strongly opposed to publication of the plan. He said:

> It was hard enough to set a monetary target for one year ahead: it was much harder for a four-year period. Even with a target *range* there was still in his view too much rigidity in the figures. He was concerned that wages might not accommodate to the declining

monetary path; and that if they did not, the pressure on interest rates and activity might well be intolerable.

Mrs Thatcher concluded the meeting by saying she understood Richardson's misgivings but she and Howe were 'convinced it would be right to publish'.[10]

Up until then, there had never really been any discussion in Cabinet about the monetarist strategy. Now, Mrs Thatcher decided she had better obtain the Cabinet's endorsement for publication of the MTFS. At a Cabinet meeting on 13 March 1980, a minority of Cabinet members, led by Ian Gilmour and Jim Prior, spoke out against publication. Fewer spoke in favour. The majority remained silent – from which Mrs Thatcher felt able to conclude that 'the balance of view in the Cabinet' favoured proceeding with publication.[11] And so, shortly afterwards, the MTFS was announced alongside Howe's 1980 budget.

This was a contractionary budget at a time when the economy was already in recession. However, with hindsight – and in contrast to the budget the following year – it probably had little or no effect on the path of GDP, and thus did not in itself make the recession any worse.[12] This is because public spending turned out significantly higher, and revenue significantly lower, than in the budget. On the other hand, this would mean higher government borrowing, which would make it all the more difficult to achieve the target for the money supply in 1980/81.

Further setbacks

For the three months April to June 1980, £M3 grew at a relatively modest rate – such that Governor Richardson was able to advise Mrs Thatcher that monetary growth was now running at only a shade above its target range. While it might be better to wait for another month to see if the improved money figures were being sustained, he felt the balance of risk was in favour of a modest reduction in Base Rate to provide some relief for the corporate sector. He recommended a reduction in Base Rate from 17 to 16 per cent, and this was agreed and implemented on 3 July.[13]

Richardson's optimism on the money supply figures turned out to be wide of the mark. The July figures were very bad – in large part due to the ending of the 'corset', the impact of which the Bank had greatly underestimated. Its ending caused a flood of money back into the banks, just as some had warned, adding around 4 per cent to £M3. By the autumn, £M3 was growing way over its target range again. Just as in the previous year, the money supply was proving unstable and unpredictable, and an unreliable indicator of monetary conditions.

The annual inflation rate, having reached a peak of 22 per cent in May 1980, at last began to come down. But worryingly, for both inflation and unemployment, wages and salaries were still rising fast (the percentage rise for 1980 as a whole would come out at nearly 20 per cent). The squeeze on profit margins in the private sector, which had been declining for several years, was getting ever tighter, and unemployment started to increase rapidly. By the end of 1980 the economy was operating at 8 per cent below its capacity. Both the Confederation of British Industry (CBI) and the Trades Union Congress (TUC) were making powerful presentations on behalf of their members for the government to ease up. There was an especially fiery meeting between Mrs Thatcher and the TUC General Council on 14 October 1980.

From the USA, the 'old' Keynesian, John Kenneth Galbraith, couldn't resist writing:

> Britain has, in effect, volunteered to be the Friedmanite guinea pig. There could be no better choice. Britain's political and social institutions are solid and neither Englishmen, Scots nor even the Welsh take readily to the streets. ... British phlegm is a good antidote for anger, but so is an adequate system of unemployment insurance.[14]

Mrs Thatcher spent her summer holiday in 1980 in Switzerland, where she met the Swiss monetarist, Karl Brunner. Brunner pressed on her the advantages of monetary base control (MBC), and on her return she demanded renewed action on the part of the Bank of England and the Treasury to introduce it. After the publication of the Green Paper on MBC in March 1980,[15] and with Howe, Lawson and Richardson all opposed to it, MBC had seemed to be fading as an idea. But with the money supply now accelerating and again running ahead of target, and with Mrs Thatcher fired up by her discussion with Brunner (she saw him again with his monetarist colleague Alan Meltzer in London on 30 September), MBC was now very much back on the agenda.

Around this time, I remember her saying to me: 'Why on earth can't the Bank of England simply turn off the money tap?' I responded by explaining that, if she meant the Bank should stop printing bank notes and refuse to supply the banks with notes and coins when they needed them, this would surely cause a run on the banks and cause interest rates to go through the roof. She wasn't convinced, and insisted that there must be a better way to control the money supply than relying on interest rates and limiting government borrowing.

Immediately after her return from Switzerland, and having been advised of what she called the 'disastrous' money supply figures for July, she summoned Howe and Richardson. It was a stormy meeting. She told them that her Swiss contacts had advised her that our money supply was completely out of control and that, although the strategy was correct, it was not being properly implemented. The banks seemed to be, in her words, 'shovelling money out' in spite of the high interest rates, with the Bank of England making it too easy for them by 'functioning as lender of first resort, not last resort'. Public spending and government borrowing also seemed out of control. The Bank of England, in her view, was unwilling to implement the government's strategy, preferring – as she put it at a later meeting – to pursue an interest rate policy rather than a policy to control the money supply.

In response, Howe said that public spending was proceeding more or less as planned, with the notable exception of defence spending, which was running well ahead of budget. There were shortfalls on the revenue side that mostly explained the overshoot in government borrowing. But the 'picture was not a cause for alarm'. (In retrospect, this was a surprising statement: government borrowing as a percentage of GDP for the whole financial year eventually overshot the budget forecast by 2 percentage points.) Richardson said that Mrs Thatcher did not 'properly understand' the reasons for the overshoot in the money supply. The high level of bank lending to companies was due to their desperate need for cash, which they were unable to replenish in the capital market. A clearly dissatisfied Mrs Thatcher concluded the meeting by requesting urgent work on how to get the monetary growth back within the 7–11 per cent target range, including whether to limit the banks' lending and deposit taking by implementing MBC.[16]

Mrs Thatcher instructed me to set up a series of 'monetary seminars' to be chaired by herself, with Howe, Lawson and Richardson and their respective advisers.[17] My records of these seminars show the discussion going into immense detail on many aspects of monetary policy, including the many issues around MBC. They show just how determined Mrs Thatcher was to get the monetarist plan implemented, and the work and effort she was prepared to put into it herself. What the records don't quite capture is her frustration at not being able to persuade the serried ranks of men (there wasn't a single other woman at any of the meetings) of the virtues of MBC, or the resultant fraying of tempers. On her part, the latter was all too obvious; with the others, it was barely disguised. Eventually, she felt bound to concede in the face of the weight of opinion that was against MBC. Although she would never entirely give up on the idea, she had the good sense not to override the Treasury and the Bank on a matter in which she, inevitably, lacked the necessary expertise. Without a monetary expert on her staff at this stage (Alan Walters didn't arrive until January 1981), she was basically on her own. She was able to count on a degree of behind-the-scenes support from the Treasury's Peter Middleton, but his support was more tactical than substantive. Although some minor changes were agreed on the way the Bank of England would operate in future, which could, in theory, be a precursor to MBC, no one seriously thought MBC would ever happen.

It was left to the Bank of England and the Treasury to soldier on with the conventional, and not very satisfactory, tools for controlling the money supply – interest rates, limits to government borrowing and sales of public debt to non-banks. The failure of these, taken together, to bring monetary growth back within target led to many more difficult meetings with Howe and Richardson. Howe was accustomed to these from their time together in Opposition and found ways of putting up with it – on one occasion, he opened his red box and was signing papers until the storm subsided. (Being treated by Mrs Thatcher like this over many years would be one factor in his decision in 1990 to resign from the Cabinet.)

Richardson found it more difficult to ignore Mrs Thatcher's slings and arrows. Often briefed by Gordon Pepper,[18] sometimes in person, more often in writing, she took an intense interest in the Bank's operations without ever having a good understanding of what these actually involved. She would have one-on-one meetings with Richardson (with myself as note-taker), without Howe or anyone else from the Treasury in attendance, and would often start these meeting by flattering him in some way – he was a handsome man and she liked the company of handsome men. She would then switch into attack mode, complaining bitterly about how the Bank was handling its gilts sales or money market operations, and handing out too much cash to the banks. Richardson would respond by carefully explaining how the Bank was operating to maintain stability and cost-effectiveness in the gilts market, and rebutting the criticisms of Pepper and others, while also advising her that his task was made difficult by the government's excessive borrowing. But he tended to make scant headway, and would often leave a chastened and crest-fallen figure.

Richardson was not an enthusiast for the government's monetarist approach – his deputy McMahon, executive director Fforde and senior adviser Goodhart were well known for their opposition – and Richardson gave higher priority than Mrs Thatcher to the problems of industry and unemployment. But her treatment of this highly intelligent banker and public servant was shabby. After one particularly stormy meeting, he telephoned me – it was an unusual thing in those more hierarchical days for the governor to ring a middle-ranking civil servant like myself – to express his despair and to ask what he could do to improve their relationship. According to a note by Richardson's assistant, I told him that 'uncomfortable meetings' had happened before and that 'he should not be alarmed'.

By the second half of 1980 it was clear that the private sector was being hit exceptionally hard by the government's policies, and harder than the public sector, where nationalised industries were still being cushioned by large subsidies and the Civil Service had yet to suffer any significant cut-backs. This was ironic given the government's commitment to revive the fortunes of private business and bear down on spending in the public sector. In 1979/80 and 1980/81, government borrowing overshot by billions of pounds compared with the Treasury's projections. The recession was partly responsible for this, but so, too, was overspending by government on subsidies and Civil Service pay, and the slow start to privatisation. All this made Mrs Thatcher very unhappy. She complained bitterly, but the extra spending seemed unstoppable. In September 1981, she sacked Christopher Soames, the Cabinet minister responsible for Civil Service pay, who she felt had been too willing to compromise with the Civil Service trade unions.

This meant that in order to prevent the money supply from expanding even faster, there had to be reduced lending to the private sector and larger sales of government debt. Both required higher interest rates. On the face of it, even when the Bank of England's Base Rate was at 17 per cent in the early part of 1980, interest rates in real terms were still negative if compared with the *current* rate of inflation. But this was misleading. During 1980, on account of the recession and the high exchange rate, borrowers were beginning to look at an *expected* substantial fall in inflation, which meant, on a forward-looking basis, real interest rates were positive and far higher than they had been for many years. One estimate had real interest rates, as experienced by exporters, for the first quarter of 1980 as high as 8 per cent.[19]

Businesses certainly felt that the high interest rates were causing impossible strains on their finances. I know this from personal experience since, in late 1980, my wife's family-run textile business in West Yorkshire was forced into liquidation, never to reopen. This was the fate of thousands of businesses up and down the country.[20]

The high exchange rate was also causing serious problems, and Mrs Thatcher was concerned about this. Robin Ibbs,[21] an incomer from the private sector as the head of the Central Policy Review Staff in the Cabinet Office, was constantly bringing this to her attention, arguing that the exchange rate should be capped even if this meant injecting more sterling into the system and increasing £M3. The dollar rate reached a peak of US$2.43

in late 1980, up from US$2.06 on election day, with unit costs in industry also having risen much faster than the UK's main competitors'. UK unit labour costs expressed in sterling, relative to our main trading partners', increased by an estimated 56 per cent in the two years to the first quarter of 1981.[22] The sterling rate had clearly overshot a rate that could allow British industry to effectively compete in overseas markets.

By the autumn of 1980, Mrs Thatcher was finally feeling conflicted on what should be done. On the one hand, her determination to bear down on monetary growth remained as strong as ever. On the other hand, she was becoming increasingly concerned about the plight of industry.

These conflicting considerations came into sharp relief in deciding what to do with the loss-making, state-owned vehicle manufacturer, British Leyland (BL). BL had more than 50 plants, with a production capacity of more than one million cars and trucks a year, and a workforce of around 150,000. Michael Edwardes, its feisty chairman and chief executive since 1977, had begun to turn the business around – closing unprofitable plants, getting rid of archaic work practices, enforcing lower pay settlements, entering into an alliance with the Japanese car-maker Honda. But the company's commercial viability – made a good deal worse by sterling's appreciation – remained in considerable doubt. In January 1981, Edwardes confronted the government with a stark choice: either continue to fund his restructuring plans, or the company would have to go into liquidation. Keith Joseph, Mrs Thatcher's ideological soulmate and the Cabinet minister with lead responsibility for BL, argued for liquidation. So did Trade Secretary John Nott, and so did John Hoskyns. For Mrs Thatcher, however, the prospective loss of such a significant chunk of the country's manufacturing capacity and of so many jobs, plus the short-term financial cost of liquidation for the government, were too much; she opted to support Edwardes' plan, and the funding to go with it. (The BL story did not end well: an unsatisfactory privatisation in the late 1980s and later, the sale of all its surviving parts to foreign vehicle manufacturers.)

A few months earlier, in October 1980, Mrs Thatcher had requested a paper from Treasury Permanent Secretary Wass that would 'explore ways of mitigating the adverse conditions under which British industry is operating'. Wass produced a wide-ranging review,[23] with six possible options:

- Controls on inward flows of foreign exchange
- Modest cut in interest rates with tightening of fiscal policy
- Large cut in interest rates
- Explicit exchange rate target (at a lower level)
- Significant tax switch – higher personal taxes and lower taxes for companies
- Pay freeze.

Brunner had commended the first of these to Mrs Thatcher when she met with him in Switzerland in August. He told her that Switzerland had had a good experience with such controls in keeping down its exchange rate. In his paper, Wass recognised that the last four of these would be incompatible with the government's existing economic strategy. He did not recommend any of them, but included them as a matter of completeness. As for the first two, he advised that inward controls would be administratively complicated and were unlikely to be effective for the UK. Regarding the second, he suggested a 2 per cent cut in Base Rate – to be accompanied a mix of tax increases and spending cuts. The idea, promoted within the Treasury by Middleton and Burns, was to stick with the monetary targets but switch some of the pain from the private sector to the public sector. A similar rationale would underpin the very substantial fiscal tightening in the 1981 budget.

Mrs Thatcher met with Howe and Wass on 12 November to discuss the paper. Earlier that day, she had had a stormy meeting with the president and director general of the CBI. The director general, Terence Beckett, a former chief executive of Ford of Britain who had recently told his membership that he was up for a 'bare-knuckle' fight with the government, demanded an immediate Base Rate reduction of 4 percentage points and a lower sterling exchange rate. Given the dire economic backdrop and the limited options available, her meeting with Howe and Wass was not a happy one either. But Mrs Thatcher accepted Wass's advice and agreed that the only feasible option was a reduction in Base Rate, with some offsetting action on the fiscal side.[24] She was no fan of Wass because of his well-known scepticism about the monetarist strategy, but she respected and valued his expertise, and on this occasion I remember her thanking him warmly for his advice.

On 24 November, Howe announced a mini-budget more or less reflecting what he and Mrs Thatcher had agreed – a supplementary tax payable by North Sea oil companies, some spending cuts and an increase in National Insurance contributions (NICs) payable by employees; and an immediate 2 per cent cut in Base Rate. However, the spending cuts and the NICs increase would not come into effect until the following April, and therefore they wouldn't be of any help in curbing monetary growth over the next few months. In his statement, Howe said that he expected monetary growth to slow, but acknowledged that it was likely to exceed its 7–11 per cent target range for the year. This was an under-statement to say the least: monetary growth in 1980/81 ended up at over 18 per cent.

Mrs Thatcher was not the only person in higher Conservative circles at this time to be feeling the conflict between their support for the monetarist strategy and the need to shield the private sector from its consequences. In the same month as Howe's mini-budget, Alfred Sherman, director of Keith Joseph's think tank the Centre for Policy Studies (CPS), invited the Swiss economist Professor Jürg Niehans to visit the UK and advise on what was to be done. Niehans was suggested by Alan Walters, who was still in the USA, and had taught alongside Niehans at Johns Hopkins University.

Niehans focused on the appreciation of sterling. A common view, although no longer the Treasury's, was that sterling's overshoot was largely due to North Sea oil. Niehans disagreed. He said it was due mainly to the tightness of monetary policy. The figures for £M3 had misled us into thinking that monetary policy was loose. He told one official that our focus on £M3 was 'like watching a man scalding to death in the bath, and running in hotter and hotter water, because the thermometer he was reading had the scale upside down'.[25]

Niehans said that we really should have been watching M1 (cash and current account deposits) and the monetary base (M0), both of which had been growing much more slowly.

He recommended that in the short run the existing monetary target for £M3 be discarded altogether in favour of an exchange rate target – he suggested a ceiling of US$2.15 against sterling, compared with the then existing rate of around US$2.40. This would have to be achieved by lowering interest rates and by intervention in the foreign exchange markets, even though both would mean faster monetary growth. Once the exchange rate had stabilised at a lower level, we could go back to monetary targets, but the category of money chosen should not be £M3 because – in his view – it bore little relationship to prices and money GDP, and couldn't be readily controlled. Inflexible targeting, such as we were attempting to implement, ran the risk that important information about output and the exchange rate was being neglected (he put into words exactly how I had been feeling for quite a while). If there was to be a monetary target, it should be for M0, which at least the authorities could control. He failed to say exactly how M0 could be relevant for predicting or controlling inflation.

Niehans's views should not have come as a surprise to anyone who had read an article he had published earlier that year on the overshooting of the Swiss franc in a little-known Irish journal. I suspect few people had. In that article he had praised the Swiss authorities' ditching of monetary targets in 1978 in favour of intervention in the foreign exchange market to keep the exchange rate from rising, and he was relaxed about the resultant rapid monetary expansion. He proposed a modified monetarist framework as follows: 'Set the long-run trend of the money supply for price stability; permit medium-term deviations from this trend to counteract fluctuations in output and employment; and use short-term interventions to dampen over-shooting of the exchange rate.'[26]

He produced a lengthy report that was eventually published not by the CPS – because its contents were deemed too alarming for ministers – but at Rochester University in the USA. According to Hoskyns, Niehans told him: 'If the government goes on with the present monetary squeeze, you won't just have a recession, you'll have a slump.' Hoskyns himself commented in his diary: 'We have accidentally engineered a major recession' and 'done the economy a great deal of damage by mistake'.[27] (It is curious that

Hoskyns, nonetheless, was among the most hawkish in arguing for a deflationary budget two months later.)

Niehans's views were passed on to Howe and Lawson at the Treasury and to Mrs Thatcher. They found his conclusions decidedly uncomfortable. Mrs Thatcher was furious that Sherman had invited Niehans to advise without consulting the Treasury and her own advisers first. His findings, if made public, would undermine the position of Howe and herself. The government had invested a great deal in the MTFS. The targets for and control of £M3 were the centrepiece of the MTFS. If they switched so soon to another monetary aggregate, they would lose credibility with the markets, and £M3 was important as an anchor for determining the appropriateness (or not) of the level of government borrowing. Nor for similar reasons, even for the short run, could they switch to an exchange rate target. They had said repeatedly that you couldn't attempt to control the exchange rate without an undesirable loss of control of the monetary aggregates: the monetary targets had to come first.

1981 budget

The November mini-budget and Niehans's report set the scene for Howe's March 1981 budget.[28] The challenge would be for him to present a budget that was somehow compatible with the ongoing plan for monetary growth as set out in the MTFS, while enabling, if possible, a further reduction in Base Rate. In other words, there was to be no loosening of policy overall, but further help for companies through lower interest rates.

It was clear by now that the PSBR for 1980/81, due to the depth of the recession and to overspending by government departments, was going to come out at roughly £5 billion (2 per cent of GDP) higher than in the MTFS, and the Treasury was forecasting a similar 2 per cent of GDP overshoot for the coming year. Urged on by Hoskyns and Walters, and also by Wolfson, Mrs Thatcher was determined that the PSBR should be brought back into line with the MTFS. All three advisers talked among themselves about resigning unless this happened.

Howe was also determined on a sizeable reduction in the PSBR, but he thought a £5 billion cut was neither feasible politically, nor desirable economically, as it would involve too much of a deflationary shock. Mrs Thatcher, too, was worried about the political risks, which, she complained, neither Walters nor Hoskyns understood. She and Howe eventually settled on a PSBR reduction that equated to about 1.5 per cent of GDP, consisting mainly of personal tax increases, with some minor spending cuts. Walters and Hoskyns made known their disappointment to her, but decided to stay on.

I played a modest part in persuading Mrs Thatcher not to go along with the more hawkish line proposed by Walters and Hoskyns. In a cautionary but hardly vigorous briefing note prior to the final decision, I advised: 'The short-term deflationary effect [of such a large PSBR reduction] may arguably be too deflationary. We need to consider carefully the trade-off between the deflation caused by interest rates not falling, and the deflation which would come from [budgetary] overkill.' The budget was accompanied by a further 2 per cent reduction in the Bank of England's Base Rate. This was followed, as Niehans predicted, by a weakening of the exchange rate, which gave manufacturing industry a measure of relief.

Three hundred and sixty-four academic economists signed a letter to *The Times* roundly criticising the budget for doing irreparable damage to the economy. They wrote that there was 'no basis in economic theory or supporting evidence' for the policy that the budget was seeking to implement. The letter was co-drafted by one of my former Cambridge lecturers, Frank Hahn. It was signed not just by the government's more outspoken critics like Kaldor, but also by moderates like James Meade. They were right to complain. In the second quarter of 1981 GDP was 6 per cent lower than it had been two years before, and manufacturing output was 17 per cent lower. The rate of unemployment was now at 10 per cent, double what it had been in the second quarter of 1979. The prospect for inflation, on the other hand, was by now looking much better. There was therefore no need to remove further spending power from the economy.

Mrs Thatcher and Howe, and their monetarist supporters, denied that the budget was deflationary because, they argued, it made possible the further fall in interest rates and improved private sector confidence. The economy did start a slow recovery in the second half of 1981, but this was in spite of, not because of, the budget. Although the budget was presented as a means not only of getting the MTFS back on track but also, through the interest rate cut, in helping the private sector, in reality it removed around 1 per cent of spending from the economy, and thus it meant that GDP over the coming year or so would be around 1 per cent lower than it otherwise would have been. It was by any account a seriously deflationary and destabilising budget.[29]

In retrospect, the deflation in the budget was all the more extraordinary given that the economy was still in recession, and was operating a long way below its full potential.[30] Part of the motivation was concern about growing public debt, although as a proportion of GDP it was less than 50 per cent (compared with around 100 per cent today), and there was little evidence that a higher PSBR couldn't have been funded without causing more inflation. But the main driving force was the continued obsession with the monetary targets. The easing of monetary policy was supposed to provide some offset to the fiscal deflation, but any such offset was nullified when the 2 per cent reduction in Base Rate, which accompanied the budget, was reversed in September, and then increased by a further 2 per cent in October in order to halt a run on the pound.

In a reassessment of the 1981 budget many years later, Ray Barrell, a former head of economic forecasting at the National Institute of Economic and Social Research (NIESR), argued that the 364 economists who had signed the letter to *The Times* had been excessively alarmist about the budget's effects. This was because, in his view, they had implicitly assumed 'multipliers' in respect of the tax increases and spending cuts that were a good deal higher than actually existed at the time. He nonetheless concluded that the budget had had a significantly deflationary impact. He estimated that economic growth in 1981/82 was reduced by between three quarters of 1 per cent and one percentage point compared with what would have happened with a neutral budget, although a neutral budget would have somewhat postponed the full drop in inflation over the following two years.[31]

In the year or two after the 1981 budget, it was seen by some of the government's supporters as a great victory for Mrs Thatcher and Howe – so much so that their closest respective allies competed in claiming its paternity. This was because the budget did achieve a marked reduction in the ratio of the PSBR to GDP, and because the economy did start to grow again in the second half of the year. In reality, however, the overall policy stance made the recovery more anaemic than it otherwise would have been. Inflation probably would not have come down as rapidly as it did over the next couple of years, but nor would unemployment have spiralled eventually to over 3 million. Unemployment did not need to reach this level to bring wage inflation down to an acceptable level. With a less deflationary budget, low single-digit inflation could still have been achieved over a slightly longer period, but without the further surge in unemployment.

8

Ending the experiment

To most people outside government, and many inside, the controversial 1981 budget looked like the consolidation of monetarism in the UK. And that is how Mrs Thatcher was inclined to see it at the time. In reality, the 1981 budget was the last big policy event in which monetarism was the guiding principle. It marked the end of the period of hard monetarism. After that, for the next few years it would be a softer, more pragmatic monetarism that would guide policy; and then, by the early 1990s, it had disappeared altogether. (This is not to say that monetary *policy* would be downgraded and disappear: on the contrary, as we shall see, monetary policy – that is to say, mainly interest rate adjustments – would become entrenched as the key instrument for controlling inflation.)

After all the difficulties in implementing the monetarist strategy, the change was bound to come sooner or later. There were growing doubts within the Treasury that it would be possible to carry on as before. Nigel Lawson, one of the chief architects of the medium-term financial strategy (MTFS), was losing confidence in the monetarist approach and the emphasis on controlling the money supply that went with it. In the last memorandum he wrote to Geoffrey Howe in September 1981 before leaving the Treasury to become secretary of state for energy, he pointed to the 'increasing evidence of the weakness of £M3 as a reliable proxy for underlying monetary conditions, without any great confidence being able to be attached to any of the other monetary aggregates. This clearly strengthens the case for moving over to an exchange rate discipline.'[1]

Howe himself was casting about for monetary variables to target other than £M3 – questioning whether £M3 should have been chosen as the target variable in the first place, and whether a narrower aggregate such as M1 wouldn't have been more appropriate. However, he decided that too much had been invested in £M3 politically and with the financial markets so that he couldn't make a change now.[2] Nor was he ready to think seriously, as Lawson was suggesting, about a switch to a fixed exchange rate.

In 1981 there was a growing chorus of criticism in academia, in the media, in Parliament and within the Cabinet. Of these, criticism from the academics was the least troublesome – the views of the 364 economists on the budget in their letter to *The Times* were treated with scorn by Mrs Thatcher's redoubtable press secretary, Bernard Ingham, and they made little or no impression on her. She wasn't interested in criticisms coming from academic economists, whom she viewed mostly as tarred with Keynesian and left-wing ideas.

Mrs Thatcher rarely read a newspaper. She relied instead on daily press summaries from Ingham, if he could persuade her to read them. She took it for granted that most of the press would be against the budget, as they had been against the whole monetarist project from the start. Less easy to ignore, however, was the changing tone and coverage of *The Times*. Under William Rees-Mogg's editorship, the newspaper had been the main standard-bearer on behalf of monetarism in the media. In March 1981, Rees-Mogg retired from the editorship, to be succeeded by Harold Evans from *The Sunday Times*. Evans was a Thatcher critic, and it was no coincidence that the paper almost immediately came out with a main editorial critical of the budget: 'The time has come for monetary and fiscal policies to be adjusted. … Little more is to be gained by squeezing the system.'[3]

The Times continued to carry commentary pieces by monetarists such as Patrick Minford and Tim Congdon, but it was giving increasing space to the critics. Soon after the budget, Alec Cairncross, a former government chief economic adviser, contributed a sober but powerful piece entitled 'Two cheerless years of monetarism'.[4] In July 1981, David Blake, the paper's economics editor, wrote a piece entitled 'Why has monetarism failed?' Referring to the recently published annual report of the Swiss-based Bank for International Settlements and its references to the UK, he described the latter as a 'devastating critique of what can go wrong when a government puts all its eggs in a monetarist basket'.[5]

In Parliament, the Labour Opposition, after the signal failure of their policies in 1978/79, were in no position to mount a convincing challenge, and even less so when, in early 1981, four senior members of the Labour Party – the 'Gang of Four'[6] – quit the party to form the Social Democratic Party (SDP). The challenge came more from within the Conservative Party. In February 1981, the House of Commons Treasury Select Committee, chaired by Edward du Cann, a former chair of the Conservative Party who had played a part in Mrs Thatcher's elevation to the leadership in 1975, published a scathing report on the government's monetary policy. It pointed to the lack of evidence of a direct causal link from the money supply to inflation; the high costs in terms of unemployment from the tight monetary policy being pursued; the limitations of £M3 as an indicator of monetary conditions; and the undue rigidity of the MTFS.[7]

The most serious challenge, however, came from within government itself. From the very first there had been doubters among senior ministers – although they had never been able to form themselves into a coherent group. But now, the doubters were growing in number. Remarkably, over the government's first two years in power, there had never been a proper discussion in Cabinet of the economic strategy. Following pressure from several Cabinet members, such a discussion was arranged for 17 June.

In his presentation to Cabinet, Howe took credit for the fact that inflation was now down to 12 per cent from its peak of 22 per cent the previous year, and that the rate of *increase* in unemployment was now slowing down, but he didn't offer any early prospect of unemployment actually falling or of a speedy economic recovery. He asked Cabinet to endorse the government's 'present general approach', by which he meant the continued effort to bear down on inflation through curbing monetary growth and the public sector borrowing requirement (PSBR), and to improve the supply side of the economy.

Although there were references in the discussion to unemployment having reached a 'deeply disturbing' level, with evidence of it producing crime and disorder in some areas, the criticism was relatively muted, and not many ministers spoke. Mrs Thatcher felt able to sum up by saying that the Cabinet supported the 'present economic policy, and in particular for giving continuing priority to the reduction of inflation'.[8]

I attended that meeting, and I could tell from their body language that many Cabinet members remained deeply unhappy. This became all too evident a month later at a Cabinet meeting on 23 July. It had been billed as a meeting to discuss public spending and options for further cuts, but it turned into a repeat, and much franker, debate on the economic strategy. This time, every Cabinet member spoke, and a large majority spoke out against the strategy. Howe offered an unconvincing defence and had little support from anyone else, except from Keith Joseph and from his new and inexperienced deputy at the Treasury, Leon Brittan.[9] Lawson was not yet a member of the Cabinet and was therefore not there to help. The official minutes of the meeting mention 'hopelessness, despair and rioting', and 'the tolerance of society [being] stretched near its limit', but they fail to capture fully the strength of the opposition to the strategy as expressed that day.[10]

Mrs Thatcher said little but watched with growing fury as one after another of her colleagues attacked the strategy. She expected criticism from the well-known 'Wets' – Jim Prior, Ian Gilmour, Peter Walker, Michael Heseltine and Christopher Soames. What she less expected was their being joined by Foreign Secretary Peter Carrington, Leader of the House of Commons Frances Pym and Lord Chancellor Quintin Hogg (Lord Hailsham) – who had all, until then, kept themselves on the side-lines in regard to economic policy. Hailsham plunged the dagger in deep when he likened the strategy to President Hoover's failure to stop the US economy from being engulfed by the Great Depression. What upset Mrs Thatcher even more was the criticism from ministers like John Nott, John Biffen and David Howell, each of whom had originally been members of her inner economic circle and strongly supportive of the strategy.

She and Howe were saved by her de facto deputy, Home Secretary Willie Whitelaw, who kept quiet until the end. I used to brief him when he stood in for Mrs Thatcher at Prime Minister's Questions during her occasional absences from London when Parliament was sitting, and I knew from these always enjoyable briefing sessions that he was no fan of the strategy. The consummate peace-maker within Cabinet, much valued for that and much else by Mrs Thatcher, he opted not to voice his doubts on this occasion – in the interests of preventing a possible terminal rupture within Cabinet. He told his colleagues to be patient and stand behind their chancellor and their leader.

I could tell from watching Mrs Thatcher throughout the meeting that she was badly shaken. She told me immediately afterwards that there would have to be Cabinet changes – which she followed up a couple of months later by demoting Prior and dismissing Gilmour and Soames. But with all the criticism, and with Howe having put up an unconvincing case, she felt for the first time seriously isolated and less inclined to press ahead with the strategy regardless. She still believed that reducing the growth of the monetary supply was crucial, but she was starting to realise that it was all rather more complicated and difficult than she had earlier imagined, and that her political capital was being eroded.

On 20 August 1981, Mrs Thatcher's two senior policy advisers, John Hoskyns and David Wolfson, together with speechwriter Ronnie Millar, submitted a paper to her entitled 'Your political survival' (the drafting was clearly by Hoskyns). It was mainly a critique of her style of working and leadership, which they blamed for many of the government's mistakes and failures so far. They said she should spend more time thinking strategically, listen to what others had to say, and be more encouraging and collegiate, and less critical, with Cabinet colleagues. They wrote:

> Your own credibility and prestige are draining away very fast. ... You will have to change, totally, the way you think and work, both alone and with your colleagues. This can be done only if you can first bring yourself to:
> - Admit that you, like others, have made mistakes
> - Recognize that you have a lot to learn in certain areas and therefore
> - Ask for help from those who can offer it.

They advised that she should read the paper at least twice, and then, 'if you spent a day talking through what's gone wrong in the last two years, you must be in a better position to see that things work better in the next two years'. If she didn't change her ways, they wrote, the Conservatives would lose the next election, or she would be ousted as leader before then.[11]

It wasn't a helpful intervention. It failed to give credit to one of her great strengths – which was leading from the front. Asking her to be more encouraging and collegiate with her colleagues ignored the fact that it was hard for her to do so when they were pushing back against her radicalism. How could she be more collegiate with Prior, for example, when he wanted to go slow on trade union reform; or with Soames when he was, in her view, being soft on the Civil Service unions? The advisers were correct in arguing she should be more willing to listen to people with contrary views. Yet, in regard to the biggest failure to date – the monetarist approach to tackling inflation – they were not in a good position to say this, since they had fully signed up to it.

All three thought they knew her well enough to get away with writing in such stark – some would say insolent – terms. Principal Private Secretary Clive Whitmore intercepted the paper, and rightly thought otherwise. He decided that it would be counterproductive for her to see it. Instead, he took her through it orally, and without the advisers present. She still found their views deeply hurtful. They increased her sense of isolation when her position needed bolstering at this particularly difficult time. It's doubtful whether they had any effect on her style of working and leadership. More likely, it was a factor in Hoskyns's increasing marginalisation from her inner circle until he resigned the following year.

Returning to our main theme, and moving forward, Howe's March 1982 budget signalled a clear distancing from the hard monetarism of earlier years. Although some argued that there should have been some loosening of fiscal policy to aid recovery from the recession, at least there was no repeat of the severe tightening in the previous year's budget – and this, despite the fact that the growth of £M3 had been continuing to run ahead of its target range. There were revisions to the MTFS that included the target range for £M3 being raised by three percentage points for each of the following two years, and the new ranges were also to apply to M1 and PSL2 (which included deposits with building societies as well as banks). The inclusion of three monetary aggregates, each with their different properties, suggested that the targets were there for tracking rather than for control purposes – since, with the instruments at the Treasury's and the Bank of England's disposal, it wasn't possible to try to control all three simultaneously within the same target ranges. Howe spoke in general terms about 'maintaining a monetary environment conducive to the reduction of inflation', and this would include 'not ignoring the behaviour of the exchange rate'. In a nod to James Meade's preference for targeting money GDP rather than the money supply, the budget statement for the first time included projections for money GDP.

These changes marked a very significant down-grading of the monetarist approach. The upward revisions to the target ranges implied a sanctioning of the monetary overshoot of the previous two years – since there was to be no attempt to claw back the overshoot. The reference to the exchange rate, coming after the intervention the previous September and October to stop the exchange from falling, together with the mention of other indicators including money GDP, suggested that the money supply was no longer going to be the near-exclusive focus for macroeconomic policy as it had been previously. *The New York Times*'s correspondent in London wrote: 'The Thatcher government [has] in effect buried the monetarist strategy.'[12] This was an exaggeration, but he was correct in suggesting that the period of hard monetarism was well and truly over.

The softening of the monetarist approach became even more pronounced after Nigel Lawson became chancellor of the exchequer in 1983. In his memoirs he described his 1984 Mansion House speech as his 'last significant utterance as an unreconstructed parochial monetarist'.[13] Each year until 1989, when he resigned as chancellor, he would pay obeisance in his annual budget statements to sound money as the cornerstone of his macroeconomic policy, but the money supply and monetary targets became less and less important. In 1987, £M3 was dropped altogether as a target and replaced by M0, but this, as with £M3 over the previous few years, was to be for monitoring and not for control purposes. Even 'pragmatic monetary targetry', as Charles Goodhart named it, was coming to an end because of the instability and unpredictability of the demand for holding money, as well as uncertainty about the causal link between the money supply and inflation.

Instead of trying to control the money supply as the primary means of controlling inflation, Lawson now believed that inflation could best be kept under control by returning to a semi-fixed exchange rate. (As discussed in Chapter 6, this had, in fact, been his preference before the general election in 1979.) Accordingly, he would make on-and-off attempts throughout his chancellorship to persuade Mrs Thatcher that the UK should join the European Exchange Rate Mechanism (ERM). He never managed to persuade her.

For her part, Mrs Thatcher never lost her conviction, made clear in her memoirs,[14] that inflation was caused by excessive monetary growth, and that controlling the money supply was the best, and only, way of controlling inflation. But after the shift from hard to soft monetarism starting in 1982, she never sought to reimpose a hard monetarist regime. This was for several reasons. First of all, with inflation down to less than 5 per cent by 1983, counter-inflation policy no longer had the same urgency as before. Second, after the experience of 1979–81, she must have lost some of the brimming confidence, which she once had, in the supposed efficacy and the certainties of a hard monetarist regime – although she would never admit it publicly. Third, as we shall see in Chapter 12, she could no longer count on the same confidence in the policy that some of the monetarist economists had once had. As early as 1980, even Friedman himself had cast doubt on the regime when he told the Treasury Select Committee that the effect of interest rates on the money supply was 'highly erratic and undependable'.[15]

Lastly, and perhaps most important of all, while she felt able to block Lawson's efforts to join the ERM, she must have known that she could not force him to revert to a hard monetarism in which he no longer believed – any more than she had been able to force monetary base control (MBC) on him and Howe in 1980. Mrs Thatcher had an enormous admiration for Lawson: his acute intelligence and economic and financial expertise, his stabilising of the public finances while also finding space to reduce taxes, his commitment to sound money and to free market principles, and his critical role in devising and promoting many of the supply-side reforms that were to make up the 'Thatcher revolution'. She could not afford to lose him – which would have been the outcome had she tried to force her continuing monetarist views on him. The result was a semi-truce, but also from time to time considerable tension, which – as explained in Chapter 11 – would eventually blow up and cause Lawson in 1989 to resign.

9

Counting the cost

It was well understood by monetarists and Keynesians alike that, incomes policy having failed, and with little prospect of it being reintroduced, there would have to be some deflation of demand and increased unemployment if inflation was to be brought under control. Increased unemployment would be needed to create slack in the labour market, and thus to persuade employees to accept lower pay settlements; and reduced demand would also put pressure on businesses to increase their prices by only the minimum needed to remain profitable. So an increase in unemployment was not unexpected. What surprised many – and these certainly included Mrs Thatcher – was the magnitude of the increase.

To give just one example – in November 1979, when the hard monetarist approach was well under way, the monetarist-leaning forecasters, Alan Budd and Geoffrey Dicks at the London Business School, published a forecast for unemployment of 1.7 million for 1982; in actuality, unemployment came out over 1 million higher, at 2.9 million, in that year. By contrast, their 1979 forecast of inflation in 1982 was almost correct – 8.1 per cent compared with actual inflation in 1982 at 8.6 per cent. In other words, the reduction in inflation was 'bought' at a much higher cost than they had expected.[1]

Andrew Britton, a former senior economist at the Treasury and then for over a decade director of the National Institute of Economic and Social Research (NIESR), in his authoritative account of the period, concluded that the 'conquest of inflation in the early 1980s ... was won at an exceptionally heavy cost in terms of unemployment and output lost'.[2] Leading economic journalist Sam Brittan, who was generally sympathetic to the government's monetarist strategy, agreed with another economist writer that the rising unemployment needed to achieve the inflation gains was a 'horrible scar'.[3]

In this chapter, I consider three questions: How great was the cost? What were the contributory factors that gave rise to the cost? And was it unavoidable?

The cost

There's no doubting that British society made a heavy sacrifice for the reduction in inflation. Monetarists had predicted that the short-term trade-off between higher unemployment and lower inflation would be modest. In his evidence to the House of Commons Treasury Select Committee in 1980, Milton Friedman wrote: 'I conclude that only a modest reduction in output and employment will be a side effect of reducing inflation to single figures by 1982.'[4] Patrick Minford wrote that, provided 'policies are properly understood when they are announced and implemented, the disturbance to output and employment from reduction in the money supply and in the PSBR would be minimal'.[5] David Laidler wrote: 'One would expect a reduction of five percentage points in the inflation rate to be yielded, as a first-round effect, by a one percentage point increase in unemployment' – although he qualified this by saying that he 'would not stake much on the quantitative precision of this'.[6]

It certainly didn't work out like that. The trade-off between higher unemployment and lower inflation was much worse than the monetarists expected. Between 1979 and 1983, as shown in Table 1, the rate of inflation fell by 8.8 percentage points, while the rate of unemployment increased by 6.1 percentage points, with absolute numbers of those unemployed increasing by 1.7 million. There was a 'bulge' in the unemployment rate over the four years of 17 percentage points – that is, the cumulative total of the increased unemployment rate in excess of the rate prevailing in 1979. This is a measure of the sacrifice in terms of additional unemployment to achieve the 8.8 percentage point reduction in inflation over the four years, which translates into a so-called 'sacrifice ratio' of 1.9. It means that, to achieve a one percentage point reduction in the inflation rate, there had to be the equivalent of a one percentage point increase in the rate of unemployment (approximately an extra 250,000 without jobs) lasting almost two years.[7] This is many times greater than the sacrifice ratio implied, for example, by Laidler in his evidence to the Treasury Select Committee.

An alternative approach is to look at the sacrifice in terms of lost GDP, as measured by the gap between actual GDP and what GDP would have been if it had followed its historical trend from 1979 onwards. Based again on the figures in Table 1, and taking the trend growth of output as 1.3 per cent per year (the trend growth rate for the period 1973 to 1979), the gap over the four years 1979 to 1983 sums to approximately 17.5 percentage points, just about the same 'bulge' as for unemployment. The loss of output over the four years, compared with output if it had continued on trend, was roughly £200 billion at today's prices.

Admittedly, these ratios can only offer a rough guide to what was lost in terms of jobs and output in order to bring inflation down. There are possible biases in both directions. On the one hand, the figures *understate* the sacrifice. The rate of unemployment carried on after 1983 until early 1987 at over 11 per cent, and unemployment continuing at this level achieved barely any additional benefit by way of further reduction in the inflation rate. In many towns and cities there were not the jobs to go back to because the factories where workers had once been employed had closed down altogether. Another influence, almost certainly, on the continuing very high rate of unemployment was that workers who had been unemployed for some time lost their skills and motivation. Employers opted to go for efficiency improvements rather than rehire – good for productivity, but not so good for unemployment.

On the other hand, even if the government had not been intent on curbing inflation, unemployment would have been rising anyway. The base year for the calculations is 1979, which was the peak year of the mid to late 1970s economic cycle. Consequently, there probably would have been a slowing of growth in the early 1980s anyway, and the economy was further affected by a world recession in 1980–82. Moreover, a good many of the lost jobs were in industries such as shipbuilding, steel, textiles, clothing and footwear, and coal mining, which were in long-term decline. In other words, a significant portion of the extra unemployment was 'in the works' anyway. In that sense, the sacrifice figures overstate the actual sacrifice that was incurred.

The reasons

Whatever these qualifications, it is clear that the job and output sacrifice was large. What were the reasons for this?

First of all, the cost of bringing inflation down was made significantly greater by the government's own actions in *increasing* the rate of inflation in its first year. By this I mean the nearly doubling of VAT in the 1979 budget, the Clegg pay awards for the public services and the increase in nationalised industry prices – and especially the first two. Each of these may have been desirable in their own right, but they meant that the deflation and the extra unemployment had to be greater than would otherwise have been necessary in order to achieve the actual drop in inflation.

In retrospect, the near doubling of VAT was a terrible mistake – and Mrs Thatcher was right to have been sceptical when Geoffrey Howe first mooted it to her. The theory was that, as it was a one-off, it would 'drop out' from the inflation rate after one year. In a crude sense, of course, it did. But in the meantime, it had a baneful influence on pay negotiations and in the pay settlements that resulted. It was hoped that trade unions would take into account the offset in the reduced income taxes – and for that very purpose a taxes and prices index was invented by the Treasury that combined the two. But in practice, it was the current and recent inflation rate that influenced the unions in their pay bargaining. It undoubtedly contributed to the disastrously high 1979/80 pay settlements – disastrous, that is to say, for the government's fight against inflation. It thus got to a considerable degree 'embedded' into inflation and was not just a one-off that fully dropped out a year later.

The VAT increase added 3.5 per cent to the inflation rate when it was introduced in 1979. If we assume conservatively that, say, half of it got embedded into inflation as a result of higher pay settlements, the cost of reversing its impact on inflation – based on the 1.9 sacrifice ratio calculated above – would have accounted for approximately one-fifth of the 17 percentage point 'bulge' in unemployment over the four years.

The pay awards for public service employees after the general election, based on Professor Clegg's recommendations, included 20 per cent pay increases for nearly 500,000 nurses and midwives and 18 per cent for 600,000 teachers, and increases in excess of 10 per cent for other groups. While these awards did not affect prices directly, they, too, would have influenced pay negotiations in the private sector, as well as adding substantially to public expenditure and borrowing. In her election campaign, Mrs Thatcher had unwisely, and – in view of the size of her election victory – unnecessarily, committed herself to fully honouring whatever Professor Clegg recommended.

While these actions by the government increased the eventual cost of bringing inflation down, it was the 1980 and 1981 recession that basically made possible the decline in inflation from 1980 onwards. Insofar as the recession was necessary in order to achieve lower inflation, it is, in a sense, immaterial as to how and why it came about. Yet the part that government played in causing the recession, however necessary it may have been from the point of view of bringing down inflation, was certainly of great interest at the time, and it continues to be a matter of political and historical interest to this day.

We know, of course, that the restrictive monetary and fiscal policies contributed to the recession. But there were other factors that were outside the government's control, namely the doubling of oil prices in 1979 following the revolution in Iran, and the world recession in 1980–82. The doubling of oil prices was estimated by London Business School forecasters to have reduced UK GDP by as much as 1.6 per cent in 1980 compared with what it otherwise would have been, as well as increasing UK inflation by 2.8 percentage points.[8] The world recession was estimated by the same forecasters to have reduced UK GDP in 1981 by 3.7 per cent, compared with what would have happened if the world recession had not occurred.[9] According to Andrew Britton's calculations, roughly half of the fall in GDP between 1979 and 1981 was due to the raising of interest rates and the tightening of fiscal policy.[10] The London Business School forecasters came to a similar view.[11]

Over the same two years, the number of unemployed increased by 1.2 million. If the effect of government policy on unemployment was in the same proportion as the effect on GDP, then government policies might have accounted for about 600,000 of the additional unemployed. This is more or less in line with other estimates that were made in the aftermath of the recession. In early 1982, Samuel Brittan wrote that 'short-term management might at most have added about half a million to the unemployment figures' between 1979 and 1981. He cited other studies suggesting between 500,000 and 700,000.[12]

The number of unemployed continued to increase by a further 600,000 by 1984. With the economy continuing to operate at well below its potential, it's reasonable to assume that a good portion of this further increase was due to deficiency of aggregate demand in the economy caused by a continuation of the government's restrictive macroeconomic policies, which were driven, in turn, by a determination not to allow inflation to take off again.

Was the cost inevitable?

By the late 1970s, there was more or less a consensus among economists that, over the long term, there was no such thing as a choice between low unemployment and high inflation, or high unemployment and low inflation. There was only one feasible level of unemployment in the long term, irrespective of the rate of inflation. This was Friedman's natural rate, the rate at which inflation remained stable, and this rate was determined by structural factors such as the flexibility of the labour market, the tax and benefit system and the housing market. However, even monetarists were in agreement that, over the short term, there *was* a trade-off between inflation and unemployment. In particular, lowering inflation did involve an increase in unemployment until the inflation goal had been achieved. The short-term unemployment costs would be higher, the greater the desired reduction in inflation, and the faster it was intended to achieve this lower inflation rate.

Without ever being stated explicitly, the Thatcher government's goal was to get the inflation rate down to low single-digit figures over a period of about five years, and to do so gradually. (This was implicit in the targets for £M3 in the MTFS.) Starting from an inflation rate of just over 10 per cent, this, on the face of it, should not have seemed too daunting, *except* that there was rising inflation in the system from the pay settlements over the previous Winter of Discontent, and this was greatly exacerbated, as we have seen, by the VAT increase, the Clegg pay awards, and the oil price increase. So, to achieve the inflation goal, there had to be a substantial squeeze and a far-from-gradual reduction in inflation from 1980 onwards if single-digit inflation was to be achieved on the same timescale.

But the economy was already under considerable downward pressure on account of the oil price increase, high interest rates, the high exchange rate and the world recession. Crucially, by March 1981, there was evidence of pay settlements over the previous few months falling rapidly – Howe referred to this in his budget speech – and monthly inflation was on a downward path. It did not require a further substantial deflation of money expenditure for this to continue. If a little more time had been spent looking at what was actually happening to pay settlements and to inflation, and less time being preoccupied with the monetary aggregates, we might have realised this.

With a less restrictive budget, inflation probably would not have come down so fast, and the eventual benefits of lower inflation would have been postponed. According to the natural rate of unemployment theory, unless the natural rate could somehow have been brought down, the cumulative costs in terms of higher unemployment might not have been any different: the costs would just have been stretched out. But that would have been beneficial in both political and economic terms.

Of course, we do not know precisely what would have happened to unemployment if monetary and fiscal policy, taken together, had been less restrictive. Based on the same proportionate trade-off between the increase in the rate of unemployment and the reduction in the rate of inflation that actually occurred between 1979 and 1983, if the unemployment rate had increased to, say, 10 per cent rather than 11.5 per cent (a difference of 400,000 in terms of jobs), then the inflation rate in 1983 might have been about 7 per cent rather than 4.6 per cent. A 10 per cent unemployment rate would still have been in excess of Stephen Nickells's estimate of 9.5 per cent for the natural rate of unemployment for the period, so in theory at least, there would still have been 'enough' unemployment for inflation to continue decelerating.

This purely arithmetic calculation may understate the benefits of a more gradualist approach after inflation peaked in 1980. Alan Budd and Geoffrey Dicks wrote that 'it is better to proceed slowly since this gives more time for all parts of the economy to adjust to the lower rate of inflation. ... If the inflation rate falls too rapidly, real wages are too high and unemployment rises.'[13] Given a little more time, another reason why inflation might have come down without so much additional unemployment is that the government's measures to improve the supply side of the economy and, in effect, to reduce the natural unemployment rate, should have begun to make an impact.[14] On the other hand, in his memoirs Lawson argued that a more gradualist policy wouldn't have worked because, from a high inflation starting point, it required a sharp shock to break high inflation expectations.[15]

The 1981 budget did have the desired effect on inflation, but the further increase in unemployment over the next two years was truly shocking and created exceptional hardship and strain in communities across the land, and especially in the Midlands and the North. The 'scar' became even more horrible.

Apart from avoiding the VAT increase, not paying out fully on the Clegg pay awards or a less deflationary 1981 budget, were there other things that the government could have done to reduce inflation at lower cost?

One was practical, although its effect would not have been immediate. The government could and should have moved more quickly to identify and implement measures to help reduce the natural rate of unemployment – that is to say, the rate of unemployment needed to bring the rate of inflation down. Trade union reform was the obvious one (and I discuss this in the next chapter), but there were other measures such as improved training for young people and for unemployed people, improvements in the housing market, changes in the tax and benefit system to incentivise the return to work, and deregulation and greater competition in product markets. All of these issues would be addressed over time, but too slowly. Mrs Thatcher would have liked to have moved faster, but there wasn't the will or the capacity among her ministerial colleagues. The second was more theoretical than practical – namely an incomes policy, either agreed or imposed. Budd and Dicks, significantly both monetarist in their thinking, wrote that:

> an incomes policy which held pay increases down to 10 per cent, for example, in the 1979/80 pay round could greatly have reduced the consequent rise in unemployment. Since such a figure would have been consistent with monetary policy (unlike the Labour government's ill-fated 5 per cent target in 1978/79), there need have been no pay explosion when the incomes policy ended.[16]

It would have prevented in 1979/80 what they called 'the disastrous discrepancy between pay settlements and the inflation rate consistent with the government's monetary policy'. They concluded that 'in general it is reasonable to believe that an incomes policy can play a transitional role in bringing wage settlements into line with monetary policy, although there are costs in terms of the distortions of relative pay'.[17]

These views expressed exactly what I felt at the time. However, for Mrs Thatcher, an incomes policy was intellectually and politically a non-starter. But in any case, even if constructed on a more sensible basis than in the last year of the Callaghan/Healey policy, it is hard to imagine the trade unions being willing to accept such a policy from her government.

Mrs Thatcher's attitude

Mrs Thatcher was undoubtedly surprised and upset by the rise in unemployment in the early 1980s. She had been led to believe by Milton Friedman and most of the British monetarists that the rise in unemployment consequent on bringing inflation down would be small and temporary. It turned out to be neither small nor temporary. It is an interesting question whether, had she been told in 1979 that the unemployment rate was likely to more than double and the numbers out of work might increase by 2 million, she would have wanted to adjust the economic strategy. The answer is that it probably wouldn't have made any difference. To start with, like other enthusiasts for monetarism, she wouldn't have believed the numbers. But second, thanks to her 'primitivist' understanding of monetarism, she implicitly believed that there really was no trade-off between unemployment and inflation, even in the short term. That is one of the reasons why she invented and would repeat the mantra 'There is no alternative'. And as for the option of a more gradualist approach after the inflation explosion in her first year in office, it is unlikely that she would have been content to aim for an inflation rate as high as, say, 7 per cent for 1983, which might well be an election year.

The most one can say is that she might have been spurred into moving faster to curb the power of the unions and to accelerate supply-side measures to bring forward the improvement in the real economy. And if I had been able to convince her that the VAT increase would cost jobs as well as increasing inflation, she might have been more robust in her initial opposition to it.

The Canadian economist Harry Johnson had once said in an address to the American Economic Association that what distinguishes Keynesians from monetarists is that the former care about unemployment and the latter do not. It would be untrue to say that Mrs Thatcher didn't care about unemployment. In her speech to the Conservative Party annual conference in 1980, she said:

> The level of unemployment in our country today is a human tragedy. Let me make it clear beyond doubt. I am profoundly concerned about unemployment. Human dignity and self-respect are undermined when men and women are condemned to idleness. The waste of a country's most precious assets – the talent and energy of its people – makes it the bounden duty of Government to seek a real and lasting cure.[18]

But this was the same speech in which she declaimed: 'The lady is not for turning.' There was no question in her mind of changing tack on the broad policy. This was partly because she was under the false impression, from the accelerating money supply figures, that monetary policy was overly loose. It was also because she was convinced that curbing inflation was imperative – morally, politically and economically – and that being less robust on inflation would do nothing, even in the short term, to preserve jobs.

When she talked about it, she would say that the rising unemployment was not the government's fault: it was the fault of the trade unions for not moderating their wage demands and the employers for giving in to them – although, in the public sector, this meant her own ministers. To what extent she fully appreciated the effect unemployment had on communities is doubtful. She spent very little time visiting the worst affected areas in the North and the Midlands or in Scotland and Wales. The civil disturbances in Brixton, Liverpool and other cities that took place in 1981 were attributed by many to the rising unemployment among young people and minority ethnic groups (the unemployment rate for both groups was approximately double the national rate). She disagreed: the riots were due, in her view, to the failure of community leaders and to moral weakness.

In July 1980, when confidence in the strategy was starting to wear thin both inside and outside government, Mrs Thatcher asked me to organise a meeting of academic economists with her at Chequers to review the situation. She suggested various economists she knew were sympathetic to the government's overall approach: Patrick Minford, Brian Griffiths, Jim Ball, Douglas Hague and Christopher Foster.[19] She didn't want any of the government's critics. She reluctantly agreed to my suggestion that we invite my former tutor at Cambridge, Robin Matthews. He was about to become professor of political economy at Cambridge, the most prestigious chair at that university, which had once been held by Alfred Marshall, and was one of the government's more moderate critics – unlike James Meade, he didn't sign the famous letter to *The Times* criticising the 1981 budget. He was an expert on the long-run performance of the British economy as well as being a fine macroeconomist.

At the meeting, Matthews expressed concern that by not doing enough on the supply side of the economy – he mentioned in particular the imperfections in the housing market – the government was promising too much too soon. He was also worried about the hit to manufacturing from an overvalued exchange rate, and suggested that the government should 'talk the rate down'.[20] A shy man, he made little impact on Mrs Thatcher. But nor did Griffiths, someone she knew well, who expressed serious concern about the rising tide of unemployment. As so often with meetings with outsiders on matters relating to the strategy, she was looking for validation of her already fixed views rather than for new insights.[21]

10

Mrs Thatcher and the trade unions

Whether Mrs Thatcher had adopted monetarism or a more eclectic approach for tackling inflation, there's no doubt that the power imbalance between trade unions and employers that she inherited from Labour was going to make it all the more difficult. Even politicians on the centre-left recognised this, although they rarely spoke openly about it. While this issue is a slight diversion from the main topic of this book, it is, nonetheless, highly relevant.

Mrs Thatcher was ambiguous in her views on the labour market. When in her 'primitivist' monetarist mode of thinking, she believed that reducing the growth of the money supply would seamlessly bear down on wage settlements, and thereby quickly translate into lower price inflation. If the government made plain its monetary plan, and made sure to implement it, the trade unions would quickly adjust their wage-bargaining behaviour. Although he knew rather little about British trade unions, this was Milton Friedman's view. And Mrs Thatcher wanted to believe it.

Practically speaking, however, she was much less optimistic. She feared that inflationary pay settlements would continue, even if the Treasury and the Bank of England managed to get the money supply under control. And this could only mean the worst of both worlds: continuing high inflation combined with lower output and more unemployment.

It was this latter view that made her determined to bring about major reforms to the way the trade unions were able to operate and to reduce their bargaining power and influence. There was a political element in this, too: she was determined to avoid a situation wherein, as had happened with the Heath and Callaghan governments, the unions could potentially bring her government down through widespread strike action.

Mrs Thatcher fully understood the unsettling fact that since the 1960s inflation and unemployment had been rising together, and that higher and higher unemployment seemed to be required for inflation to be curbed. Although she refrained from describing it in these terms, the natural rate of unemployment had been inexorably on the rise. She believed instinctively – and this, too, was the firm view of her senior policy adviser, John Hoskyns – that trade union power was the major part of the problem.

Later research by Stephen Nickell and Jan van Ours showed that her instincts were correct. They estimated the natural rate of unemployment (or 'equilibrium' rate of unemployment, as they called it) at 3.8 per cent for the years 1969 to 1973, rising to 7.5 per cent for 1974 to 1981, and 9.5 per cent for the period 1981 to 1986. They concluded that the principal reason for this trend was the increase in trade union bargaining power vis-à-vis employers. By the late 1990s, the natural rate of unemployment, on their estimates, had fallen to under 6 per cent, and much the most important reason for this was the substantial reduction in the unions' bargaining power due to the 1980s trade union reform legislation and the decline in union representation in the private sector. The other significant factors were the toughening up of the benefit system, starting in 1983, and lower employment taxes, but taken together their effect was less than half the effect of the reduction in union power.[1]

This was consistent with the view of James Meade. He argued that, without reforms to wage bargaining, unemployment would have to rise to an unacceptably high level if inflation was to be brought down.[2] Mrs Thatcher implicitly accepted this, but she and her ministers moved too slowly on trade union reform to prevent it from happening.

Scholars on the left have tended to see Mrs Thatcher's determination to reduce trade union power as part of a neoliberal agenda aimed at rebalancing class and economic power in favour of capital – in the words of two of these scholars, 'the restoration of capital's class power over labour that has been restrained under the Keynesian social compact'.[3] But they were not alone. In an interview in the early 1990s, Alan Budd said he was worried there had been those who had never believed in monetarism as a way of combating inflation but who regarded it as a good way of creating unemployment and reducing the strength of the working class.[4]

This was not what motivated Mrs Thatcher. For her, except when she was in her 'primitivist' monetarist mode, unemployment was a sad, although necessary, consequence of the attack on inflation, and lower wage and salary inflation was necessary for industry to stay profitable and invest. Profits in British industry were at a dangerously low level; wages and salaries had been taking an increased share of national income. There had to be a rebalancing of the wage–profit share.

This was not just some pro-capitalist prejudice on her part. It was the Marxian economist, Andrew Glyn, who a few years earlier had identified the declining share of profits in national income since the 1950s – after many decades in which its share had been more or less stable. Glyn had attributed this decline to the increasing power of organised labour, and predicted that, unless it was reversed, the British economy would be in serious trouble.[5] Thus, in Mrs Thatcher's view, reducing the pay-bargaining power of the trade unions was necessary for combating inflation *and* for enabling industry to make adequate profits. She thought that the balance of power had shifted too far in favour of the trade unions at the expense of employers, but was often also highly critical of the latter for not standing up to the unions, and for their poor record with regard to investment and innovation.

Engaging with the trade unions

Mrs Thatcher had made it clear well before the general election that she wasn't interested in engaging the trade unions in any form of incomes policy. The trade unions had made it even clearer that they wouldn't be interested either.

Keith Joseph and Mrs Thatcher's monetarist contacts had warned her against having any truck with incomes policy on both doctrinal and practical grounds, and it was pretty much ruled out in the Conservative Party's election manifesto. The unions' unwillingness to cooperate with the Callaghan government over the 1978/79 winter would have made her even more wary of going down the incomes policy route. Asked at a press conference shortly before the election whether she would seek the cooperation of the unions, she replied that she 'expected the trade union leaders to cooperate' with the government. She meant – although it seemed wishful thinking at the time, and turned out to be – cooperation on trade union reform.

Whatever the recent experience of the Labour government with the unions, I personally found it hard to believe that Mrs Thatcher wouldn't want to establish at least some form of personal communication with them – to explain her policies and try to influence their behaviour in the coming pay round. Also, there were some in her Cabinet, especially her employment secretary, Jim Prior, who still were interested in trying for some kind of agreement on wages as the only way of achieving reduced inflation without a large hike in unemployment.

Ken Stowe, the principal private secretary in her first few months in office, suggested to Mrs Thatcher that she should meet with Len Murray, the general secretary of the Trades Union Congress (TUC). She agreed to do so, with great reluctance. The meeting was not a success. She was polite, but made no effort to reach out. She told Murray that, with the return to free collective bargaining, she hoped the trade unions would take into account the government's determination to bear down on inflation. She said that her plans for legislation on trade union reform were 'small and moderate' and would 'not follow the path of 1971'.[6] It was clear that Murray didn't believe her and left very dejected. He was keen, however, on further contact, and suggested that she meet with the TUC's economic committee, which she agreed to do.

The latter meeting took place a month later. It was a disaster. Murray presented a scorching critique of the recent budget and of the government's whole approach. Mrs Thatcher answered in equally trenchant terms.[7] Howe and Prior, who were also present, looked on uneasily. It was clear there wasn't going to be any cooperation between Mrs Thatcher and the unions, or even peaceful coexistence: the scene was set for the confrontations to come.

In her first week in office, German Chancellor Helmut Schmidt came to London for bilateral talks. He told Mrs Thatcher that he spent 200 hours a year in conversations with trade union leaders, such conversations being key to Germany's economic success. He believed that, by persuading union leaders to take into account the macroeconomic and employment implications of the wage bargains they struck with employers, he was able to secure lower inflation and lower unemployment. Mrs Thatcher expressed no serious interest: her response was merely to agree that inviting union leaders to dinner occasionally might be useful.

Howe and Prior together made a further effort before the summer was out to engage with trade union leaders on the economy. They suggested a National Economic Forum consisting of representatives from government, the unions, business and consumers. The aim would be to educate, disseminate and, if possible, agree on the main problems facing the economy and their solution. Crucially, this would include, on the lines advocated especially by monetarist economists, getting union and business leaders to understand the seriousness of the government's counter-inflation policy, with a view to reducing their inflation expectations, and thereby hastening the actual reduction in inflation and at minimum cost in terms of unemployment. Mrs Thatcher vetoed it on the grounds that trying to 'agree' was bound to mean the government compromising on its policies and the whole thing might look like a back door to an incomes policy.[8] In the light of their bruising first encounters with Mrs Thatcher, union leaders weren't interested in the idea either.

Wage inflation was, nonetheless, high on Mrs Thatcher's mind from her very first day in office when she saw the Cabinet Office briefing. She was alarmed at the prospects of large pay settlements for teachers, civil servants and other public servants that would follow in the wake of the Clegg Commission's recommendations. She asked to see Professor Clegg and tried to persuade him to come in with lower figures. Clegg, a courtly academic with strong connections to the Labour Party, stood his ground and said he would stick closely to his terms of reference, which was to make recommendations on the basis of comparability with the private sector. The Clegg recommendations, which during the election campaign she had said the government would honour, were to cause major problems for the budget deficit, and for inflation, over the next two years.

Whether with a more positive approach from Mrs Thatcher the trade unions would ever have come to terms with the government's economic strategy is questionable. My own view is that she should, nonetheless, have made a greater effort to reach out to them. Even if it had only made a small difference in terms of influencing their approach to wage bargaining and other economic reforms that the government were intent on, it would have been worth trying.

Trade union reform

Mrs Thatcher was frustrated by the slow start on the part of her employment secretary, Jim Prior, in moving ahead with trade union reform. Apart from monetary policy, failure to make an early impact in this area of policy was what caused her the greatest angst during my two-and-a-half years working for her. Prior was in favour of trade union reform but wished to go about it in a way and on a time line that would minimise the risk of industrial strife. It was surprising that she had appointed him to this post, since his views were well known from before the election when he had been Opposition spokesperson on industrial relations and the trade unions. I recall numerous meetings between him and Mrs Thatcher when she would push for faster and more radical action on issues such as the 'closed shop', secondary picketing, strike ballots and trade union immunities, and he would push back. Her contests with him included an impromptu visit to Prior's department, as she put it, to 'see what they are all doing'. His expert senior adviser on trade union reform, Donald Derx, became Mrs Thatcher's least favourite civil servant. She believed, unfairly, that he was holding Prior back. Strangely, she never wanted her policy adviser, John Hoskyns, to be present at her meetings with Prior. Hoskyns found this intensely frustrating – his views on trade union reform were well informed and even more radical than hers. But Mrs Thatcher didn't want him to make the running with Prior on the issue. She felt he had a poor grasp of politics, and she wanted to be in control.

Mrs Thatcher would have done better to have had Hoskyns alongside her, for she was disappointed with the scope of the first legislation on trade union reform, the Employment Act of

1980, and showed her displeasure by transferring Prior to the Northern Ireland Office in September 1981. She appointed in his stead her close ally Norman Tebbit, who brought to fruition the more radical Employment Act of 1982. The most important provisions of this Act were to do with secondary picketing, sympathy strikes and with restricting the immunities from civil action that the unions had hitherto enjoyed. In introducing the bill in Parliament, Tebbit said that the intention was to 'redress the imbalance of bargaining power to which the legislation of the previous government had contributed so significantly'. Judging from the furious response of various trade union leaders, they were seriously concerned that the legislation was going to reduce their power. There is little doubt that it did.

The legislation in 1980 and 1982, declining union membership (which had peaked in 1980), high unemployment and the defeat of the striking coal miners in 1984 – these all contributed to reduced union militancy, and eventually helped to make possible in the 1990s the combination of low inflation and significantly lower unemployment in that decade. It was logical that, given the experience of the 1970s and in the absence of an incomes policy of some kind, the trade unions would have to be weakened if inflation was to be suppressed, and without doing too much damage to the real economy. In that sense, Mrs Thatcher's desire to move faster than Prior on trade union reform was correct. Whether it was politically feasible was another matter. Prior, with the backing of the Confederation of British Industry (CBI), believed a gradualist approach was for the best in terms of achieving trade union acceptance. And she was not above the need for caution herself.

Thus, in early 1980, there was a serious strike in the steel industry that was ended with an inflation–busting pay increase of 16 per cent, which Mrs Thatcher personally approved. Even more seriously, in early 1981 there was a threatened national coal strike over plans to close 23 highly uneconomic pits. The National Coal Board and her energy minister, David Howell, were minded to press ahead with the closures. But after discovering that coal stocks at the power stations were too low for electricity supplies to endure a lengthy strike, and after much heart-searching, she decided that the planned closures should be cancelled.

She felt this badly, and soon set in hand a covert, but hardly secret, plan to gradually increase the power stations' coal stocks so that, when the next clash with the miners came, the government would be better placed to stand up to them. The build-up of coal stocks, together with the legislation on picketing, sympathy strikes and civil immunities, enabled the government to stand firm against the miners in 1984 without compromising on the pit closures. The violence on the picket lines involving the miners and the police has negatively coloured Mrs Thatcher's reputation ever since. Yet the defeat of the mineworkers' union sent an unmistakable and important signal that government policy was no longer to be blocked by trade union power as it had been in the 1970s.

The earlier climb-down in 1981 was a humiliation for Howell, and his political career never recovered. His misjudgement was to believe that Mrs Thatcher was ready to take the miners on at that time. She blamed him for the debacle, and moved him from the energy department to the transport department later in the year, and from the Cabinet altogether in 1983. She should have blamed herself, too, for not working more closely with him and giving him more support as this mini-crisis developed. She had lost confidence in his ability to oversee the management of the industry; I was taken aback by the ruthless way in which she treated him, especially since he had been one of the minority in the Cabinet who, in its early stages, had strongly supported the monetarist strategy.

In the wake of the 1981 climb-down, Mrs Thatcher asked me for suggestions on how Howell's department could be strengthened. I suggested that former diplomat John Guinness, now working in the Cabinet Office, should be inserted into the department at a senior level. Guinness's patrician style was unusual in the 1980s Home Civil Service, and not one that Mrs Thatcher found appealing, but I was able to persuade her that his mental agility and policy competence were of the highest order, and his move to the department was a great success. He would, in due course, become permanent secretary.

Prior was on the liberal wing of the Conservative Party, and he was appalled by the rising tide of unemployment. Ironically, however, it was his caution on trade union reform that indirectly helped to cause it. It was introduced too slowly. Until the reforms began to bite, it had to be left to rising unemployment to bring wage inflation down. The trade unions had shown, with the Winter of Discontent, that they would not work with Callaghan and Labour; and it was even less likely that they would work with Mrs Thatcher and the Conservatives. Therefore, Concerted Action on the lines recommended to her by Chancellor Schmidt was not a serious option. For tackling inflation, until trade union reform began to have an impact, it had to be left to high unemployment to do most of the heavy lifting.

11

The quest for an alternative anchor

Soon after Nigel Lawson became chancellor in 1983, and after I had spent 18 months on secondment to an investment bank (one of the first such secondments from the Treasury), I was appointed undersecretary at the Treasury heading up the Treasury's work first on finance economics, and then on monetary policy and financial institutions. I worked with some exceptionally talented individuals. Among these, Rachel Lomax would later become chief of staff to the president of the World Bank, permanent secretary in more than one government department, and then a deputy governor of the Bank of England. David Willetts would be a highly capable minister of state for universities and science in David Cameron's coalition government, and would write an important book on intergenerational inequality.[1] Martin Hall went on to senior positions in the private finance sector, and achieved a doctorate in Crusader Studies at London University.

In those days, the Bank of England *advised* on all key matters involving the conduct of monetary policy, especially on interest rates and public debt management. But it was the chancellor of the exchequer, and the prime minister, who *decided*. The Bank's advice was mediated through the permanent secretary (Peter Middleton), one of his deputies (Frank Cassell), and my monetary policy group.

The government's approach to monetary policy, now that the money supply was no longer the lodestar, had to be an eclectic one. Instead of focusing mainly on unpredictable and unstable money supply figures, a much wider range of indicators were looked at: price and wage inflation, the exchange rate, data on output and employment, and so on. Containing inflation remained a top priority, but output and unemployment were no longer ignored, as had been pretty much the case with monetary policy in monetarism's heyday during Mrs Thatcher's first two years in office.

Lawson and the Exchange Rate Mechanism

This eclectic approach seemed to be working reasonably well. Although unemployment remained exceptionally high, inflation was now down to around 5 per cent and the economy was growing. Lawson, however, wasn't satisfied. He regretted the absence of a money or nominal anchor for policy making and for influencing wage bargaining and price setting, and he was worried about the instability in exchange rates – not just for sterling, but for other countries' exchange rates too.

Partly due to the strong dollar, sterling dropped to an unprecedented low of US$1.05 to the pound in early 1985. Such instability, in his view, was bad for the UK's exporters and importers. Large fluctuations in exchange rates more generally were also bad for the world economy. He was therefore a strong supporter of greater cooperation between the leading finance ministries and central banks to reduce these exchange rate ups and downs – notably with the so-called Plaza Accord in 1985, which was aimed at securing a depreciation of the dollar[2] – and the Louvre Accord 17 months later, the aim of which was to stop the dollar from falling any further and to stabilise the currency markets more generally.

As for sterling itself, Lawson did not think a return to a fixed exchange rate was desirable or feasible, but he increasingly felt that, for the sake of greater exchange rate stability, and so as to provide a new nominal anchor in place of the money supply, joining the European Exchange Rate Mechanism (ERM) would be an attractive solution.

In a series of fraught meetings in 1985, Lawson tried to persuade Mrs Thatcher that we should join the ERM.[3] She refused. The main reason was that she was still attached emotionally and intellectually to the control of the money supply as the first priority: joining the ERM would formally mean abandoning this in favour of controlling the exchange rate. In the light of what she had learned from the Friedmanites, she also believed that floating exchange rates were preferable, both in principle and from a practical point of view. Although there was a degree of flexibility built into the ERM arrangements, she was suspicious that joining would lock the UK into a semi-fixed exchange rate regime. And finally, she didn't want UK monetary policy to be dictated to by the Bundesbank.

Over the next few years, Mrs Thatcher was unmovable on the issue. The tenor of the meetings in 1985 and the depth of her opposition undoubtedly damaged her relationship with Lawson; it made it near impossible for them to discuss what was a central question of macroeconomic policy; and it would eventually be the root cause of his departure.

Lawson found her intransigence highly frustrating – so much so that in March 1987 he adopted a policy, albeit never announced, of 'shadowing' the Deutschmark (DM). He instructed the Bank of England to intervene in the foreign exchange market to maintain the sterling/DM rate at just under 3 DM to the pound. The DM was in a period of weakness at this time, so it involved the Bank making very substantial purchases of DMs and dollars in the foreign exchange market to prevent sterling from rising above 3 DM. Lawson did this partly by way of fulfilling his obligations under the Louvre Accord, but his main purpose was to achieve a stable alignment with the DM, and thus achieve the same benefits as if the UK was a member of the ERM, and in the hope that it would lead to the UK joining.

It is a moot question, much debated then and since, as to how much Mrs Thatcher knew about this covert policy.[4] It appears that Lawson never actually discussed it with her. It is clear that she knew in a general sense that his policy was to stabilise the sterling/DM rate – she would have inferred this from seeing the Bank's large purchases of DM in its regular reporting on the foreign exchange market, and it was referred to in minutes addressed to her by my successor (but three) as private secretary, David Norgrove.[5] But she probably wasn't aware that Lawson had set the Bank of England a specific exchange rate target – not to allow the rate to move above DM 3.

Given her views on the ERM and her strong preference for floating over pegged exchange rates, why didn't Mrs Thatcher challenge Lawson on the issue? It was partly because it was a subject both of them found hard to discuss, and if he felt he could get away with it, it was a subject Lawson didn't wish to discuss with her. Maybe, because Lawson's reputation was riding high in the wake of a tax-cutting budget that had contributed to the Conservatives' victory in the May 1987 General Election, she didn't feel able to seriously challenge him. But putting to one side her instinctive preference to leave the exchange rate to find its own level, she may also have been perversely pleased that the Bank of England was building up its reserves of DMs and dollars against a time when they might be needed to defend the pound.

In an interview in early November 1987, Mrs Thatcher was challenged on the DM shadowing. She professed not to know about it. But now it was effectively out in the open, she did engage Lawson on the issue. The monetarist Brian Griffiths, in his role as head of her policy unit, had been warning her of the inflationary consequences of the Bank of England boosting the money supply via its purchases of DMs. Lawson would later claim that the Bank's purchases of DM did not inflate the money supply because they were 'sterilised' by additional sales of gilts. However, he ignored the fact that the low interest rates needed to keep sterling below DM 3 inflated bank lending.[6]

Mrs Thatcher told Lawson to back off and only continue with the shadowing if it could be done without large-scale intervention. By early March 1988, with continued upward pressure on sterling, it was clear that this was no longer possible, and on Mrs Thatcher's instruction, Lawson discontinued the policy, and there was a return to managed floating.

In 1987, and again in 1988, GDP grew at an unsustainable rate of 5 per cent, and although there remained a margin of slack in the economy, in the latter part of 1988 inflation re-emerged as a serious problem. These years were to be dubbed the 'Lawson boom' years. Mrs Thatcher would later blame the inflation on his policy of shadowing the DM and for losing sight of the need to control the money supply. A more plausible explanation is that the Treasury mistakenly forecast a slowing of growth in 1988, and – taking advantage of a forecast budget surplus for the first time in years – Lawson decided it was safe to announce substantial tax cuts in his budget (notably a cut in the higher rate of income tax from 60 to 40 per cent and a cut in the basic rate from 27 to 25 per cent), and he also kept interest rates at too low a level. These were the main reasons why the economy overheated and inflation accelerated. The faster growth in the money supply may have contributed, but it was not the main cause.

Then, in November 1988, Lawson tried a different tack. Unbeknown to very few at the time even within the upper echelons of the Treasury, he wrote to Mrs Thatcher, proposing to give statutory independence to the Bank of England, and making it responsible for the conduct of monetary policy and preserving the value of the pound. His models were the US Federal Reserve Bank, the Bundesbank and the National Bank of Switzerland. The scheme he had in mind would be closely matched by the Labour government in 1997, when they actually did make the Bank operationally independent. He argued that Bank independence would 'provide a beneficial jolt in inflationary expectations and would help to lock into the body politic of this country a permanent anti-inflationary force'.[7]

Mrs Thatcher rejected the proposal out of hand for two reasons. First, as she wrote, with inflation on the rise again it would be an 'admission of failure of resolve on our part' and an 'abdication by the Chancellor when he is at his most vulnerable'. Second, she did not wish to give up her own and the Treasury's control over interest rates.[8]

After this further setback, and despite the disappointing experience eventually with shadowing the DM, Lawson remained convinced that the best option for providing a nominal policy anchor was to join the ERM. With inflation on the rise, he felt all the more that being linked through the ERM to the discipline of the Bundesbank would be helpful, as well as for exchange rate stability. In the summer of 1989, he once again tried to convince Mrs Thatcher – this time in alliance with the foreign secretary, Geoffrey Howe. I had by now returned from my posting in Washington, and with the Foreign & Commonwealth Office's (FCO) John Kerr, I was tasked with drafting the paper they would submit to her. I was happy to do this as I was in favour of ERM entry. It was in the run-up to a summit of European leaders in Madrid where Mrs Thatcher was going to be asked once again to state her intentions with regard to joining the ERM. When she saw the paper, she felt she was being cornered into making an immediate decision, and would have none of it.

Alan Walters had returned from the USA to Downing Street in May 1989 as Mrs Thatcher's economic adviser once more. While she was away in Malaysia in October later that year, attending a Commonwealth Heads of Government Meeting (CHOGM), media reports emerged that he had been denouncing Lawson's departure from monetary targets and preference for a targeted exchange rate and joining the ERM. I was attending the meeting in my role as permanent secretary of the Overseas Development Administration (ODA). Mrs Thatcher asked me for my opinion. I told her that, whatever the rights and wrongs of the disagreement between the two on the policy, if Walters was to continue as her adviser, Lawson would consider his position untenable. She told me I was exaggerating.

Mrs Thatcher had no intention of losing Walters, and Lawson resigned. So ended the ministerial career of one of the UK's brightest and most accomplished reformist chancellors. Unwilling to be caught up in the political furore that would surely follow, Walters resigned immediately afterwards and returned to the USA.

Mrs Thatcher was a great admirer of Lawson for many of the things he did as chancellor. As late as 1988 she described him as 'unassailable' and 'my brilliant chancellor'. She had felt confident enough in his judgement to go along with the gradual down-grading of the monetarist holy grail. But in her heart, and egged on by Alan Walters and by Brian Griffiths, she never really lost her obsession with monetarism and controlling the money supply. It is sad, although perhaps inevitable, that she and Lawson eventually fell out essentially on this question.

Joining the ERM

Paradoxically, after Lawson's resignation, his successor as chancellor, John Major, was able to persuade Mrs Thatcher that joining the ERM would be a good idea after all. Although he had previously served in the Treasury as minister in charge of public spending, he had never been closely engaged in the ERM debates. He quickly convinced himself that there was no going back to monetary targets, and that joining the ERM combined the advantages of an external financial discipline and greater exchange rate stability without the rigidity of a fixed rate. There was also growing domestic political pressure, especially from employers' organisations such as the Confederation of British Industry (CBI), for the UK to join.

Over the summer of 1990, with greater patience and posing less challenge than Lawson, Major got Mrs Thatcher reluctantly to agree that joining the ERM was desirable and inevitable. Mrs Thatcher needed one final sweetener – that there would be an interest rate cut on the day of joining, which was to be 5 October 1990, just before the Conservative Party's annual conference. The Treasury and the Bank of England were unhappy with the interest rate cut because they thought it would give the wrong signal that this was a political deal rather than a decision to join justified on its economic merits. Major, who would just six weeks later succeed Mrs Thatcher as prime minister, ruled that it was worth it to get Mrs Thatcher over the line.

Joining the ERM didn't work out well. In the late summer of 1992, sterling found itself at the bottom of its agreed ERM band. The UK was obliged under the terms of the ERM not to allow sterling to fall outside its band, and the Bank of England was having to spend large amounts of foreign exchange in order to prevent sterling from doing so. Other ERM members' currencies were under pressure too. In early September, Italy was forced to withdraw.

Political uncertainties – and especially over whether France would be able to sign the Maastricht Treaty[9] – was one factor behind these difficulties. But the main reason was to do with German reunification in 1991. The German government spent massively to support the integration of the two Germanys, and this necessitated extremely high interest rates in Germany to maintain the value of the DM and keep German inflation under control. This, in turn, required high interest rates in other ERM members if they were to stay within their ERM bands. For the UK, it meant a prolongation of the recession that had ensued after the 'Lawson boom'. Former Conservative minister Norman Tebbit would call the ERM the 'eternal recession mechanism'.

John Major, and his chancellor Norman Lamont, made repeated requests to the Germans to lower their interest rates so that UK interest rates could be reduced. After the Italian withdrawal in early September, currency speculators turned against sterling. At a disastrous meeting of European finance ministers and central bank governors in Bath, Lamont pleaded with the Bundesbank governor to reduce the Bundesbank's key lending rate. The Bundesbank governor refused.

One option at that point could have been for the government to have sought a general realignment of currencies within the ERM system, to include a devaluation of sterling. Germany would have been willing to seriously consider such a realignment. But the Treasury judged that a devaluation would not allow UK interest rates to fall: they would still be in hock to German rates. Major and Lamont also considered that a devaluation would put paid to the government's credibility in managing the economy.

On 16 September 1992, a day that would go down in UK history as 'Black Wednesday', Base Rate was raised from 10 to 12 per cent in the morning. A further three percentage point increase was promised for later in the day. The Bank of England spent billions of dollars and other currencies in propping up sterling that day. But these measures failed to stem the speculative tide, and before the second Base Rate increase had been implemented, the government suspended UK membership of the ERM, never to return. The economic cost of the Bank of England's failed intervention was later estimated by the Treasury at £3.3 billion.

Exit from the ERM was accompanied by an immediate depreciation of sterling, exactly what Major and Lamont had sought to avoid, and in due course by lower interest rates. Both of these enabled the economy to recover and unemployment to fall quite swiftly and without reigniting inflation. But the chaotic and costly nature of the exit was to be regarded for many years as a symbol of the Conservative government's mismanagement of the economy, just as the IMF loan had been considered a symbol of Labour's economic mismanagement back in 1976. It undoubtedly played a part in the Conservatives' loss to Labour at the 1997 General Election.

Mrs Thatcher's long-standing scepticism about the ERM and not wishing to be at the mercy of the Bundesbank now seemed to be fully vindicated, and Lawson's long-held enthusiasm for it to be misplaced. In his memoirs he blamed the UK's departure on not having joined in calmer times back in 1985, when he had recommended joining; on German mishandling of the economic consequences of reunification; on the Bundesbank for failing to fulfil its own ERM obligations to assist other members in staying within their ERM bands; and on the misguided drive on the part of some ERM members towards monetary union. In spite of all these mishaps, he stuck to his belief that an exchange rate anchor for managing the economy was better than a money supply anchor.[10]

Whatever the case for the UK originally joining and the reasons for our departure, the UK's brief membership did help to bring inflation down – from over 10 per cent before joining in 1990 to 3.5 per cent when we left – even though it meant interest rates staying too high for too long.

Inflation targeting

After the UK dropped out of the ERM, an exchange rate anchor was no longer available, and a money supply anchor was long past its sell-by date. A decision had to be taken on what to do next by way of finding an alternative. Inflation targeting had been successfully pioneered in New Zealand in 1990, and then in 1991 by Canada. This is what the Treasury quickly opted for. Rather than using interest rates for targeting either the money supply or the exchange rate, the idea now was to use interest rates to achieve an explicit target for inflation.

Essentially, this meant using interest rates to influence the level of aggregate demand in the economy. To combat rising inflation, interest rates would be raised so as to bear down on consumer and investment spending, and this would put downward pressure on prices. Reduced spending would also mean reduced output and employment, and with fewer jobs, there should be moderation in wage and salary settlements, and therefore reduced inflation through that route, too. If inflation got too low, which at that time seemed unlikely, but would become an issue in the 2010s, interest rates would be reduced and would work in reverse.

In the period up to 1997, the inflation target was set as a range of 1–4 per cent. Zero or negative inflation was to be avoided since it might encourage consumers to postpone their spending. After 1997, when the Bank of England became operationally independent and was given sole responsibility for achieving the target, it was set at a single point of 2.5 per cent. In 2003, the target was reduced to 2 per cent.

The Treasury opted for an inflation target rather than a money GDP target, as advocated by James Meade (see Chapter 4), for several reasons. Data on prices is available more quickly than data on GDP; unlike GDP data, price data are never revised; and an inflation target is likely to be better understood and therefore more credible in terms of influencing expectations. To meet Meade's concern that, with an inflation target, higher inflation caused by a one-off supply shock might lead to too sharp a policy response, it was accepted that the Bank of England had a degree of discretion as to how rapidly it needed to get back on track to meet the target.

Inflation targeting has continued to the present day. In the period up to the Global Financial Crisis (GFC) in 2007, it proved a considerable success. Low inflation, low unemployment and steady growth were achieved in most years (see Figures A7–A9 in the Appendix). It worked well when Ken Clarke was chancellor between 1992 and 1997 and Eddie George was governor of the Bank of England – their monthly meetings on monetary policy were affectionately named the 'Ken and Eddie show'. The success of inflation targeting was further enhanced by the Bank of England's independence in 1997. Divorced from the vagaries and imperatives of politics, monetary policy – with its aim of achieving and maintaining low inflation – now had greater credibility than in previous times.

Success in achieving low inflation with steady growth in the early 2000s may have led to a certain complacency in the UK and elsewhere that all was well on the macroeconomic front. It was not, as the GFC was to rudely show – with the collapse or near-collapse of banks across the world and a sharp downturn in economic activity. The GFC's principal cause was reckless lending by banks and other lenders in the USA for so-called sub-prime mortgages (mortgages for people with poor credit-worthiness); the parcelling up of such lending into mortgage-backed securities and their onward sale to other banks in the USA and in other countries, including the UK; and finally, a major downturn in the US housing market, which resulted in insolvency for many borrowers and lenders. The fault lay principally with lenders and regulators in the USA, with some help from the Federal Reserve Bank, in keeping interest rates at too low a level.

The UK banking system could not have been isolated from the banking crisis in the USA. But the continuing drive for financial liberalisation (which had been right to begin with, back in the 1980s under Geoffrey Howe and Nigel Lawson's leadership, but later went too far), inadequate monitoring and supervision of the banks and poor decision making on the part of the bankers in investing in the dodgy, mortgage-backed US securities – all these made things worse in the UK than they otherwise would have been.

As we shall see in Chapter 13, inflation targeting in the period after the GFC was arguably *too* successful. Inflation was held at a very low level, but there was insufficient demand in the economy to enable a satisfactory recovery. In stark contrast, as I will go on to discuss in Chapter 14, inflation targeting was unable to prevent the sharp spike in inflation in 2022 as a result of Brexit, Covid-19 and higher energy and commodity prices due to the war in Ukraine.

12

The monetarists
and the critics look back

By the mid to late 1980s, Mrs Thatcher's unsuccessful experiment with hard monetarism – to be precise, the experiment with trying to control the money supply for the purpose of bringing down inflation – was finished, and a matter for the economic historians. In this chapter, I review the responses of some of the monetarists and some of their critics looking back.

The monetarists

In her memoirs, Mrs Thatcher appears to be in denial. In a chapter entitled 'Floaters and fixers', she writes: 'The only effective way to control inflation is to use interest rates to control the money supply.'[1] She also writes: 'Our success in bringing down inflation in our first term from a rate of 10 per cent (and rising) to under 4 per cent (and falling) had been achieved by controlling the money supply.'[2] This is, of course, misleading. Nigel Lawson in his memoirs would describe this as 'the myth of a golden monetarist age'. He pointed out that over the eight years for which monetary targets had been set, they had been breached in all but two years.[3] Inflation was, in fact, brought down by deflating the economy and by reducing the wage-bargaining power of the trade unions, not by controlling the money supply. Mrs Thatcher also says nothing about the enormous sacrifice in terms of lost output and unemployment, and whether inflation could have been brought down more efficiently and at lower cost. In relation to the £M3 figures, she claims that 'of course, we never just looked at monetary figures to gauge what was happening. We also looked at the real world around us.'[4] This may have been true – in fact, it was true later, but in her first two years in office, when hard monetarism prevailed, it was all too rare.

Lawson argued that, while the monetary targets had been missed, a 'tight monetary policy had brought down inflation largely, though not exclusively, via the exchange rate'. In other words, the policy objective had been achieved but not through curbing monetary growth. The 'spirit of the strategy' had worked, if not its content.[5] In his 1985 Mansion House speech, he admitted to the great difficulty he and Geoffrey Howe had had with £M3 as a monetary target because of its waywardness in relation to prices and incomes. In saying these things, he was implicitly accepting that the monetarist approach had been wrong.

Looking back ten years later, Mrs Thatcher's principal policy adviser, John Hoskyns, told an interviewer that the monetarist policy 'did a great deal of damage to the economy. ... They were trying to do it right but got it wrong.'[6]

What were the reactions of the British monetarist experts? With varying degrees of *mea culpa*, they all admitted the policy had not gone to plan. In his account of the period, Walters gives a relatively sunny description of what happened. This was a bit surprising, given his support for Jürg Niehans's criticisms in early 1981. 'It is difficult', he wrote, 'to exaggerate the importance of ... the MTFS [medium-term financial strategy].' The fact that the monetary targets and the public sector borrowing requirement (PSBR) projections contained in the MTFS had been serially overrun did not particularly worry him. It was the framework and commitment to financial discipline that mattered, whether or not the targets were adhered to. This is hard to reconcile with his and the other monetarists' view that published targets would enhance the credibility of the government's counter-inflation policies: how could this be so if the targets were overrun year after year? He conceded, however, that £M3 had proved seriously misleading, and that efforts to bring it back on track had led in 1980 to a 'very severe monetary squeeze'.[7]

David Laidler was much more critical – critical of the government's 'clumsy' implementation of the monetarist plan, and critical of himself and his fellow monetarists for faulty analysis and over-optimism. The clumsy implementation included: failure to take into account the VAT increase and the abolition of the 'corset' in the setting of the monetary targets; and failure to introduce a control system (that is, monetary base control, MBC), which would have enabled the Treasury and the Bank of England to control the growth of the money supply more effectively than reliance on interest rates, adjustments to government borrowing and sales of public debt.[8]

He and his fellow monetarist academics had been over-optimistic about the stability of the demand for money function (that is, the velocity of circulation). In a Deloitte, Haskins & Sells lecture at Cardiff University in 1988, Jim Ball stated that the instability in the relationship between broad money and money GDP had made the broad money target 'pretty silly'. Separately, he wrote: 'The crude focus on the broad measure of money, M3, in the Government's first eighteen months was disastrous (I say without hindsight) particularly as it was accompanied by a further major expansion in the public sector borrowing requirement.'[9] His former colleague at the London Business School, Alan Budd, originally an optimist on the stability of velocity, would admit many years later in an interview with a researcher that the use of monetary targets 'didn't really work, because the relationship between the growth of the money supply and the growth of the economy was too loose. ... No reasonable person would think you can control the economy through monetary targets.'[10]

The monetarists had, furthermore, been over-optimistic about the ability to bring down inflation without impacting too heavily on output and employment. According to Ball, they all knew that bringing down the great inflation of the 1970s would have significant adverse side effects on real income and employment, but 'none of us expected the deep and prolonged depression that ensued. ... The result of the misleading £M3 numbers was a monetary stance that was supposed to be gradualist, but was, in practice far from it. ... Monetary policy was inadvertently too tight.'[11]

Tim Congdon, on the other hand, argued that the monetarist strategy had, by and large, been a success. Comparing the situation in 1984 and 1985 with the corresponding years a decade earlier, he pointed to better outcomes on inflation, output and the balance of payments. Apart from his rather arbitrary choice of years for comparison, he conveniently left out the fact that unemployment was 2 million higher in 1984 and 1985 than ten years earlier, merely suggesting that higher unemployment 'may have been inevitable'. He believed that Lawson should have persisted with monetary targets rather than dropping them as he did in the late 1980s; had he done so, Congdon argued, the inflationary boom of those years would have been avoided.[12]

Unlike several of the other monetarists, Congdon was a consistent supporter of £M3 as the target variable, and he had no time for MBC. He felt that the strategy had been unnecessarily thrown off track by the Treasury's failure to foresee that the liberalisation of the financial system, including the ending of the 'corset', although desirable in themselves, would lead to the release of pent-up demand for credit from the banks, making the monetary targets much harder to achieve. He was also critical of the government for its part in actually causing higher inflation – that is to say, the VAT increase and the deliberate raising of public sector prices, and the high public sector pay settlements. In regard to the latter, he wrote: 'Text book versions of monetarism ... are silent about the problem of public sector inflation.'[13]

Gordon Pepper argued that monetarism hadn't failed; it had never really been tried. With co-author Michael Oliver, he wrote that 'the experiment during the 1980s was mainly an exercise in political monetarism and not control of the money supply'.[14] By 'political monetarism', he meant that the government had announced monetary targets in order to reduce inflationary expectations, and persuade the financial markets and wage bargainers that they were serious about containing inflation. But they hadn't been serious about controlling the money supply and meeting the monetary targets, because they had failed to adopt MBC. His particular gripe was that the government had focused almost exclusively on the *demand* side – on the demand for credit and the demand for holding money – and had done nothing with regard to the *supply* of money.

The government had, of course, rejected MBC, and it was true that the monetary targets had been serially exceeded. But it wasn't true that the government hadn't *tried* to control the money supply. In fact, they had tried very hard – in fact, too hard – through using high interest rates to reduce the demand for money and the demand for bank loans. Pepper failed to say what might have happened to the real economy and to unemployment if MBC *had* been adopted and had succeeded in containing the £M3 within the targets set.[15] Inflation might have reduced faster, but interest rates would almost certainly have been higher still, and the impact on the real economy would have been even more damaging.

Patrick Minford had been in favour of £M3 as the target variable, but in retrospect he said this had been a mistake: the monetary base (M0) should have been chosen, which 'was unaffected by deregulation and told a quite different story of sharply tightening monetary conditions'. As a result, 'policy turned out to be more fiercely contractionary than the gradualism intended; it was closer to shock tactics than gradualism'. But that didn't worry him. He would actually have preferred less gradualism and more shock. He argued – and had a model that purportedly proved this – that a better result for both inflation and output in the medium term would have been achieved if the monetary stance in the first two years had been even tougher. Whether or not he was correct in logic, in political, practical terms, he was talking in the realm of the fairies.[16] Many years later, the great guru himself, Milton Friedman, broke cover and said: 'The use of quantity of money as a target has not been a success. I am not sure I would as of today push it as hard as I once did.'[17]

One alleged benefit of the monetarist-inflicted squeeze on the economy was that it contributed to the significantly faster rate of growth of productivity during the 1980s compared to the 1970s. GDP per head between 1979 and 1989 increased by 2.1 per cent per annum on average, compared with 1.5 per cent between 1973 and 1979. The pick-up in the growth of labour productivity in manufacturing was even more striking: 4.2 per cent compared with 0.7 per cent (the 4.2 per cent figure for 1979 to 1989 was a near reversion to the 5.0 per cent per annum increase in manufacturing productivity experienced between 1960 and 1973).[18]

There were many reasons for the improvement. The removal of industrial subsidies, privatisation, trade union reform, financial services liberalisation, tax reform, joining the European Single Market and improved management morale – these all contributed.

So, too, as far as productivity in manufacturing was concerned, did the closure of relatively inefficient firms and job shedding among those that survived. The net job losses totalling 2 million in the manufacturing sector were entirely among the unskilled. In addition, there is little doubt that fear and anxiety induced by the threat of unemployment, heightened by a less generous benefits system, resulted in changes in shop floor behaviour that had hitherto been detrimental to efficiency; and the extreme financial pressures brought about by the high exchange rate may have forced management to look harder at finding ways of saving on labour costs. In this sense (the high unemployment and the high exchange rate), the monetarist strategy *did* have a positive effect on productivity, although to describe it as a *benefit* of the monetarist strategy is perhaps going too far.

In his careful account of the Thatcher era, economic historian Nicholas Crafts wrote:

> The policy reforms of the 1980s, while imperfect and leading to disturbing outcomes in other respects, probably raised rather than lowered the long run growth potential of both the economy overall and manufacturing compared with a counterfactual of trying to continue with the (ultimately unsustainable) policies of the 1970s.[19]

The critics

There were no surprises in the comments from those who had always been critical of the monetarist strategy – relief that it was unravelling, but also criticism that the strategy had been attempted in the first place.

Samuelson's colleague at MIT, the Nobel laureate Robert Solow, who was incidentally an adversary of my supervisor, the anti-monetarist Joan Robinson, on issues other than monetarism, wrote of Friedman after he died: 'Milton Friedman's are bad for society. Fruitless debates with talented (near-)extremists waste a lot of everyone's time that could have been spent more constructively, either in research or in arguing about policy issues in a more pragmatic way.'[20]

James Tobin contributed a typically lucid essay in *The Economist* magazine in which he showed how his long-held reservations about monetarism had been confirmed by subsequent events in the USA and in Europe – and in particular, the adoption and application of unreliable monetary targets to conquer inflation and the denial of fiscal action when it was needed to bring output into line with output potential.[21]

A former Treasury chief economic adviser, Bryan Hopkin, together with Brian Reddaway and Marcus Miller (a fellow student of mine at Yale), wrote:

> We think the progenitors of the Medium Term Financial Strategy greatly under-estimated the technical difficulty of keeping to their arbitrary and over-ambitious targets and the costs of doing so: if the government had achieved the M3 target in 1980/81, the costs to the economy would have been much greater. Moreover, they had a greatly exaggerated assessment of the possibility of influencing expectations in a helpful way by government statements, which would not really be believed and which would seem of little relevance to (for example) the people negotiating a particular wage-bargain: in general, they seem to have had an over-simplified and lop-sided view of the way the economy works.[22]

Most of the academic critics conceded that deflating the economy had been necessary for inflation to be brought down, but monetarism had been the wrong approach. On the other hand, Robert Neild, one of the strongest critics at the time, later wrote: 'monetarism, despite its fallaciousness, served a useful purpose – it provided a veil for the severe deflation that was needed to stop the inflationary spiral of the 1970s'.[23]

Mrs Thatcher's most ardent critic within the Cabinet was Ian Gilmour, a former owner and editor of *The Spectator* magazine. After she dismissed him in 1981, he published a stream of scathing and elegantly written books and articles criticising virtually every aspect of her economic policies – from monetarism to privatisation, deregulation, the Poll Tax, housing policy and reforms to the welfare state. There was one exception – namely her labour legislation, which he described as a 'successful and necessary assault on trade union powers'.[24] He compared monetarism to the 4th-century heresy, Arianism: 'As with Arianism, so with monetarism. Its adoption spelt its end. The theory was safe until it was fully put into practice.'[25]

Those critics who were watching monetary developments on both sides of the Atlantic tended to be a lot kinder about the 'Volcker shock', the policy of Federal Reserve Bank chair Paul Volcker to raise US interest rates to record heights in 1981.[26] Thus, the *Financial Times* columnist Martin Wolf, an earlier critic of Mrs Thatcher's monetarism, in an obituary piece praised Volcker for winning the battle against inflation and 'ushering the long period of stable inflation that later generations now take for granted'.[27] (Wolf also rightly celebrated him for his supreme virtues as a public servant.) Yet the 'Volcker shock' caused a dip in GDP for the USA no less steep than that in the UK.

On the other hand, what made Volcker's actions seem more acceptable and necessary than the monetary squeeze in the UK was the fact that, unlike in the UK, he was acting in the face of an expansionary federal budget over which he had no control; and the US recovery after the 'shock' was speedier and more robust and thus there was less long-term damage. British critics, also, were perhaps less interested in the loss of jobs in Detroit than in Lancashire.

I got to know Paul Volcker well during my years in Washington (1985–88) as the Treasury's representative there. I admired him greatly for his wisdom and expertise, and for his public service values. Unlike Treasury Secretary James Baker, he went out of his way to be friendly and understanding of British interests – although he was less than happy when I took members of the Treasury Select Committee to see him. Tory MP Nicholas Budgen placed his feet on Volcker's table as if he was at an undergraduate dining club, Labour's Brian Sedgemore delivered an anti-American polemic, while his Labour colleague, Austin Mitchell, walked around the room taking photographs.

In retracing this story of British monetarism, I have wondered with hindsight whether – in view of the success with inflation targeting from the 1990s onwards – public targets for inflation or for money GDP might have been helpful in the early Thatcher period. As mentioned earlier, money GDP targeting was proposed by James Meade and James Tobin. In a period of high inflation and great uncertainty as to the speed at which it could be reduced, it's an open question as to whether targets for either inflation or money GDP would have helped; quite possibly not. And in a period of such turbulence, a return to a managed exchange rate through membership of the European Exchange Rate Mechanism (ERM) would not have worked either. It may well be that it would have been better in this period not to have had any explicit anchor and conducted policy on an eclectic basis, using a mixture of monetary and fiscal instruments, and having regard to the full range of economic and financial indicators.

There are no real heroes in this sorry tale. I certainly wasn't one. If anyone came close to being heroic, it was the Treasury's permanent secretary, Douglas Wass. He believed in the importance of money and credit for the management of the economy, but he never accepted the monetarist doctrine, and he didn't hide his views from ministers. He argued strongly against the first publication of a monetary target in 1976. Having had his views on this set aside by Denis Healey, he went on to conduct a brilliant negotiation with the IMF to secure a better deal for the UK than had earlier seemed possible. In 1980, he argued even more vigorously against multi-year monetary targets and their publication. Again, his views were overridden. He might have resigned at this point for a lucrative career in the City or to lead a major university, but he preferred to stay on to moderate the policy when and where he could – for example, his key advocacy of the switch from extreme monetary tightness in favour of a tighter fiscal stance in November 1980, and his moderating views in the discussions over the 1981 budget. Despite his scepticism about monetarism, he recognised that there were upsides as well as downsides from the government's policies. Referring to changes in shop floor behaviour, he was reported as saying when he retired in 1983: 'This is a surprise to me. There is a potential for productivity growth on a scale we have not had in this country.'[28]

Peter Middleton, the key Treasury official just below Wass responsible for developing and implementing the monetarist strategy, wasn't a true believer either. While never admitting it publicly, according to his own typology (see Chapter 4) he probably counted himself somewhere between a 'reluctant monetarist' and a 'disbelieving monetarist'. Gordon Pepper called him a 'political monetarist'.[29] In the best British Civil Service tradition, Middleton nonetheless applied his very considerable monetary expertise, under the political direction of Mrs Thatcher and Howe and Lawson, to doing all he possibly could to make a success of their monetarist strategy. Its failure certainly wasn't due to him. The same could be said of other key Treasury individuals, such as Rachel Lomax, who worked on monetary policy at that time.

Bank of England Governor Gordon Richardson and several of his senior advisers, especially John Fforde and Charles Goodhart, also deserve to be remembered for their consistency and resoluteness in expressing their reservations with regard to the monetarist strategy and to MBC, when others – faced by a prime minister never happy with the Bank's performance – might have been more compliant. Of course, in the view of Walters and Mrs Thatcher's other monetarist supporters, that was part of the problem. But at the end of the day, Richardson and his advisers were more right than wrong.

A few Treasury officials found engaging with the monetarist agenda more than difficult. Andrew Britton, one of the Treasury's outstanding macroeconomists, left in 1982 to become director of NIESR. As mentioned earlier, the economist Henry Neuberger left to work for the Labour Party; one of the Treasury stars of the 1970s in the administrative service went into semi-hibernation and his Treasury career ceased to flourish. Among the members of Mrs Thatcher's Cabinet, Ian Gilmour sacrificed his political career through his outspoken opposition to the policies.

13

The legacy

In the light of monetarism's failure in the early 1980s, several of the key ideas associated with it have lapsed more or less into oblivion, both in academic circles and with policy makers.

First of all, except in very general terms over the long run, inflation cannot be ascribed to changes in the money supply, however defined. The statistical and causal relationship between the amount of money in the economy and the level of prices is just too uncertain. The main drivers of inflation are excessive spending in relation to the available supply of goods and services, and costs rising faster than productivity. Changes in the money supply over the short term do not offer a useful explanation for either. There are other non-monetary factors, too, which can drive up inflation: internal or external shocks such as tax changes, supply bottlenecks caused by industrial action, labour shortages in particular sectors, or higher import prices.

Second, for similar reasons, the idea that inflation can be curbed by setting targets for the money supply, and trying to control the money supply so as to hit those targets, has entirely lapsed. In tandem, so too has interest in monetary base control (MBC).

Third, very few economists today subscribe to the more extreme monetarist notion that governments and central banks have no role to play in trying to stabilise the real economy. It is almost universally accepted now that economies cannot be relied on to remain on a stable path of their own accord. The main job of macroeconomic policy, and in particular monetary policy, is to stabilise money GDP, and thereby hold down and stabilise inflation; but it is also the job of monetary policy, providing it

161

doesn't jeopardise the primary aim of controlling inflation, to help stabilise the real economy and employment as well.

Under the Bank of England Act 1998, the Bank – in addition to its primary mandate to control inflation – has a secondary mandate to 'support the economic policy of Her Majesty's government, including its objectives for growth and employment'.[1] The Federal Reserve Bank (the Fed) in the USA has a similar dual mandate. During the Global Financial Crisis (GFC), the Bank of England and the Fed each took dramatic action on interest rates both to bolster the financial system and to help mitigate the recession. The Bank's Base Rate was reduced by a full five percentage points – from 5.5 per cent in December 2007 to 0.5 per cent in March 2009. Milton Friedman would have approved of this because the GFC was the sort of 'major disturbance in the economic system', as he put it, for which monetary intervention was justified.

Friedman had also recommended, however, that governments and central banks should desist from trying to fine-tune the economy. He thought this was unworkable and would cause more damage than good. Yet in the case of monetary policy, that is precisely what the Bank of England (and other central banks) do today. Based on its regular assessments of inflation, monetary conditions and real economic variables, the Bank of England's Monetary Policy Committee has made frequent adjustments to interest rates in recent years aimed at achieving its inflation target without unduly compromising economic growth.

Some positives

On the other hand, there are several important ideas associated with monetarism that have become more or less mainstream among academic economists and policy makers. Their retention has been generally for the good, so in that sense, not all of Friedman's influence, by any means, turned out to be negative.

First of all, money does matter from the point of view of both analysis and policy making. The money supply, however defined, proved much less useful, either as an indicator of inflationary pressure or as an instrument for controlling inflation, than the monetarists had claimed for it. Nonetheless, never again will the

UK and other market economies be viewed largely in what might be called a money or finance 'vacuum', as tended to be the case in the heyday of Keynesianism in the 1950s and 1960s.

Second, there can be no trade-off or choice, for more than a few years at most, between the rate of inflation and unemployment. To be more precise, with a rising rate of inflation, there may be a temporary reduction in unemployment, but the reduction in unemployment will never be permanent.

Third, it follows that inflation – quite apart from the social injustices it causes – can do nothing permanently to assist the real economy, and will most likely damage it. The primary objective of macroeconomic policy therefore has to be very low inflation, and this requires macroeconomic policies that do not accommodate rising inflationary pressures.

Fourth, there is a 'natural rate of unemployment' below which inflation accelerates and above which inflation decelerates. One of the main objectives of supply-side policies, especially improvements in the working of the labour market, is to reduce the natural rate of unemployment so that inflation can be stabilised at the lowest possible rate of unemployment.

Fifth, the rate of inflation *is* responsive to adjustment in interest rates, and such adjustments are the appropriate instrument for keeping inflation under control and, in most circumstances, for managing aggregate money demand. As Bank of England Governor Mervyn King said in his 2005 Mais Lecture:

> Monetary policy aimed at price stability has proved to be the key to successful management of aggregate demand. Fortunately, the theory and practice of monetary policy in the United Kingdom have changed out of all recognition in the past twenty-five years. We have moved from the Great Inflation to the Great Stability.[2]

If King had known what was coming with the GFC, the austerity years and the Covid-19 pandemic, he might not have spoken quite so positively about monetary policy's role, but he was right insofar as monetary policy is to be preferred, as long as it is working, to fiscal policy for managing aggregate demand and controlling inflation.

These, then, are the main ideas from monetarism around which there is more or less a consensus – some that have been cast aside and some that have become part of mainstream thinking on macroeconomic policy. There is one key idea, however, around which there is less consensus, which is whether macroeconomic policy, in its stabilisation role, should operate solely through monetary policy, or whether it should on occasion also rely on fiscal policy.

The role of fiscal policy

The anti-fiscalist view, which was held strongly by the monetarists, is based on one or more of the following:

- The public are sufficiently rational that, in the face of an increased budget deficit, which they will eventually have to pay for in higher taxes, they will reduce their spending and increase their savings – such as to completely neutralise the impact on the economy of the increased deficit. This was the rational expectations hypothesis. One of its chief proponents, the American economist Robert Lucas, claimed that it spelt 'the death of Keynesian economics'.[3]
- A higher deficit, by raising interest rates, *crowds out* private spending to an equivalent or possibly even greater amount. Contrariwise, a tighter fiscal stance and lower public borrowing cause interest rates to fall and thereby *crowd in* extra private spending. The effect of any change in fiscal stance (a larger or smaller deficit) is therefore, for this reason, also neutral.
- Fiscal policy is too unwieldy in terms of political decision making – being hard to initiate and hard to reverse – and its impact is too unpredictable.
- Additional public debt is undesirable because it requires servicing, and this requires higher taxes in future; it may push up interest rates; and it may have negative distributional effects. It may also limit the government's ability to borrow at a future date when the need to borrow may be greater.

The first two arguments are theoretically possible, but the vast majority of economists and policy makers today – while ready to accept that the impact of deficit spending is less than the early Keynesians postulated – give neither of them much, if any, credence.[4]

The third and fourth arguments, however, do have to be taken seriously. Most economists today take the view that if monetary policy is working and is able to have its desired stabilising effect – controlling inflation and preventing the economy from going into recession or from growing at a rate above its potential – then it is superior to fiscal policy for this purpose, and that in most circumstances, using fiscal policy as a stabiliser should be avoided. Fiscal policy is too unwieldy and too uncertain in its effects to operate in this way, and is too likely to lead to costly economic distortions.

This is the corollary of the 'golden rule' adopted by the incoming Labour government in 1997, and confirmed by succeeding governments, that – over the economic cycle – the government will only borrow to invest and not to fund current, day-to-day spending. It effectively rules out using fiscal policy to stabilise the economy.

But what if monetary policy is *not* working? Should fiscal policy then be brought into play? Many economists would argue in the affirmative. Others – who are the heirs to the monetarists in this regard – still argue that fiscal policy should be used for stabilising the economy *only* in the most extreme circumstances such as war, a pandemic or major financial crisis. This was Friedman's position. The drawbacks to trying to use fiscal policy as an instrument of macroeconomic management are so great, they argue, that in normal times it should concentrate exclusively on the provision of public goods and public services, on improving the supply side of the economy, and on welfare.

Keynes, of course, took the opposite view, which was the one I had learned at university. He didn't believe monetary policy on its own would be effective in averting even modest economic downturn because a reduction in interest rates couldn't be counted on to have much effect on aggregate spending – especially when rates reached a very low level. Governments therefore have no option, whatever the political complications, but to increase public spending or reduce taxes to maintain economic stability. He wasn't much concerned about extra public borrowing because, unless the government was obliged to borrow abroad, the extra borrowing would be exactly matched by the extra wealth and savings that the borrowing and spending created, and the extra call on the budget for the additional interest payments would be matched by the payments received by holders of the additional bonds. Even if this meant higher taxes overall, the nation as a whole would be better off and therefore able to pay the higher taxes.

Modern money theory

The so-called 'modern money theory' (MMT) developed by L. Randall Wray and others in the USA essentially takes the same view.[5] Their starting point is that we need to revert to Keynes, and accept that it is the government's job to close the gap between actual and potential output through its tax and spending policies. How any extra government borrowing is to be financed is, for them, a secondary issue. They argue that, for a country with its own currency and which hasn't adopted a fixed exchange rate, the borrowing can always be financed – if necessary, by 'printing money' (that is, funding by the central bank or by the commercial banks). MMT draws heavily on the work of Abba Lerner, one of Keynes's greatest disciples and advocates in the USA.[6]

The overall approach of MMT, with its emphasis on what is happening in the real economy and to employment and unemployment, and on the potential for using fiscal policy more actively, is a valuable corrective to the *anti-fiscalism* inherited from monetarism. Just as Harry Johnson contrasted Keynesians with monetarists years ago, MMT advocates care more about unemployment than they do about inflation. Yet contrary to what their critics say, they do not advocate extra spending and borrowing, or printing money, if it would lead to higher inflation. They would probably take greater risks with deficit financing and inflation than more orthodox economists, but they wouldn't ignore those risks. Where they are wrong, however, is in more or less ignoring the possible negative consequences of extra government borrowing, and also the issue of debt sustainability.

Almost any extra taxes needed to service the additional debt are likely to be distortionary, and may therefore hamper economic growth. Unless extremely narrowly targeted, the additional taxes are likely to be a burden on the general taxpayer rather than just on the holders of the additional debt, so there are likely to be negative distributional consequences between economic classes (the richest being holders of the additional debt and the poorer majority paying most of the additional taxes), and there *may* be an adverse distributional impact in favour of the old at the expense of the young.[7]

Debt sustainability

As for the issue of debt sustainability, this centres on the question of whether and to what extent, in the view of the financial markets, there is any probability of the government being unable to cover the interest payments on its debt, without resorting to inflation to reduce its real value. The question became all the more pertinent with the greater mobility of capital, as happened with the opening up of financial markets from the 1980s.

For every country, there is a 'debt limit', normally expressed as the ratio of public debt to GDP. This is the point at which a country effectively becomes insolvent – when it is unable to cover its interest payments and is unable to undertake any further borrowing. This was the situation of Greece in 2012. There is a much lower level of indebtedness, the 'debt threshold', where the debt level begins to have adverse effects on economic activity, to constrain a government's ability to stabilise the economy, and to put long-term debt sustainability at risk. The difference between a country's actual debt/GDP ratio and its 'debt limit' is termed its government's 'fiscal space' – the extent to which additional borrowing is feasible, if deemed necessary, albeit at rising cost.

The 'debt limit' and 'debt threshold' will differ greatly between countries – depending on many factors such as the savings propensity of their citizens, their government's prospective revenues, the history of their government honouring (or not honouring) their debts without resort to inflation, and political stability or instability. The former chief economist at the IMF, Olivier Blanchard, told an audience in Japan in 2021: 'We now understand that there is no magic number for debt-to-GDP ratios. Japan has convinced the world that it can sustain a 250% ratio of gross debt to GDP without a debt crisis.'[8]

One point, however, that Blanchard failed to bring out is that it was easier for Japan to sustain a high public debt ratio because it had, for many years, run a large surplus on its external balance of payments. Its government had therefore not had to rely on borrowing from abroad. In contrast, roughly 30 per cent of the UK's public debt in recent times has been held by overseas investors.

In 2013, IMF staff economists estimated that the UK's *debt limit* was a debt/GDP ratio of 167 per cent. Using a similar methodology, in 2011 the credit rating agency, Moody's, offered an estimate of 223 per cent; and in 2015 the Organisation for Economic Co-operation and Development (OECD) gave an estimate of 194 per cent. The OECD had suggested a *debt threshold* for all advanced OECD countries of 90 per cent.[9] An influential study by the American economists Carmen Reinhart and Kenneth Rogoff also cautioned against debt/GDP ratios rising beyond 90 per cent.[10]

The public debt/GDP ratio in the UK rose sharply during the GFC as the government spent in order to rescue the banks and to avert too sharp a recession – it rose from 36 per cent in 2007/08 to 65 per cent in 2009/10, rising further to 81 per cent in 2015/16.

In the post-GFC years, it was the government's explicit goal not to allow the debt/GDP ratio to go higher than 80 per cent. Whether this was the right thing to do has been hotly debated. These were the 'austerity years', when economic growth was sluggish and below its potential, and inflation averaged at 2 per cent – in line with the Bank of England's mandated target. There seemed to be scope for stimulating the economy without igniting inflation. The Bank of England attempted to do so through lowering Base Rate to near zero and through quantitative easing (QE) – the purchase by the Bank of gilts and commercial bonds from the public and from financial institutions. The former was aimed at keeping short-term interest rates at near zero, the latter at lowering longer-term rates.

QE seems to have been more effective in stabilising financial markets and stimulating extra spending in support of fiscal expansion in times of crisis – that is to say, during the GFC and Covid-19 crisis years – than it was in stimulating extra spending in the years *between* the two crises when fiscal policy was restrictive. Whatever its impact on spending, QE had one unfortunate side effect – that by pushing up asset prices, it increased the wealth of the owners of assets, and thus increased the inequalities between rich and poor.[11]

Many studies show that, when interest rates get to zero or close to zero (the 'zero lower bound'), monetary policy becomes less able to stimulate the economy; this is what Keynes meant by the 'liquidity trap'. So it shouldn't have been a surprise that, when interest rates reached very low levels during the austerity years, monetary policy on its own was unable to speed up the recovery.

The Treasury, under the chancellorship of George Osborne, was able to borrow in these years at exceptionally low interest rates. Even when the debt/GDP ratio reached 81 per cent in 2015/16, it was still short of the putative 90 per cent 'debt threshold', and a long, long way short of any possible 'debt limit'. Yet the Treasury opted not to use fiscal policy to provide any economic stimulus. On the contrary, government borrowing as a percentage of GDP was steadily reduced, such that fiscal policy was actually contractionary. As a percentage of GDP, the public sector borrowing requirement (PSBR) was reduced by an average of one percentage point per year between 2009/10 and 2015/16.

Many economists at the time took the view that, given the ineffectiveness of monetary policy, the very low interest rates at which government was able to borrow, and the still not excessive level of public debt, the Treasury should have set aside its concerns about debt sustainability during this period, and 'reassigned' fiscal policy to at least playing a part in ensuring an adequate level of demand in the economy. Leading Oxford economists Christopher Allsopp and David Vines, neither of them ultra-Keynesians, and both preferring monetary policy to fiscal policy for stabilising the economy providing it was working, were among those who took this view.[12] The Treasury's reluctance to use fiscal policy as an add-on to monetary policy in the austerity years in order to stimulate economic activity, and coincidentally to pay for better public services, shows that – in this respect – the long shadow of monetarism was still at work.

The Treasury under Chancellor Rishi Sunak had no such qualms about using fiscal policy to support the economy and individual livelihoods after Covid-19 arrived in the UK in early 2020, and the associated 'lockdowns' that followed. Between 2019/20 and 2020/21 the ratio of government borrowing to GDP increased by ten percentage points – from 2 per cent to 14 per cent. The public debt/GDP ratio at the end of 2022 had risen to 101 per cent. Because of the lockdowns, GDP in 2020 still suffered a fall of 11 per cent, the biggest one-year decline in several centuries.

Despite the very heavy government borrowing in these Covid-19 years, and despite the debt/GDP ratio rising well above the 'debt threshold' of 90 per cent suggested by the OECD, the cost of borrowing remained extremely low. In the two years 2020 and 2021, the yield on 10-year gilts never exceeded 1 per cent, albeit the latter was partly held down by the Bank of England's large-scale purchases of gilts under its QE programme, and the cost of the government's short-term borrowings was also less than 1 per cent.

The fiscal expansion is rightly credited with having helped to prevent a much deeper recession and much greater hardship than would otherwise have occurred. There would be a cost in terms of higher debt service in future years, but, especially given the low cost of the extra borrowings, there were few who thought this cost hadn't been worth incurring. And as Keynes would have wanted to remind us, while the higher debt service would be an additional burden on the budget, the cost to the nation collectively would be far less – since UK purchasers of the additional debt, who made up the majority, would be recipients of the higher debt service payments.

Among a few commentators, however, there was a less positive view – namely that the effective monetisation of the extra borrowing through QE would sow the seeds of a renewed inflation. In the next chapter, I will argue that this could only have played a small part in the re-emergence of inflation in 2022.

14

The return to stagflation?

By early 2023, the UK economy had largely recovered from the effects of the Covid-19 pandemic. Although trailing behind other advanced countries, GDP was back to its pre-pandemic level, and the unemployment rate was at its lowest level since 1974. On the other hand, the economy was experiencing much higher inflation than in recent years, and there was the prospect of anaemic growth or even recession. Some commentators called this a repeat of the 'stagflation' of the late 1970s and early 1980s. They also drew comparisons with the Winter of Discontent on account of the strikes across public services – with nurses, ambulance drivers, doctors, university and school teachers, and train drivers withdrawing their labour in support of higher pay.

'Stagflation' was the term coined to describe the combination of high inflation, low or negative economic growth and rising unemployment, which characterised the 1973 to 1983 decade. The two worst years were 1975 and 1980. If we just focus on 1980, inflation peaked at 22 per cent in May of that year, and averaged 18 per cent for the year as a whole. GDP declined by 2.2 per cent, and the unemployment rate averaged 6.8 per cent, rising by three percentage points to 9.6 per cent in 1981 with the unemployed total averaging 2.6 million in that year.

The stagflation of the most recent past is far more modest in terms of scale, and its causes are quite different. And the strikes by public service employees, while causing considerable disruption, have been nothing like on the scale of the Winter of Discontent. In 2022, inflation averaged 11.6 per cent – its highest level in 40 years, but still a long way short of the 1980 experience – and in 2023 inflation started to come down. The Bank of England's

Monetary Policy Report in August 2023 was now forecasting that inflation would drop to 5 per cent by the end of the year, and back to the Bank's mandated 2 per cent target in 2025.[1]

GDP in 2022 for the year as a whole actually grew by a healthy 4 per cent, with the rate of unemployment averaging just 3.7 per cent. However, during the second half of the year, GDP growth began to slow, and forecasters were expecting a small decline in GDP in 2023 and the unemployment rate rising to just over 4 per cent. By mid-2023, forecasters had become a little more optimistic on GDP growth and unemployment, with the Monetary Policy Committee now forecasting a small GDP *increase* (half of 1 per cent) for 2023. The overall picture in terms of GDP, unemployment and inflation looked considerably more benign than in 1980 and 1981.

The one area in which the latest stagflation has been less benign than 40 years ago is in regard to living standards – hence, the 'cost of living crisis'. The best measure of living standards is real household disposable income (RHDI) – that is to say, average household income after tax. On a per capita basis, over the three financial years 1979/80 to 1982/83, RHDI actually increased by 0.5 per cent. Despite the deep recession, affecting output and employment, living standards were bolstered by wages and salaries growing faster than prices and by cheaper imports due to the appreciation of sterling and lower commodity prices other than oil.

By contrast, between the three financial years 2019/20 and 2022/23, RHDI per capita *fell* by a full 3.3 per cent. This is largely explained by average earnings increasing much more slowly than prices – earnings in 2022 grew by 6.2 per cent, while inflation was over five percentage points higher. The cost of living crisis impacted especially on poorer households, since the price of essentials, especially food and energy, rose much faster than inflation overall. It brought into sharp focus the glaring gap between the wealthiest and the poorest, with income inequality getting worse between 2021 and 2022.

The hard truth is that a fall in living standards was at some point inevitable because of the deterioration in the UK's terms of trade. There was a sharp increase in the price of energy and food imports due to the war in Ukraine, and import prices were higher more generally owing to supply bottlenecks consequent on Brexit. What we produce is now worth less. Comparing 2022 with 2021, the prices *paid* by UK households for goods and services rose nearly 4 per cent faster than the prices *received* for goods and services produced in the UK. The increase in import prices, relative to export prices, has made the UK a poorer country. No leading politician seemed prepared to explain this – it was left to senior officials at the Bank of England to do so.

The causes of the latest inflation were very different from the causes of the inflation of 40 years ago. In 1980 there were certain one-off price shocks – in particular, the near-doubling of VAT and the doubling of oil prices the previous year. But the inflation was mainly driven by higher wage costs. And the inflation rate was *held down* by cheaper imports resulting from the appreciation of the sterling exchange rate and lower world commodity prices.

In 2022, in contrast to 1980, there was no help from an appreciating exchange rate or lower commodity prices. According to the economist and member of the Bank's Monetary Policy Committee Swati Dhingra, 70 per cent of the 2022 inflation was due to external factors – that is to say, increased energy and other import costs. Only 30 per cent of it was due to higher labour costs. In other words, without the external factors, inflation in 2022 would have been more like 3.5 per cent rather than close to 12 per cent.[2]

With the rate of unemployment at less than 4 per cent, the labour market was relatively tight. One factor contributing to the tightness of the labour market was the departure of European Union (EU) workers. Another factor, and probably more significant, was the fact that the number of people of working age who were classified as 'inactive' had significantly increased since before Covid-19. Since 2022, the number of 'inactive' has decreased, but as of August 2023, the increase was still 350,000 above pre-pandemic levels. Much of the increase was due to people citing long-term illness or disability. This 'loss' of workers was good for the official unemployment rate but bad for inflation, for the social security budget, and for the economy's capacity to grow.

Even though the high inflation of 2022 was set to fall back, it proved more persistent than the Bank of England had expected.

The main reason is that the Bank underestimated the tightness of the labour market and the recovery of consumer demand as people dug into savings built up during the pandemic. The result was an excess of demand over supply, such that employees in some sectors were able to secure higher earnings more in line with current price rises and companies were able to increase their profit margins – both of which had inevitable inflationary consequences.

Hardly anyone has attributed the re-emergence of this inflation to excessive monetary growth. Recent *Monetary Policy Reports* from the Bank of England contain not a single reference to the money supply. Nor did Chancellor of the Exchequer Jeremy Hunt, in his March 2023 budget speech, mention the money supply. A much quoted recent paper from across the Atlantic by former Federal Reserve Bank chair Ben Bernanke and former International Monetary Fund (IMF) chief economist Olivier Blanchard on the concurrent US inflation has no mention of monetary growth either.[3]

One notable exception is Tim Congdon, who has continued with great persistence over the past four decades to view inflation through a monetarist lens. In giving evidence to the House of Lords Economic Committee for their 2021 report on quantitative easing (QE), he warned that the massive purchase of bonds by the Bank of England during Covid-19 (its stock of bonds reached nearly £900 billion by March 2022) would necessarily expand broad money, and thereby lead to higher inflation. For him, the higher inflation that ensued is proof of this.[4]

The injection of cash into the system by the Bank via QE during Covid-19 played an important role in stabilising financial markets, keeping interest rates low and indirectly helping to fund the ballooning public sector borrowing requirement (PSBR) – even if this meant that the PSBR was being indirectly monetised and therefore adding to the expansion of the money supply. (In the year to February 2021, broad money growth reached a peak of 15 per cent.) The alternative to this indirect funding of the PSBR through the Bank's QE programme would have been higher interest rates or a lower PSBR, and an even worse recession and worse hardship.

The minority of commentators like Congdon who blame the latest inflation on QE and monetary expansion seem to ignore the fact that over two thirds of the higher inflation was generated by external shocks. And they ignore the lesson painfully learned in the early 1980s that the link between monetary growth and inflation is extremely opaque and imprecise. Their assertion that larger holdings of cash must convert into higher spending begs the question, posed many years ago by Keynesians such as my Cambridge supervisor, Joan Robinson: why should pension funds and other asset managers, in deciding to sell their holdings of bonds when interest rates reach a very low level in order to take a profit and hold cash instead until they see interest rates rising and bond prices falling again, go out and spend the cash on goods and services?

That said, the swing of the pendulum against looking at changes in the money supply in analysing inflation and for the conduct of monetary policy has perhaps gone too far. As the Radcliffe Committee opined 65 years ago, the authorities have to bear in mind, when setting interest rates, the 'whole liquidity position' of the economy – that is to say, the quantity of financial assets that can, with varying ease, be changed into ready cash – which can, in turn, influence the level of spending in the economy. The money supply is one part, although not the only part, of this 'whole liquidity', and thus changes in the money supply do deserve attention – although not in the mechanistic way that was the case in monetarism's heyday.

The Bank of England's massive purchases of bonds during Covid-19 certainly increased the amount of liquidity in the economy, and since March 2022 it has taken steps to reverse this by selling its holdings of gilts back to the financial institutions. By reducing the price of gilts and increasing their yields, this has also helped, alongside the increases in Base Rate, to increase the cost of borrowing and thus dampen private spending. As of August 2023, the Bank had reduced its stock of gilts and other bonds by about £100 billion.

Going back to the very high inflation of 1980, the response of the Thatcher government was to deflate the economy in order to put downward pressure on wages and profit margins, and also to offset the one-off price shocks. The deflation was masked by the rapid increase in the money supply, but it was very real. The effect of the rising unemployment on wages was relatively muted at first, because unemployment was significantly below its natural rate – the rate at which inflation could be expected to start decelerating – but by 1981, pay settlements and price inflation were coming down quite rapidly.

In 2022, since external shocks were the main source of the inflation, it wasn't possible or appropriate to address the inflation problem in quite the same way. The external shock to inflation couldn't be ignored; otherwise, the price rise due to higher energy and other import costs would have become embedded into higher inflation on a continuing basis. But if the Bank of England had tried to bring the inflation rate back to 2 per cent in very short order, it would have had to tighten monetary policy in an even more draconian manner than in 1980. There would have needed to be a significant *fall* in money wages and money wage costs to offset the rise in energy and other import costs. The effect would have been a serious recession.

The Bank was right therefore to make use of what Mervyn King had called its 'constrained discretion' in deciding how fast to bring inflation back down to 2 per cent, and how hard it would have to press down on aggregate demand to achieve this. The fact that the 'natural rate of unemployment' was now thought to be in the region of 4 per cent, compared with over 9 per cent in the early 1980s, meant that unemployment would not need to rise by much in order to achieve a deceleration in inflation.[5]

Whether it is right that the Bank *should* have this particular discretion is an interesting question. Many would say that the speed at which inflation is to be brought down, and the resulting path for output and employment, is a political choice, and should therefore be subject to guidance from the government.

The discretion the Bank actually applied was to choose a path for inflation that would bring the inflation rate down to 2 per cent in 2024. This is the basis on which it appeared to conduct its interest rate policy in 2022 and 2023. Between January 2021 and August 2023, the Bank's Base Rate was raised in 14 steps, from near 0 to 5.25 per cent. In fact, inflation came down more slowly than the Bank and other forecasters predicted. With hindsight, if it was going to achieve 2 per cent inflation in 2024, the Bank should probably have moved more firmly in 2022 to dampen demand.

Against this background, it was clearly important that fiscal policy, if not specifically directed at combating inflation, should be supportive of the Bank's efforts. In the autumn of 2022, when inflation had become a serious problem again, the newly appointed prime minister, Liz Truss, and her chancellor, Kwasi Kwarteng, attempted quite the reverse. Instead of supporting the Bank's efforts to dampen demand, they announced major tax cuts. They were trying to repeat Ted Heath and Anthony Barber's failed trick in 1972 – attempting to 'grow the economy out of inflation', and quite the opposite of Mrs Thatcher and Geoffrey Howe's deflation of 1980 and 1981. The result was an immediate collapse of sterling to its lowest level ever against the US dollar, a sharp increase in market interest rates, and the forced resignation of Truss and Kwarteng. Labour likened them to 'gamblers in a casino'.

The intended tax cuts were quickly cancelled by their successors, Rishi Sunak and Jeremy Hunt. This restored stability to the financial markets, but without entirely annulling the damage to the government's economic credibility – as evidenced by a continuing higher cost of borrowing than before, both for the government and for home owners. The episode showed that, even if the prime responsibility for controlling inflation is with the central bank, fiscal and monetary policy have to operate in the same direction.

Sunak and Hunt had good reason, therefore, on counter-inflationary grounds, to try to avoid additional spending to fund higher pay settlements in the public services. Yet from the point of view of recruitment and retention, and equity in relation to employees in the private sector, some additional spending on public sector pay seemed inevitable. On the other hand, higher public spending and borrowing would put upward pressure on aggregate demand, and require the Bank to increase interest rates even more. The only alternative would be public spending cuts elsewhere, or higher taxes. Not a welcome quandary a year or two in the run-up to a general election.

Keeping control of inflation is made more difficult when the economy and labour productivity are growing slowly. Slow productivity growth constrains the growth of real wages. Slow growth in GDP means there is less government revenue, and therefore less scope for tax cuts and for more spending on public services. The desire for higher wages and the pressure for higher government spending and lower taxes are more likely, in these circumstances, to result in higher inflation.

Unfortunately, there has been an unprecedented slow-down in productivity growth since the Global Financial Crisis (GFC). Nicholas Crafts and Terence Mills have estimated that, in the fourth quarter of 2018, real GDP per hour worked was only 2.0 per cent higher than in the pre-GFC peak of the fourth quarter of 2007, and in 2018 there was a shortfall of 19.7 per cent between the actual level of productivity and what it would have been on the basis of the pre-GFC productivity trend. They ascribe this extraordinary slow-down to a combination of the GFC, the waning impact of information and communication technologies, and the uncertainties and relative shrinking of highly productive exporters caused by Brexit.[6]

Five years on, the productivity situation doesn't look any better. The impact of the GFC may be less important now, but this is offset by the negative impact of Brexit being probably greater than earlier seemed likely – in terms of lower exports and investment and shortages of skilled and semi-skilled labour. There was also the withdrawal of 350,000 from the labour force, which – if not reversed – will put a continuing damper on GDP growth.

The twin problem of low GDP growth and low productivity growth is the most daunting and most important economic challenge that the British government of whatever political stripe has to address. Improved skills, increased private investment, technological innovation, improved infrastructure, better arrangements for trading with Europe, persuading 'inactive' workers to return to the labour force – these are all needed. And so, too, is better decision making on public investment spending – to ensure the best possible benefit/cost outcomes.[7] How to make all these things happen – especially how to find the necessary resources when there are such pressures on the public finances, and when private savings are typically lower than among our main competitors – is another story.

15

Epilogue

Keynes once wrote about 'madmen in authority, who hear voices in the air [and] are distilling their frenzy from some academic scribbler from a few years back'.[1] Mrs Thatcher was perfectly sane, and the economists whom she admired were no mere scribblers. Yet the doctrine of monetarism that they espoused and promoted was highly contestable as a theory, and so was the empirical evidence that they claimed for its support. She allowed herself to be persuaded that monetarism was the holy grail, and that – with the addition of supply-side measures – it was the answer to the UK's economic problems.

After the wage explosion consequent on the Winter of Discontent, there is no question but that curbing inflation required a deflation of aggregate demand and an economic slowdown. But instead of nailing their colours to the mast of monetary targets and controlling the money supply, the government should have borne down on money demand through a careful admixture of monetary and fiscal restraint – careful to ensure that the burden of restraint was not borne excessively by high interest rates and a high exchange rate, and that the overall stance of policy was not *too* deflationary: not more deflationary than was absolutely necessary to bring inflation down to an acceptable level, and at an acceptable pace.

Interest rates and the exchange rate should not have been allowed to go so high. The government should have delayed any significant *inflation-inducing* policies – however desirable they were in principle – until the rate of inflation had been brought down to a reasonable level. Thus, the VAT increase and accompanying income tax cuts should at least have been delayed; and citing the deteriorating world economic situation, despite Mrs Thatcher's pre-election pledge, the government should have held back from paying out fully on the Clegg Commission pay awards to public service workers. The reforms to trade union law should have been brought forward more quickly and more decisively so as to reduce the upward pressure on pay settlements and improve labour market flexibility. If it had been possible to obtain some understanding with the trade unions and employers on pay and prices, as some among the Conservative Party's leadership had favoured prior to the 1979 General Election, that, too, would have helped. But given Mrs Thatcher's views on the trade unions and on incomes policy, and the views of the trade union leadership on the government's policies generally, such an understanding was never really a starter.[2]

It was unfortunate, to say the least, that Mrs Thatcher became so enamoured with monetarism before the 1979 General Election; that she failed – or was not given the opportunity – to consider its possible shortcomings; and then, after the election, adopted hard monetarism and ploughed ahead with it for too long when it clearly wasn't working. Although monetarism appealed to her instinctively, it is equally a shame that the monetarist community in academia, the City and the media were so persuasive with her. I and other 'disbelievers' in the Civil Service and in the Bank of England were, in some small degree, a moderating influence, but our hands were inevitably tied by the fact that monetarism, for her, was a political endeavour, and not to be seriously questioned by officials.

After I finished working for Mrs Thatcher as her private secretary in the autumn of 1981, my contacts with her were sporadic. One such contact was on a visit to London in the autumn of 1987 from my posting as the Treasury's representative in Washington, DC. I briefed her on the collapse of equity markets in the USA (Wall Street's 'Black Monday'), which she blamed on Ronald Reagan for his neglect of the Federal budget deficit.

The only extended time I spent with her was at the biennial Commonwealth Heads of Government Meeting (CHOGM) in Malaysia in October 1989. I had, a few months previously, been appointed permanent secretary at the Overseas Development Administration (ODA) with responsibility for the aid budget.

I was there as a member of the UK delegation to provide Mrs Thatcher with advice on aid and development issues, which always featured on CHOGM agendas. I knew she had little interest in aid for development and poverty reduction. In fact, she had been encouraged by LSE's Peter Bauer, a friend and admirer, to believe that aid often did more harm than good. When I was her private secretary, she had presided over severe cuts to the aid budget and had declined my suggestion that she should meet Robert McNamara, the outstanding president of the World Bank and former US defence secretary under Presidents Kennedy and Johnson. Earlier in 1989, she had pledged UK aid to support an exceptionally costly and uneconomic hydroelectric project in Malaysia, which, two years later, when a final decision on the financing had to be taken, I would feel obliged to do my best to block.[3] I therefore expected my role as her adviser on aid at CHOGM to be somewhat dispiriting. And it was. But there was also another reason.

At every CHOGM that Mrs Thatcher attended in the 1980s, the subject of economic sanctions against South Africa would feature prominently, and the Malaysia meeting was no exception. The issue of sanctions dominated the conference, and led to a great deal of acrimony. In 1986, Mrs Thatcher had given in to Commonwealth pressure and conceded the imposition of modest 'voluntary sanctions'. Now, in 1989, led by Australia and urged on by Nelson Mandela and other African National Congress (ANC) leaders, Commonwealth members wanted to impose a tougher sanctions regime. Mrs Thatcher was opposed, she said, because the South Africans would find ways of getting round them; to the extent they did work, they would impact adversely on the black population; and they would do nothing to persuade the apartheid government to move more swiftly to democratic rule – if anything, the reverse. She was also worried, although she didn't say so publicly, that tougher sanctions would hurt the UK's commercial interests in South Africa.

John Major, newly appointed foreign secretary after her dismissal of Geoffrey Howe in July of that year, spent many gruelling hours negotiating compromise language for the end-of-meeting communiqué. This included the UK's reservations about additional sanctions, and Mrs Thatcher signed up to it. Then, an hour after its publication, she put out her own statement, albeit co-signed by Major, stating in blunter terms her personal opposition to further sanctions, paying tribute to the positive developments that were taking place in South Africa, and suggesting that Commonwealth leaders should concentrate on encouraging the South African government rather than on further punishment.

I personally disagreed with her view that tougher sanctions would make the ending of apartheid less likely. I was shocked by her breach of Commonwealth etiquette in putting out a separate statement like this. I could tell that Major felt sidelined and humiliated.[4] However, the apartheid and sanctions issue was outside my official responsibilities, and although I observed what was going on at close quarters, I kept quiet.

What I failed to appreciate at the time, because no one in her inner circle told me, was that Mrs Thatcher's rough statement against further sanctions was her input to a brilliant diplomatic exercise being led by our ambassador to South Africa, Robin Renwick. He had been trying for months to persuade Prime Minister De Klerk to release Nelson Mandela from prison. The UK's strong opposition to further sanctions would be De Klerk's 'reward' for releasing him. On 2 February 1990, De Klerk announced the unbanning of the ANC, and on 11 February Mandela was released.[5]

The last time I met Mrs Thatcher (now Lady Thatcher) was at a talk on sterling and the euro that Alan Walters gave in November 2000, in one of his rare visits to the UK. Mrs Thatcher also spoke. Surrounded by other close advisers from her time as prime minister, and in contrast to the rather frail figure she often presented in her retirement years, she was in sparkling form. She thanked Alan Walters warmly for all the work he had done in helping her to conquer inflation and achieve economic recovery. It was not an occasion for her or anyone else to dwell on what might have been done better. In any case, judging from her memoirs, I doubt she would have felt there had been anything on the macroeconomic front in the early years of her premiership for which she would have wished to express her regrets. Sadly, as this book has attempted to show, for all her positive achievements as prime minister, her tryst with monetarism was not one of them.

Appendix

Figure A1: Growth of GDP and manufacturing output, 1975–90[a]

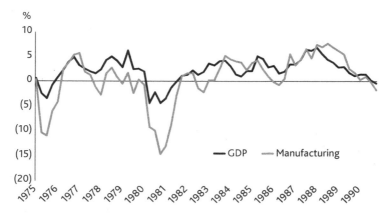

Note: [a] Quarter by quarter annual percentage growth rate.

Source: ONS, www.ons.gov.uk/economy/economicoutputandproductivity/output/timeseries/
k22a/diop; https://www.ons.gov.uk/economy/grossdomesticproductgdp/timeseries/ihyr/qna

Figure A2: Level of GDP and manufacturing output, 1975–90[a]

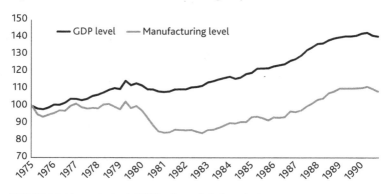

Note: [a] Quarter by quarter level of GDP and manufacturing output.

Source: ONS, www.ons.gov.uk/economy/economicoutputandproductivity/output/timeseries/
k22a/diop; https://www.ons.gov.uk/economy/grossdomesticproductgdp/timeseries/ihyr/qna

Figure A3: Rate of unemployment, 1975–90[a]

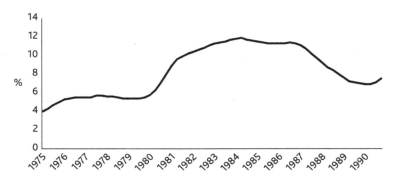

Note: [a] Quarter by quarter rate of unemployment (seasonally adjusted).

Source: ONS, www.ons.gov.uk/employmentandlabourmarket/peoplenotinwork/unemployment/timeseries/mgsx/lms

Figure A4: Rate of inflation, 1975–90[a]

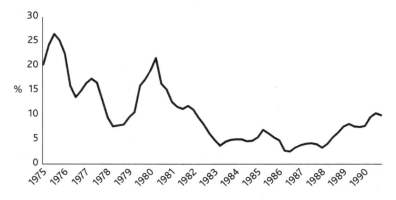

Note: [a] Annual percentage change in RPI by quarter.

Source: ONS, www.ons.gov.uk/economy/inflationandpriceindices/timeseries/czbh/mm23

Figure A5: Monetary targets and actual growth of money supply, 1979/80–1983/84

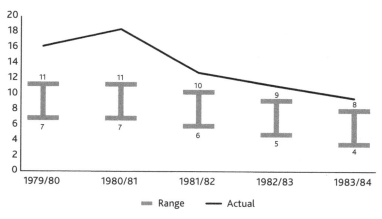

Note: Money supply in this chart refers to £M3.

Source: See Table 2

Figure A6: Velocity of circulation: £M3 and PSL2, 1963–86[a]

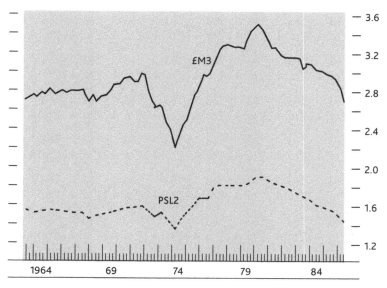

Note: [a] Ratio of money GDP to £M3 and PSL2.

Source: Bank of England (1986) 'Financial change and broad money', *Bank of England Quarterly Bulletin*, December, p 501, chart 4

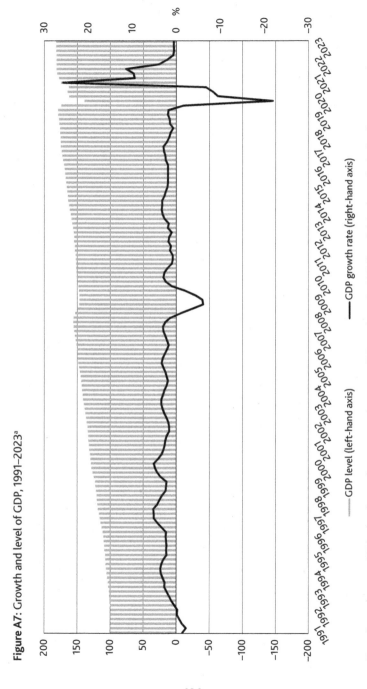

Figure A7: Growth and level of GDP, 1991–2023[a]

GDP level ((left-hand axis) ──── GDP growth rate (right-hand axis)

Note: [a] Quarter by quarter GDP levels and quarter by quarter annual percentage GDP growth rate. For 2023, the underlying data are for the first three quarters only.

Source: ONS, www.ons.gov.uk/economy/grossdomesticproductgdp/timeseries/ihyr/pn2, www.ons.gov.uk/economy/grossdomesticproductgdp/timeseries/ihyq/qna

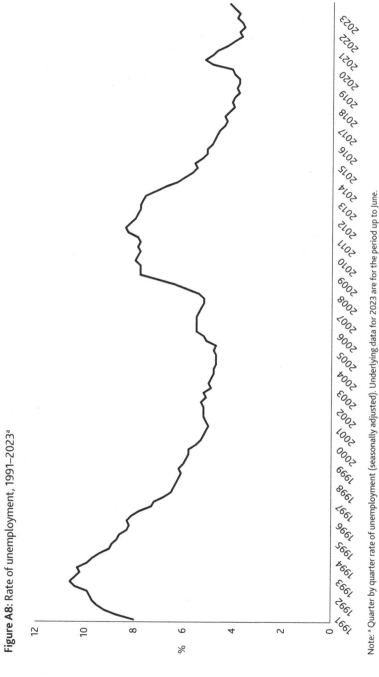

Figure A8: Rate of unemployment, 1991–2023[a]

Note: [a] Quarter by quarter rate of unemployment (seasonally adjusted). Underlying data for 2023 are for the period up to June.

Source: ONS, www.ons.gov.uk/employmentandlabourmarket/peoplenotinwork/unemployment/timeseries/mgsx/lms

Figure A9: Rate of inflation, 1991–2023[a]

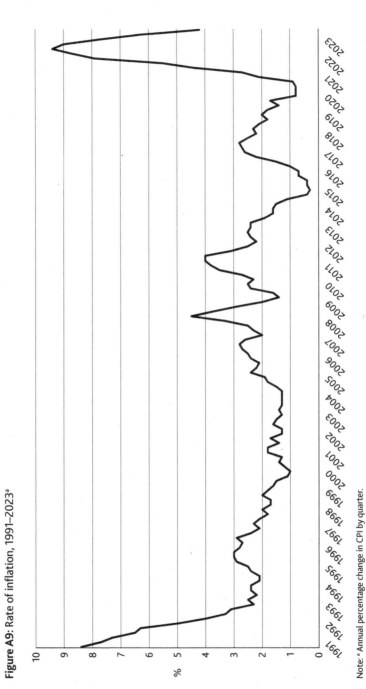

%

Note: [a] Annual percentage change in CPI by quarter.

Source: ONS, www.ons.gov.uk/economy/inflationandpriceindices/timeseries/l55o/mm23

Glossary

Base Rate

The interest rate the Bank of England charges commercial banks when they borrow from it. In the 1980s, it was known as Minimum Lending Rate. It is also known as Bank Rate.

CHOGM (Commonwealth Heads of Government Meeting)

Leaders of the Commonwealth countries meet every two years (see https://thecommon wealth.org/chogm).

Closed shop

A factory, office or other business establishment where employees must be members of a trade union.

Corset

Supplementary special deposits scheme (an instrument of monetary control) (see Chapter 5 for more information).

CPI (Consumer Price Index)

A measure of inflation published monthly by the Office for National Statistics. It measures the change in the cost of a representative sample of retail goods and services, excluding housing costs.

CPS

Centre for Policy Studies, a centre-right think tank, set up in 1974 by Sir Keith Joseph and Margaret Thatcher (see https:// cps.org.uk).

DCE (domestic credit expansion)	The expansion of lending by commercial banks to the private and public sectors.
ERM (European Exchange Rate Mechanism)	The exchange rate regime introduced by the European Economic Community in January 1979 whereby member states agreed to peg their currencies against each others'. The UK joined the ERM in 1990, and left it in 1992.
FCO (Foreign and Commonwealth Office)	The UK government department with overall responsibility for its foreign policy. Renamed the Foreign, Commonwealth and Development Office in 2020.
Fed (Federal Reserve)	The central bank of the USA.
GATT (General Agreement on Trade and Tariffs)	The international organisation set up in 1947 to promote and supervise reductions in trade barriers. It was superseded in 1995 by the World Trade Organization.
GDP (gross domestic product)	The total value, assuming unchanged prices, of all the finished goods and services produced within a country's borders.
GFC (Global Financial Crisis)	The 2007–08 financial crisis that affected banks, and their customers, across the world.
Gilts	UK government sterling-denominated bonds issued by HM Treasury.
IMF (International Monetary Fund)	Established in 1946 to oversee the international financial system and to provide assistance and advice to its member governments when their countries get into balance of payments difficulties.

M0 Currency notes and coins in circulation plus banks' reserves – that is, their till money and cash reserves with the Bank of England. Also known as the 'monetary base' or 'high-powered money'.

M1 Notes and coins in circulation plus current account deposits with banks. Also known as 'narrow money'.

M3 Notes and coins in circulation plus current account and interest-bearing accounts with banks. A slightly narrower category, called sterling M3 (£M3), excludes foreign currency deposits. Also known as 'broad money'.

MBC (monetary base control) A system of monetary control whereby the central bank aims to control the banks' liabilities (and therefore broad money) by limiting the growth of M0 (see Chapter 6 for a fuller explanation).

Money GDP GDP at current prices.

MTFS (medium-term financial strategy) The medium-term plan for the money supply and for the PSBR announced by the Conservative government in 1980, and updated annually through the 1980s.

Natural rate of unemployment The rate of unemployment at which inflation stabilises, below which it accelerates and above which it decelerates. Also known as the 'non-accelerating inflation rate of unemployment' (NAIRU) or the 'equilibrium rate of unemployment'.

NEDC (National Economic Development Council) An economic planning forum set up in 1962 to bring together management, trade unions and government, aimed at addressing the problems of UK industry. It was abolished in 1992.

NIESR (National Institute of Economic and Social Research) The UK's longest established independent economic research institute, focusing especially on macroeconomic issues.

ODA (Overseas Development Administration) The government department responsible for managing the overseas aid budget until 1997 when it was renamed the Department for International Development.

ONS (Office for National Statistics) The independent agency within the UK government responsible for collecting and publishing national statistics.

PSBR (public sector borrowing requirement) The combined deficits of central and local government and nationalised industries. It is now known as the 'public sector net cash requirement'.

PSL2 A wider measure of 'broad money': M3 (see above) plus building society deposits and National Savings.

QE (quantitative easing) The purchase of bonds by the Bank of England from the financial markets aimed at lowering medium- and long-term interest rates.

RPI (Retail Price Index) A measure of inflation published monthly by the Office for National Statistics. It measures the change in the cost of a representative sample of retail goods and services, including housing costs.

TUC (Trades Union Congress)   Federation of trade unions in England and Wales, representing the majority of trade unions, with a membership currently of about 5.5 million, down from a membership in 1979 of 13.5 million.

Velocity of circulation   Ratio of money GDP to the money supply, however defined, over a given period of time – normally one year.

Notes

Acknowledgements

[1] Wray, L.R. (2015) *Modern Money Theory: A Primer on Macroeconomics for Sovereign Monetary Systems*, Basingstoke: Palgrave Macmillan.

Chapter 1

[1] Some readers may be puzzled why in the remainder of this book I always refer to Mrs Thatcher with the prefix 'Mrs' while I don't include a masculine prefix when referring to the male characters. This simply reflects the way I always referred to her, except when I called her 'prime minister', and except among her more fervent critics, this was the way in which most people referred to her. The same convention also applied to other women in public life at that time. By contrast, men in public life were routinely referred to without any prefix.

[2] The Cabinet had 22 members, but the chief whip, Michael Jopling, also attended.

[3] Neild, R. (2014) 'The 1981 Statement by 364 Economists', in D. Needham and A. Hotson (eds) *Contractionary Fiscal Expansion: The Thatcher Government's 1981 Budget in Perspective*, Cambridge: Cambridge University Press, Chapter 1, p 8. Neild was the co-author of a statement signed by 364 economists, and published in *The Times*, which was highly critical of the 1981 budget. In this 2014 essay, he conceded that a 'short, sharp dose of deflation' had been necessary, as well as radical reform of the trade unions. But the deflation, in his view, went much too far.

[4] Thatcher, M. (1993) *The Downing Street Years*, London: HarperCollins.

Chapter 2

[1] Silk, L. (1981) 'The Thatcher plan's failure', *The New York Times*, 8 July, www.nytimes.com/1981/07/08/business/economic-scene-the-thatcher-plan-s-failure.html

[2] At the time of his resignation from the Treasury, Neuberger was head of its economic assessment unit. He would later publish a scathing critique of the Conservative government's macroeconomic policies. See Neuberger, H. (1983) 'Turning the clock back?', *Fiscal Studies*, 4(2), 43–54, https://ifs.org.uk/journals/turning-clock-back

[3] Congdon, T. (1982) 'Why has monetarism failed so far? The public sector problem', *The Banker*, 132(674), 43.

⁴ For the definition of £M3 and of other categories of the money supply, see the Glossary.

⁵ Mrs Thatcher also retained the other four private secretaries: Ken Stowe (principal private secretary), Brian Cartledge (foreign affairs), Nick Sanders (parliamentary affairs) and Mike Pattison (social affairs). But none worked in policy areas that were as diametrically different from those of the previous government.

⁶ This contrasted with Callaghan's Policy Unit, which included the economist and later leading figure in the City and chair of the BBC, Gavyn Davies.

⁷ Thatcher, M. (1993) *The Downing Street Years*, London: HarperCollins, p 46.

⁸ On his first day in office as chancellor of the exchequer in September 2022, Kwasi Kwarteng asked Tom Scholar to resign as Treasury permanent secretary. This certainly contributed to the financial markets' negative reaction to Liz Truss's and Kwasi Kwarteng's so-called 'Growth Plan'.

Chapter 3

¹ Lewis's book, *The Theory of Economic Growth*, was one of the foundational texts when I studied development economics at Yale and worked as an economist at the World Bank in the late 1960s and early 1970s (Lewis, W.A. [1955] *The Theory of Economic Growth*, London: Allen & Unwin Ltd).

² On this point, in a review article in 1933, Robinson wrote: 'He completely overlooks the significance of this discovery, and throws it out in the most casual way without pausing to remark that he has proved that output may be in disequilibrium at any number of different levels' (Robinson, J. [1933] 'The theory of money and the analysis of output', *Review of Economic Studies*, 1[1], 22–6, p 25).

³ Lekachman, R. (1966) *The Age of Keynes*, New York: Random House, p 59.

⁴ Keynes's ideas on macroeconomics and how governments should manage their economies came together in his most famous book, *The General Theory of Employment, Interest and Money* (Macmillan, 1936).

⁵ In the simple Keynesian model, the fiscal multiplier operates as follows: the private recipients of extra government spending spend part of the money they receive, and the recipients of that extra private spending spend part of the money they receive, and so on. The other part goes into savings, into taxes and into imports. In the original Keynesian model, the extent of these 'leakages' determines the size of the multiplier. The same applies in a similar manner to tax cuts. However, actual experience over the past decades shows that the size of the multiplier is much less than the size thus implied. Economists at the IMF have reported that, in 'normal times' (that is, other than when there is a major economic downturn), fiscal multipliers in the advanced countries in recent decades have been in the range of 0 and 1. The main reasons for multipliers being lower than in the Keynesian model are: the existence of automatic fiscal stabilisers, flexible exchange rates, higher (or lower) interest rates that may arise from a fiscal expansion (or contraction), and confidence factors that may affect private spending (see Batini, N., Eyraud, L., Forni, L. and Weber, A. [2014] *Fiscal Multipliers:*

Size, Determinants, and Use in Macroeconomic Projections, Technical Notes and Manuals, Fiscal Affairs Department, IMF, September, www.imf.org.external/pubs/ft/tnm1404.pdf).

[6] The 'target' rate was the rate of unemployment necessary to allow for shifting demand for labour between firms and industries ('frictional unemployment'), below which wage inflation was thought likely to increase.

[7] Keynes, J.M. (1931) *Essays in Persuasion*, Basingstoke: Macmillan, p 78.

[8] Keynes, J.M. (1923) *A Tract on Monetary Reform*, Basingstoke: Macmillan, p 17.

[9] Keynes, J.M. (1923) *A Tract on Monetary Reform*, Basingstoke: Macmillan, p 40.

[10] Lerner, A. (1964) 'Keynesian Economics in the Sixties', in R. Lekachman (ed) *Keynes' General Theory: Reports of Three Decades*, New York: St Martin's, pp 227–8, p 227.

[11] Nickell, S. (1990) 'Inflation and the UK labour market', *Oxford Review of Economic Policy*, 6(4), 26–35.

[12] Modigliani, F. (1977) 'The monetarist controversy or should we forsake stabilization policies?', *The American Economic Review*, 67(2), 1–19.

[13] Council of Economic Advisers (1961) 'The American economy in 1961: Problems and policies', www.jfklibrary.org/asset-viewer/archives/JFKPOF/073/JFKPOF-073-002, p 52.

[14] The quantity theory is encapsulated in the equation MV=PT where M is the quantity of money (however defined), V is the velocity circulation for that particular definition of the money supply, P is the average price level, and T is the output of goods and services in volume terms.

[15] Radcliffe, C. (1959) *Report of the Committee on the Working of the Monetary System* (Radcliffe Report), London: HMSO. Radcliffe was a senior judge. The nine Committee members included only two professional economists, Alec Cairncross and Richard Sayers. They did, however, take copious evidence from professional economists. The most influential of these for drawing up their final report was Cambridge's Richard Kahn. Paul Samuelson wrote of the Committee's findings: 'The unanimous conclusion of this distinguished group of British academics and men of finance was, in the end, that money as such did not matter.' He was only slightly exaggerating (Samuelson, P. [1970] 'Monetarism Objectively Evaluated', in P. Samuelson (ed) *Readings in Economics*, New York: McGraw-Hill, p 145).

[16] Samuelson, P. (1961) *Economics: An Introductory Analysis* (5th edn), New York: McGraw-Hill.

[17] Friedman, M. and Schwartz, A.J. (1963) *A Monetary History of the United States 1867–1960*, Princeton, NJ: Princeton University Press.

[18] See Ericsson, N.R., Hendry, D.F. and Hood, S.B. (2017) *Milton Friedman and Data Adjustment*, IFDP (International Finance Discussion Papers) Notes 2017-05-15, Board of Governors of the US Federal Reserve System.

[19] Mrs Thatcher's intellectual mentor, Keith Joseph, would echo this point in a speech in 1976 when he said an over-large public sector 'could play havoc with the best designed monetary policy'. See Joseph, K. (1976)

'Monetarism is not enough', Stockton Lecture, London: Centre for Policy Studies, https://cps.org.uk/wp-content/uploads/2021/07/111028102723-MonetarismisNotEnough1976.pdf

[20] Friedman, M. (1968) 'The role of monetary policy', *The American Economic Review*, LVIII(1), 1–17, p 14.

[21] Friedman, M. (1968) 'The role of monetary policy', *The American Economic Review*, LVIII(1), 1–17, p 14.

[22] Friedman, M. (1969) *The Optimum Quantity of Money, And Other Essays*, London: Macmillan.

[23] Friedman's reasoning, in contrast to that of Keynes, was that he believed that aggregate spending in all its forms is relatively *responsive* to interest rate changes, and that the demand for money (that is, velocity) is relatively *unresponsive* to interest rate changes. On these two points, at least in regard to the US economy, he was vindicated by later research. But this research also showed that the effect of interest rate changes only works through gradually, and that, in the short term, interest rates cannot be relied on to stabilise the economy. See Modigliani, F. (1977) 'The monetarist controversy or should we forsake stabilization policies?', *The American Economic Review*, 67(2), 1–19.

Chapter 4

[1] I joined the government's Administrative Service rather than the Economic Service as a 'late entrant' because I didn't feel I had the technical skills to flourish as an economist in a world where econometrics and forecasting models were becoming increasingly important, and because I wanted to be involved in policy work.

[2] See www.britishpoliticalspeech.org/speech-archive.htm?speech=174

[3] Friedman, M. (1968) 'The role of monetary policy', *The American Economic Review*, LVIII(1), pp 1–17. The address is now best known for Friedman's articulation of the 'natural rate of unemployment' hypothesis.

[4] Neild, R. (2014) 'The 1981 Statement by 364 Economists', in D. Needham and A. Hotson (eds) *Expansionary Fiscal Contraction: The Thatcher Government's 1981 Budget in Perspective*, Cambridge: Cambridge University Press, Chapter 1, p 8.

[5] Friedman, M. (1970) 'A theoretical framework for monetary analysis', *Journal of Political Economy*, 78(2), 193–238.

[6] Friedman, M. (1970) 'Monetarism, Yes', in P. Samuelson (ed) *Readings in Economics*, New York: McGraw-Hill, p 384.

[7] Friedman, M. (1970) 'The Quantity Theory of Money Vindicated', in P. Samuelson (ed) *Readings in Economics*, New York: McGraw-Hill, p 142.

[8] They could do this through open market operations – the purchasing and selling of government bonds from and to the banks – and by limiting the amount of cash they were willing to lend to the banks.

[9] Samuelson, P.A. (1970) 'Monetarism Objectively Evaluated', in P. Samuelson (ed) *Readings in Economics*, New York: McGraw-Hill, pp 145–54. This essay provides an excellent summary critique of Friedman's monetarism.

10 Wapshott, N. (2021) *Samuelson Friedman: The Battle Over the Free Market*, New York: W.W. Norton & Co, p 212.

11 Tobin, J. (1965) 'The monetary interpretation of history: A review article', *The American Economic Review*, 55(3), 464–85, p 480.

12 Tobin, J. (1980) *Monetary Policy – Minutes of Evidence*, House of Commons Treasury and Civil Service Committee, Session 1980–81, Volume 2, London: HMSO, p 215 (reprinted 1981).

13 Samuelson, P. (1970) *Readings in Economics*, New York: McGraw-Hill, p 146.

14 Johnson, H. (1971) 'The Keynesian revolution and the monetarist counter-revolution', *The American Economic Review*, 61(2), 1–14, p 13.

15 Johnson, H. (1971) 'The Keynesian revolution and the monetarist counter-revolution', *The American Economic Review*, 61(2), 1–14, p 12.

16 Volcker, P. (1989) 'The contributions and limitations of "monetary" analysis', *Quarterly Review*, Special Issue, 75th anniversary, 35–41, p 36.

17 Volcker, P. (1978) 'The role of monetary targets in an age of inflation', *Journal of Monetary Economics*, 4(2), 329–39, p 332.

18 Volcker, P. (1978) 'The role of monetary targets in an age of inflation', *Journal of Monetary Economics*, 4(2), 329–39, p 330.

19 Volcker, P. (1978) 'The role of monetary targets in an age of inflation', *Journal of Monetary Economics*, 4(2), 329–39, p 330.

20 Volcker, P. (1978) 'The role of monetary targets in an age of inflation', *Journal of Monetary Economics*, 4(2), 329–39, p 333.

21 Wapshott, N. (2021) *Samuelson Friedman: The Battle Over the Free Market*, New York: W.W. Norton & Co, p 212.

22 Kaldor, N. (1970) '"The new monetarism" 1969–1970', *Lloyds Bank Review*, July.

23 Robinson, J. (1970) 'Quantity theories old and new', *Journal of Money, Credit and Banking*, 2(4), 504–12.

24 Griffiths, B. (1976) *Inflation: The Price of Prosperity*, London: Weidenfeld & Nicolson. Griffiths argued that, if rapid inflation was allowed to continue, it would put prosperity seriously at risk, and 'even the future of capitalism, [and] the very existence of a free society'.

25 In his memoirs, Rees-Mogg wrote: 'We had created the forum for which the Chicago School of ideas could be propagated, challenged and accepted in Britain' (Rees-Mogg, W. [2011] *Memoirs*, London: HarperPress).

26 The bank liberalisation was implemented under a policy called Competition and Credit Control. One of its effects was to allow banks to raise deposit rates in relation to their lending rates. In the early aftermath of the new policy, until the banks became more fully competitive in their rate setting, this often led to 'round-tripping' – that is to say, large customers would borrow from one bank and place the money on deposit with another bank. Another effect was 'reintermediation' – the process whereby the banks recaptured a share of the lending, which, because of the controls, had been undertaken through non-banking channels.

27 Walters and Laidler were the two leading researchers in the UK on these relationships historically. Walters had researched the demand for money

relationship for the UK for the period 1867 to 1961, and in 1966 had published his findings. He, with co-author Noel Kavanagh, wrote: 'The evidence for the UK suggests some long run stability [in the demand for holding money] combined with very large variations in the short run' (Kavanagh, N. and Walters, A. [1966] 'The demand for money function in the United Kingdom, 1877–1961', *Bulletin of the Oxford Institute of Economics & Statistics*, 28[2], 93–116, p 104). In 1981, Laidler wrote: 'The demand for money seems to be more stable over time than the early critics of monetarism suggested. … Shifts in it have been not of sufficient magnitude seriously to undermine the long run relationship between money and money income' (Laidler, D. [1981] 'Monetarism: An interpretation and an assessment', *The Economic Journal*, 91[361], 1–28, p 25).

28 Walters, A. (1986) *Britain's Economic Renaissance: Margaret Thatcher's Reforms 1979–84*, Oxford: Oxford University Press, p 111.

29 It is more complicated than this insofar as changes in the public's and banks' holdings of notes and coins, and changes in the balance of payments, also have to be incorporated.

30 Burns, T. and Ball, J. (1976) 'The inflationary mechanism in the UK economy', *The American Economic Review*, 66(4), 467–84. In 1979 and 1980 the money supply expanded rapidly, yet the exchange rate *appreciated*. The advent of North Sea oil and high interest rates clearly 'overrode' any effect the rapid monetary growth might have had on the exchange rate the other way.

31 Minford, P. (1980) *Third Report from the Treasury and Civil Service Committee, Session 1980–81, Volume 2, Minutes of Evidence*, London: HMSO, p 14.

32 Brittan, S. (1975) *Second Thoughts on Full Employment Policy*, London: Centre for Policy Studies. As things turned out, the UK got the unemployment early on, *and* it continued at a high level for several years.

33 Griffiths, B. (1976) *Inflation: The Price of Prosperity*, London: Littlehampton Book Services, p 46.

34 Friedman, M. and Schwartz, A.J. (1982) *Monetary Trends in the United States and the United Kingdom: Their Relation to Income, Prices, and Interest Rates, 1867–1975*, NBER (National Bureau of Economic Research), Chicago, IL: University of Chicago Press.

35 Congdon, T. (1983) 'Has Friedman got it wrong?', *The Banker*, July, p 157.

36 Meade's Stockholm Lecture was published in *The Economic Journal* (Meade, J.E. [1978] 'The meaning of "internal balance"', *The Economic Journal*, 88[351], 423–35 [Stockholm Lecture]). See also his critique of monetarism in Meade, J.E. (1981) 'Comments on the papers by Professors Laidler and Tobin', *The Economic Journal*, 91(361), 49–55. In this latter article, he classified monetarists in a series of categories, including himself as a 'Keynesian monetarist'.

37 Burns, T. (1981) *Economic Policy and Prospects*, Taylor and Francis Online (www.tandfonline.com).

38 Brittan had proposed as early as 1975 that the Treasury should set a target for money GDP, but he also suggested that it would be best achieved through setting a path for the money supply (Brittan, S. [1975] *Second Thoughts on*

Full Employment Policy, London: Centre for Policy Studies). Later, in 1982, he dropped the idea of monetary targets and, like Meade, opted for targeting money GDP through instruments other than the money supply.

39 Meade, J.E. (1982) *Wage-Fixing*, London: Allen & Unwin.

40 Meade, J.E. (1978) 'The meaning of "internal balance"', *The Economic Journal*, 88(351), 423–35 (Stockholm Lecture), p 428.

41 Nigel Lawson, in his memoirs, mentioned money GDP as a possible objective, but dismissed it on account of the time lag in publishing first estimates and because first estimates were subject to revision. He also argued that money GDP was 'too removed from the instruments the policy maker has at his disposal' (Lawson, N. [1992] *The View from No 11: Memoirs of a Tory Radical*, London: Bantam Press, pp 416–17).

42 Middleton, P. (1989) 'Economic policy formulation in the Treasury in the post-war period', NIESR Jubilee Lecture, *National Institute Economic Review* (see https://journals.sagepub.com/doi/abs/10.1177/002795018912700104). Denis Healey, in his memoirs, called himself and Treasury officials 'unbelieving monetarists'.

43 Gilmour, I. (1996) *Dancing with Dogma: Britain under Thatcherism*, London: Pocket Books.

44 Keegan, W. (1984) *Mrs Thatcher's Economic Experiment*, London: Penguin Press.

45 Keegan, W. (2019) 'In my view', *The Observer*, 28 July.

Chapter 5

1 Tony Benn was secretary of state for energy. Leader of the left-wing anti-European Community, anti-IMF faction within the Cabinet, he was a constant thorn in Callaghan's side throughout his premiership.

2 Launched in 1975 with the worthy aim of improving productivity in manufacturing, it amounted to little more than a collection of studies and talking shops. Under the aegis of the National Economic Development Council (NEDC), a tripartite body involving government, trade unions and employers, it involved many discussions in Sector Working Parties, and monthly top-level meetings between ministers, and trade union and business leaders. I spent 16 months in 1977 and 1978 responsible for the Treasury's input to the Industrial Strategy. It is hard to claim that it had many concrete results.

3 For a useful discussion of the slowly emerging monetarism under Labour and under the Conservatives, see Needham, D.J. (2015) 'Britain's money supply experiment, 1971–73', *The English Historical Review*, 130(542), 89–122.

4 Needham, D.J. (2015) 'Britain's money supply experiment, 1971–73', *The English Historical Review*, 130(542), 89–122, p 91.

5 Goodhart, C.A.E. and Crockett, A.D. (1970) 'The importance of money', *Bank of England Quarterly Bulletin*, 10, 159–98.

6 House of Commons (1975) *Hansard*, vol 890, 15 April.

7 Congdon, T. (1976) 'Money supply growth rate guideline is 12%', *The Times*, 23 July.

[8]   Healey, D. (1989) *The Time of My Life*, London: Michael Joseph, p 491.

[9]   There was no requirement in the 1976 IMF agreement to limit monetary expansion as such. However, there was an agreed limit on DCE, and since DCE is the main credit counterpart to £M3 expansion (the other is the balance of payments surplus or deficit), the limits agreed for DCE meant, by implication, given the agreed forecast for the balance of payments, a limit on monetary growth.

[10] These included Deputy Governor Kit McMahon, John Fforde and Charles Goodhart.

[11] Richardson, G. (1978) 'Reflections on the conduct of monetary policy – the first Mais lecture', *Bank of England Quarterly Bulletin*, 1 March, City University, www.bankofengland.co.uk/-/media/boe/files/quarterly-bulletin/1978/reflections-on-the-conduct-of-monetary-policy.pdf

[12] Richardson, G. (1978) 'Reflections on the conduct of monetary policy – the first Mais lecture', *Bank of England Quarterly Bulletin*, 1 March, City University, www.bankofengland.co.uk/-/media/boe/files/quarterly-bulletin/1978/reflections-on-the-conduct-of-monetary-policy.pdf, p 34.

[13] The credit counterparts of an increase in M3 are: an increase in the banks' credit advances to the private sector *plus* the public sector borrowing requirement (PSBR) *minus* sales of public debt to non-banks *minus* overseas financing of public and private deficits.

[14] If the PSBR was larger, the volume of gilts purchased by the banks was likely to be larger, which would increase the size of their balance sheets, and therefore M3.

[15] This was the scheme whereby banks had to pay a swingeing penalty to the Bank of England if their interest-bearing deposits exceeded a certain level. It was devised by Charles Goodhart at the Bank of England. It worked well in constricting some of the lending (in particular, the 'round-tripping') that had boosted monetary growth artificially. At the same time, it drove a considerable amount of intermediation out of the banks, so that when the 'corset' was removed in 1980, it contributed to the massive growth of £M3 in that year.

[16] Wass, D. (2008) *Decline to Fall – The Making of British Macro-Economic Policy and the 1976 IMF Crisis*, Oxford: Oxford University Press, p 213.

[17] Representing the governments of France, Germany, the UK and the USA.

[18] The proposals were contained in a White Paper, *In Place of Strife*, Cmnd 3888 (1969). They were the work of Harold Wilson and his secretary of state for employment and productivity, Barbara Castle. Callaghan, who was home secretary, led the opposition to the proposals in Cabinet.

Chapter 6

[1]   ERG members on the pro-monetarist side, or tending in that direction, were Joseph himself, John Nott, John Biffen, Nigel Lawson and David Howell; firmly on the anti-monetarist side were Jim Prior and Ian Gilmour, who were old-fashioned Keynesians and advocates of prices and incomes policy.

[2]   For Lawson's views at this time, see his memoirs: Lawson, N. (1992) *The View from No 11: Memoirs of a Tory Radical*, London: Bantam Press, p 421.

[3]   Howe, G., Joseph, K., Prior, J. and Howell, D. (1977) *The Right Approach to the Economy: Outline of an Economic Strategy for the Next Conservative Government*, London: Conservative Party Central Office, October, p 7.

[4]   Howe, G., Joseph, K., Prior, J. and Howell, D. (1977) *The Right Approach to the Economy: Outline of an Economic Strategy for the Next Conservative Government*, London: Conservative Party Central Office, October, p 11.

[5]   Howe, G., Joseph, K., Prior, J. and Howell, D. (1977) *The Right Approach to the Economy: Outline of an Economic Strategy for the Next Conservative Government*, London: Conservative Party Central Office, October, pp 5, 12.

[6]   In fact, there were to be two bands – 2.25 per cent and 6 per cent. The UK was offered the wider band. Most of the joining members opted for the narrower band.

[7]   In 1986, when I was posted to Washington, DC, I had dinner with Tony Blair, at that time a junior member of Labour's Treasury team. He made exactly the same point: it would be good for an incoming Labour government, in the event of Labour winning the upcoming 1987 General Election, if the Conservative government decided to join the ERM ahead of the election.

[8]   Letter from Howe to Thatcher, 31 October 1978 (www.margaretthatcher.org).

[9]   See Thatcher, M. (1993) *The Downing Street Years*, London: HarperCollins.

[10] After their meeting, Friedman wrote to Ralph Harris, Director of the Institute of Economic Affairs, as follows: 'She is a very attractive and interesting lady. Whether she has the capabilities that Britain so badly needs at this time, I must confess, seems to me still an open question' (www.margaretthatcher.org).

[11] On the lack of science in economics, Mrs Thatcher was correct. My Cambridge supervisor, the brilliant Keynesian Joan Robinson, once wrote that 'economics is a branch of theology'. James Meade, in his 1977 Stockholm Lecture, when he received the Nobel Prize, described political economy as lying 'somewhere between the visions of literature and the precision of Natural Science' (see Chapter 4).

[12] Friedman, M. (1980) 'Monetarism: A reply to the critics', *The Times*, 3 March.

[13] In a television interview in February 1985 (*A Week in Politics*, Channel 4), Peter Jay asked Mrs Thatcher whether the unemployment rate (then at over 3 million) had reached its natural rate. She replied that the natural rate 'was not a doctrine to which I ever subscribed'. In answer to a parliamentary question from Michael Foot on 28 March 1981, she said that the natural rate 'is an academic concept, invented some time ago. I have never agreed with it or thought it sound'.

[14] This aspect of her working methods, her attention to detail, was generally praised by commentators, but it had its disadvantages when it blocked out attention to wider questions. This was captured, unkindly, but not altogether unfairly, by Ian Gilmour. Never on the same wave length personally or

ideologically, he would write: 'She was mistress of the irrelevant detail' (Gilmour, I. [1996] *Dancing with Dogma*, London: Pocket Books).

[15] Moore, C. (2013) *Margaret Thatcher: The Authorized Biography, Volume One: Not for Turning*, London: Allen Lane, p 425.

[16] Hayek, F. (1945) *The Road to Serfdom*, London: Routledge.

[17] Congdon, T. (1978) *Monetarism: An Essay in Definitions*, London: Centre for Policy Studies.

[18] Ortega y Gasset, J. (reissue 1994) *The Revolt of the Masses*, New York: W.W. Norton & Co.

[19] Hayek, F. (1984) 'An interview with A.F. Hayek', Libertarianism, 1 May, www.libertarianism.org/publications/essays/interview-f-hayek

[20] Hoskyns, J. and Strauss, N. (1977) *Stepping Stones*, London: Centre for Policy Studies, https://cps.org.uk/research/stepping-stones (attached to a letter from Hoskyns to Thatcher, 14 November 1977). In Hoskyns's letter, he told her to read the report twice and get back to him if she had any questions (www.margaretthatcher.org).

[21] Hoskyns's frustrations are vividly portrayed in his book (Hoskyns, J. [2000] *Just in Time: Inside the Thatcher Revolution*, London: Aurum Press).

[22] At the Conservative Party conference in 2016, Theresa May said: 'If you believe you are a citizen of the world, you are a citizen of nowhere.'

[23] Crafts, N. (2013) 'The economic legacy of Mrs Thatcher', VOX EU, Centre for Economic Policy Research Policy Portal, https://voxeu.org/article/economic-legacy-mrs-thatcher

[24] H.H. Asquith, David Lloyd George, Andrew Bonar Law, Stanley Baldwin, Neville Chamberlain, Winston Churchill, Harold Macmillan and Jim Callaghan had all served as chancellors of the exchequer; Ted Heath had held several Cabinet positions with large economic responsibilities; Harold Wilson had been shadow chancellor and had an education in economics.

[25] From time to time I also had to stand in for the private secretary for foreign affairs. For example, on 28 December 1979, I was the note-taker on the call between President Carter and Mrs Thatcher when he informed her of the Soviet invasion of Afghanistan.

[26] Letter from Lankester to the Treasury, 12 July 1979, PREM 19/38 f17 (www.margaretthatcher.org/document/114988).

[27] In her memoirs, Mrs Thatcher wrote: 'We were better prepared for taking the required economic decisions than any previous Opposition' (Thatcher, M. [1993] *The Downing Street Years*, New York: HarperCollins, p 42). If this was true, it said more about the lack of preparation on the part of earlier Opposition parties.

[28] Hotson, A. (2017) *Respectable Banking: The Search for Stability in London's Money and Banking Markets since 1695*, Cambridge: Cambridge University Press, p 142.

[29] Open market operations involve the Bank of England buying and selling Treasury bills and other government securities from and to the banks. Until the 1990s, this was done via the Discount Houses (see following note).

30   The Discount Houses, of which there were about a dozen, provided an efficient market in Treasury bills and other short-dated government bonds, which was of benefit to the Treasury and the Bank of England. But also, for reasons mostly lost in history, it was to them and them alone, and not to the clearing banks, that the Bank of England acted as lender of last resort. The Discount Houses could always borrow from the Bank of England, if they were short of cash, at Base Rate; and the banks could always obtain cash from the Discount Houses, either by reducing their outstanding advances to them or by selling them Treasury bills or other short-term securities. Through these tortuous but normally smooth-running arrangements, the Bank of England was able to influence the clearing banks' borrowing and lending rates in line with whatever was the prevailing Base Rate.

31   In his memoirs, Lawson described MBC as an issue of 'passionate interest to a small number of people and mind-numbing gobbledygook to many others' (Lawson, N. [1992] *The View from No 11: Memoirs of a Tory Radical*, London: Bantam Press, p 77).

32   Foot, M.D.K.W. (1981) 'Monetary Targets: Their Nature and Record in the Major Economies', in B. Griffiths and G.E. Wood (eds) *Monetary Targets*, London: Palgrave Macmillan, pp 13–61.

33   Lawson, N. (1992) *The View from No 11: Memoirs of a Tory Radical*, London: Bantam Press, pp 13–46.

34   The 'corset' was anti-competitive because it only applied to the clearing banks, and therefore put them at a disadvantage compared with other deposit-taking institutions.

35   Memorandum from Margaret Thatcher to Geoffrey Howe, 25 June 1979 (www.margaretthatcher.org).

Chapter 7

1   Their proposal for a medium-term financial plan was first set out in Burns, T. and Budd, A. (1977) 'Economic viewpoint: How much reflation?', *Economic Outlook*, October, 2(1), 7–11, London Business School with Gower Publishing.

2   Brittan, S. (1980) 'Lombard: A low surprise in the PSBR', *Financial Times*, 22 February.

3   Friedman, M. (1980) 'Memorandum submitted to the Treasury and Civil Service Committee', *Memoranda on Monetary Policy*, Session 1979/80, July, London: HMSO, p 56.

4   For a given monetary target, the higher the PSBR, the higher the interest rates would have to be in order sell more gilts to non-banks, and thereby to limit the amount of government borrowing from the banks. More government borrowing from the banks meant an increase in £M3.

5   See, for example, Beenstock, M. (1980) *Response to Questionnaire on Monetary Policy*, House of Commons Treasury and Civil Service Committee, Session 1979–80, Volume 2, London: HMSO, p 60.

[6]   When the 'corset' was in operation, businesses found it convenient to offer credits between each other rather than using the intermediation of the banks. Reintermediation, after the abolition of the 'corset', was the reversal of this process, bringing such credit creation back inside the banking system.

[7]   Memorandum from Berrill to Lankester, 25 February 1980 (www. margaretthatcher.org). When I was a student at Cambridge, Berrill was a fellow of King's College. He gave superb lectures on British economic history.

[8]   Memorandum from Goodhart to the Bank of England Governor's private secretary, 24 October 1979 (www.margaretthatcher.org).

[9]   Biffen to Thatcher, 3 March 1980 (www.margaretthatcher.org).

[10]   Record of meeting (Lankester to Wiggins, 10 March 1980) (www. margaretthatcher.org).

[11]   Minutes of Cabinet held on 13 March 1980 (www.margaretthatcher.org).

[12]   See Britton, A. (1991) *Macroeconomic Policy in Britain 1974–87*, Cambridge: Cambridge University Press, p 220 and table 14.10.

[13]   Record of a meeting between Thatcher, Howe and Richardson (Lankester to Wiggins, 3 July 1980) (www.margaretthatcher.org).

[14]   Galbraith, J. (1980) *The Observer*, 31 August.

[15]   HM Treasury and Bank of England (1980) *Monetary Control*, Consultation paper presented by HM Treasury and the Bank of England to Parliament by the Chancellor of the Exchequer, Cmnd 7858, London: HMSO.

[16]   Record of a meeting held at 10 Downing Street, 3 September 1980 (www. margaretthatcher.org).

[17]   These 'seminars' took place on 8 September, 18 September, 13 October and 17 November. For the seminar on 8 September, neither Richardson nor his deputy, Kit McMahon, were available as they were out of the country. They sent along in their stead two senior executive directors, John Fforde and Eddie George (who would become governor in 1993). Fforde was well known for his anti-monetarist views, which he did not disguise at the meeting. Mrs Thatcher was not amused, and was furious at the absence of both the governor and the deputy governor.

[18]   She stopped seeing Pepper after I warned her that she was unwittingly sharing market-sensitive information with him. Pepper was conscious of this himself and was, I think, quite relieved when the meetings stopped.

[19]   Backhouse. R. (2002) 'The macroeconomics of Margaret Thatcher', *Journal of the History of Economic Thought*, 24(3), 313–34, p 324.

[20]   A few weeks after my wife's family's textile business closed, Mrs Thatcher asked me out of the blue how it was doing. When I told her it had gone into liquidation, she was visibly shocked. She asked me if anything could be done to save the business. I told her it was too late. But in any case, quite apart from the fact that the Department of Trade and Industry, under Keith Joseph, had severely cut back its support for companies in difficulty, it obviously wouldn't have been appropriate for me to have been involved in any rescue effort.

21 Ibbs had been a senior director at the major chemical company ICI, and later became chair of Lloyds Bank.

22 Backhouse. R. (2002) 'The macroeconomics of Margaret Thatcher', *Journal of the History of Economic Thought*, 24(3), 313–34, p 324.

23 The Wass paper, entitled *Policy Options*, can be found at www. margaretthatcher.org (letter from Wiggins to Lankester, 7 November 1980).

24 Record of meeting, Lankester to chancellor's private secretary, 13 November 1980 (www.margaretthatcher.org).

25 Britton, A. (1991) *Macroeconomic Policy in Britain 1974–87*, Cambridge: Cambridge University Press, p 107.

26 Niehans, J. (1980) 'Monetary policy with overshooting exchange rates', *The Economic and Social Review*, 11(4), 281–300.

27 Hoskyns, J. (2000) *Just in Time: Inside the Thatcher Revolution*, London: Aurum, pp 263, 269.

28 For a more detailed account of the decision-making on the 1981 budget, see Lankester, T. (2014) 'The 1981 Budget: How Did It Come About?', in D. Needham and A. Hotson (eds) *Expansionary Fiscal Contraction: The Thatcher Government's 1981 Budget in Perspective*, Cambridge: Cambridge University Press, Chapter 2. The title of this book was misleading since the 1981 budget was 'contractionary' not 'expansionary'.

29 For an analysis of the effects of the 1981 budget, see Britton, A. (1991) *Macroeconomic Policy in Britain 1974–87*, Cambridge: Cambridge University Press, pp 193–226. According to Britton's detailed analysis of fiscal policy over the period 1974 to 1987, fiscal policy – with one big exception – 'hardly changed at all the amplitude of output fluctuations. It was, on balance, neither stabilizing nor destabilizing' (p 220). The big exception was the 1981 budget.

30 In the fourth quarter of 1980, GDP had fallen by 1.1 per cent, and it fell by a further 0.2 per cent in the first quarter of 1981, although the latter figure was not actually known at the time the budget was being prepared.

31 Barrell, R. (2014) 'Macroeconomic Policy and the 1981 Budget: Changing the Trend', in D. Needham and A. Hotson (eds) *Expansionary Fiscal Contraction: The Thatcher Government's 1981 Budget in Perspective*, Cambridge: Cambridge University Press.

Chapter 8

1 Lawson, N. (1992) *The View from No 11: Memoirs of a Tory Radical*, London: Bantam Press, p 112.

2 Walters would later claim that he (Walters) would have preferred M1 as the target aggregate from the start, notwithstanding its disadvantages. He wrote that the choice of £M3 had been a 'remarkable capitulation of monetarist principle to institutional continuity' (Walters, A. [1986] *Britain's Economic Renaissance: Margaret Thatcher's Reforms 1979–84*, Oxford: Oxford University Press, p 118). This was a strange comment, since part of his reputation was based on having identified the rapid growth of M3 as the cause of the mid-1970s inflation explosion.

3   *The Times*, Editorial, 31 March 1981.
4   Cairncross, A. (1981) 'Two cheerless years of monetarism', *The Times*, 27 March.
5   Blake, D. (1981) 'Why has monetarism failed?', *The Times*, 13 July.
6   The 'Gang of Four' were Roy Jenkins, David Owen, Shirley Williams and Bill Rodgers. All former Cabinet ministers, they quit the Labour Party in response to Labour's lurch to the left after the 1979 General Election defeat.
7   House of Commons Treasury and Civil Service Committee (1980/81) *Report on Monetary Policy*, HC 163, London: HMSO.
8   Minutes of Cabinet, with limited circulation, annex, 17 June 1981 (www.margaretthatcher.org). The Cabinet's most vocal critic behind the scenes, Ian Gilmour, was not present at this meeting, but tellingly, he *was* present at the meeting on 23 July.
9   Leon Brittan was a lawyer and brother of the *Financial Times's* Sam Brittan, but with none of the latter's economic expertise.
10 Minutes of Cabinet, 23 July 1981 (www.margaretthatcher.org). Cabinet Secretary Robert Armstrong clearly didn't want to broadcast across Whitehall the strength of the opposition to the strategy, with the attendant risk of leaks.
11 The Hoskyns/Wolfson/Millar paper, complete with Whitmore's marginalia, can be found on www.margaretthatcher.org (letter from Wolfson to Thatcher, dated 20 August 1981).
12 Rattner, S. (1982) 'Monetarism in Britain', *The New York Times*, 21 March.
13 Lawson, N. (1992) *The View from No 11: Memoirs of a Tory Radical*, London: Bantam Press, p 464.
14 See Chapter XXIV ('Floaters and Fixers') in Thatcher, M. (1993) *Margaret Thatcher: The Downing Street Years*, London: HarperCollins.
15 Friedman, M. (1980) 'Memorandum submitted to the Treasury and Civil Service Committee', *Memoranda on Monetary Policy*, Session 1979/80, July, London: HMSO.

Chapter 9

1   Budd, A. and Dicks, G. (1982) 'The costs and benefits of cutting inflation', Oxford Economics, *Economic Outlook*, London Business School with Gower Publishing, October, p 24.
2   Britton, A. (1991) *Macroeconomic Policy in Britain 1974–87*, Cambridge: Cambridge University Press, p 304.
3   Brittan, S. (1982) 'The "Thatcher effect" revealed', *Financial Times*, 14 January.
4   Friedman, M. (1980) *Memoranda on Monetary Policy – Answers to Questionnaire on Monetary Policy*, House of Commons Treasury and Civil Service Committee, Session 1979–80, Volume 1, London: HMSO, p 61 (reprinted 1981).
5   Minford, P. (1980) *Memoranda on Monetary Policy – Answers to Questionnaire on Monetary Policy*, House of Commons Treasury and Civil Service Committee, Session 1979–80, Volume 1, London: HMSO, p 142 (reprinted 1981).

6 Laidler, D. (1980) *Memoranda on Monetary Policy – Memorandum Entitled Notes on Gradualism*, House of Commons Treasury and Civil Service Committee, Session 1979–80, Volume 1, London: HMSO, p 51 (reprinted 1981).

7 The sacrifice ratio is the point-years of unemployment required to reduce inflation by one percentage point. See Buiter, W.H. and Miller, M.H. (1983) *Changing the Rules: Economic Consequences of the Thatcher Regime*, Brookings Papers on Economic Activity, No 2, pp 341–3. Their estimate of the sacrifice ratio for the four years 1979 to 1983 was 2.3 – slightly higher than my figure of 1.9. This is because they were using unemployment rates that were later revised downwards.

8 Budd, A., Dicks, G., Gosling, T. and Robinson, B. (1981) 'The recession of 1980 and its causes', Oxford Economics, *Economic Outlook*, London Business School with Gower Publishing, October, p 32.

9 Budd, A. and Dicks, G. (1982) 'The costs and benefits of cutting inflation', Oxford Economics, *Economic Outlook*, London Business School with Gower Publishing, October, p 25.

10 Britton, A. (1991) *Macroeconomic Policy in Britain 1974–87*, Cambridge: Cambridge University Press, pp 181, 220.

11 Budd, A. and Dicks, G. (1982) 'The costs and benefits of cutting inflation', Oxford Economics, *Economic Outlook*, London Business School with Gower Publishing, October, p 25.

12 Brittan, S. (1982) 'The "Thatcher effect" revealed', *Financial Times*, 14 January.

13 Budd, A. and Dicks, G. (1982) 'The costs and benefits of cutting inflation', Oxford Economics, *Economic Outlook*, London Business School with Gower Publishing, October, p 21.

14 Calculated applying the same proportionate trade-off between unemployment and inflation as that which actually occurred.

15 Lawson, N. (1992) *The View from No 11: Memoirs of a Tory Radical*, London: Bantam Press, p 63.

16 Budd, A. and Dicks, G. (1982) 'The costs and benefits of cutting inflation', Oxford Economics, *Economic Outlook*, London Business School with Gower Publishing, October, p 9.

17 Budd, A. and Dicks, G. (1982) 'The costs and benefits of cutting inflation', Oxford Economics, *Economic Outlook*, London Business School with Gower Publishing, October, p 9.

18 Thatcher, M. (1980) Speech to Conservative Party Conference, 10 October, www.margaretthatcher.org/document/104431

19 Douglas Hague was Professor of Economics at Manchester Business School, and a personal friend and admirer of Mrs Thatcher. Christopher Foster made his name as a transport economist, and advised Labour and Conservative governments over several decades on many aspects of government policy. He was a strong supporter of privatisation and trade union reform, and a key adviser on the 'Poll Tax' and on railway privatisation.

20 'Talking the rate down' meant the Bank of England or the Treasury indicating that they'd like to see a lower exchange rate. To be successful,

it would normally need to be accompanied by intervention in the foreign exchange market – which would mean selling sterling and inflating the money supply. But on occasion, it had worked without the latter.

21 Lankester record of meeting at Chequers, 13 July 1980 (www.margaretthatcher.org).

Chapter 10

1 Nickell, S. and van Ours, J. (2000) 'The Netherlands and the United Kingdom: A European unemployment miracle?', *Economic Policy*, 15(30), 135–80.

2 Meade and his colleagues at Cambridge developed simulations that showed, if reformed wage arrangements had been in place, inflation could have been brought down at roughly the same pace as was actually achieved, with unemployment rising to roughly 7 per cent rather than to the actual rate of near 12 per cent. They didn't explain what exactly these reformed arrangements would have consisted of; they merely said that they would ensure a situation in which wages would 'become insensitive to prices, changing only with reference to unemployment'. See Weale, M., Blake, A., Christodoulakis, N., Meade, J. and Vines, D. (1989) *Macroeconomic Policy: Inflation, Wealth and the Exchange Rate*, London: Unwin Hyman (especially Figure 9.1(d)).

3 Hung, H.-F. and Thompson, D. (2016) 'Money supply, class power, and inflation: Monetarism reassessed', *American Sociological Review*, 81(3), 447–66. These and other writers of similar Marxian bent interpreted not just the trade union reform policies through a capital versus labour lens but also the whole monetarist approach, which, they argued, favoured capital over labour.

4 BBC 2 (1992) *Pandora's Box*, Episode 3 [documentary].

5 Glyn, A., with Sutcliffe, R. (1972) *British Capitalism, Workers and the Profit Squeeze*, London: Penguin Books. Glyn was one of the few economists three decades later who predicted a 'hard landing' as a result of globalisation and excessive financial liberalisation in the USA and elsewhere (Glyn, A. [2006] *Capitalism Unleashed: Finance, Globalization, and Welfare*, Oxford: Oxford University Press).

6 Record of meeting, 31 May 1979, PREM 19/69 F352 (www.margaretthatcher.org).

7 Record of meeting, 25 June 1979, PREM 19/25 f87 (www.margaretthatcher.org).

8 PREM 19/37 f17 and minutes of sub-committee of Cabinet known as the E Committee, 17 July 1979 (www.margaretthatcher.org).

Chapter 11

1 Willetts, D. (2010) *The Pinch: How the Baby Boomers Took Their Children's Future – And Why They Should Give It Back*, London: Atlantic Books.

2 I had recently moved to Washington, DC as the Treasury representative there – economic minister at the embassy, and UK executive director on the

boards of the International Monetary Fund (IMF) and World Bank. I was with Lawson at the Plaza Hotel in New York in September 1985 when he signed up to the Plaza Accord. The preparations for the meeting of finance ministers were so sensitive that I was instructed by Lawson not to inform Oliver Wright, the British ambassador to the USA, who was now formally my line manager. When he read about the Accord the next day in *The New York Times*, he wasn't pleased.

3   These meetings are well documented in Chapter 13 of Charles Moore's biography (Moore, C. [2013] *Margaret Thatcher: The Authorized Biography, Volume Two: Not for Turning*, London: Allen Lane).

4   For a detailed account of the 'shadowing' episode, see James, H. (2020) *Making a Modern Central Bank: The Bank of England 1979–2003*, Cambridge: Cambridge University Press, pp 161–76.

5   On 14 October 1987, David Norgrove sent her a note entitled 'Intervention' in which he referred to 'intervention in the past 24 hours of $660 million, much of it in DM', and he reported that Lawson had agreed with the Bank that 'it would be wrong … to allow sterling to rise against the DM'. An earlier note from Norgrove dated 8 May informed her that 'the Chancellor has persuaded [the Bank] that intervention should continue as necessary' to stop the sterling exchange rate from rising (www.margaretthatcher.org).

6   Lawson, N. (1992) *The View from No 11: Memoirs of a Tory Radical*, London: Bantam Press, p 788.

7   Memorandum from Lawson to Thatcher, 25 November 1988 (www. margaretthatcher.org).

8   On their exchanges on this issue, see the memorandum from Lawson to Thatcher dated 25 November 1988 and her jottings thereon (www. margaretthatcher.org); and also Lawson, N. (1993) *The View from No 11: Memoirs of a Tory Radical*, London: Bantam Press, pp 867–73; Thatcher, M. (1993) *The Downing Street Years*, London: HarperCollins, pp 706–7.

9   The Maastricht Treaty, which came into effect in November 1993, laid the foundation for greater integration between the EC member states and for the EU as it is today. France held a referendum on it on 20 September 1992, with a vote of just 51 per cent in favour.

10   Lawson, N. (1993) *The View from No 11: Memoirs of a Tory Radical*, London: Bantam Press, Chapter 81.

Chapter 12

1   Thatcher, M. (1993) *The Downing Street Years*, London: HarperCollins, p 690.

2   Thatcher, M. (1993) *The Downing Street Years*, London: HarperCollins, p 688.

3   Lawson, N. (1992) *The View from No 11: Memoirs of a Tory Radical*, London: Bantam Press, p 447.

4   Thatcher, M. (1993) *The Downing Street Years*, London: HarperCollins, p 126.

5   Lawson, N. (1992) *The View from No 11: Memoirs of a Tory Radical*, London: Bantam Press, pp 413, 481.

6   BBC 2 (1992) *Pandora's Box*, Episode 3 [documentary].

7   Walters, A. (1986) *Britain's Economic Renaissance: Margaret Thatcher's Reforms 1979–84*, Oxford: Oxford University Press, pp 83, 143.

8   Laidler, D. (1985) 'Monetary policy in Britain: Successes and shortcomings', *Oxford Review of Economic Policy*, 1(1), 35–43.

9   Ball, J. (1989) 'Economic viewpoint – Economic policy: fact and ambition', *Economic Outlook*, 14(1), 27.

10 Quoted in Davis, A. (2022) *Bankruptcy, Bubbles and Bailouts: The Inside History of the Treasury since 1976*, Manchester: Manchester University Press.

11 Ball, J. (1989) 'Economic viewpoint – Economic policy: fact and ambition', *Economic Outlook*, 14(1), 27.

12 Congdon, T. (1992) *Reflections on Monetarism: Britain's Vain Search for a Successful Economic Strategy*, Cheltenham: Edward Elgar Publishing, p 112.

13 Congdon, T. (1982) 'Why has monetarism failed? The public sector problem', *The Banker*, 132(674), 48.

14 Pepper, G. and Oliver, M. (2001) *Monetarism under Thatcher: Lessons for the Future*, Cheltenham: Edward Elgar, p 36.

15 For Pepper's critique, see Pepper, G. (1998) *Inside Thatcher's Monetarist Revolution*, Basingstoke: Macmillan Press; and also Pepper, G. and Oliver, M. (2001) *Monetarism under Thatcher: Lessons for the Future*, Cheltenham: Edward Elgar. Both these books are heavily geared toward rerunning the arguments for and against MBC, for which Pepper had been one of the leading advocates.

16 Minford, P. (1990) 'Inflation and monetary policy', *Oxford Review of Economic Policy*, 6(4), 62–76. Minford was at least being consistent: at the Chequers meeting of economists in July 1980, he had advised Mrs Thatcher that she should aim to achieve money growth at the lower end of the target range.

17 Quoted in London, S. (2003) 'Milton Friedman – the long view: The legendary economist tells Simon London about his unswerving passions for shareholder supremacy and sand dabs', *Financial Times*, 7 June.

18 Crafts, N. (1996) 'Deindustrialisation and economic growth', *The Economic Journal*, 106(434), 172–83.

19 Crafts, N. (1996) 'Deindustrialisation and economic growth', *The Economic Journal*, 106(434), 172–83, p 178.

20 Solow, R. (2013) 'Why is there no Milton Friedman today?', *Econ Journal Watch*, 10(2), 215. Solow and Robinson were in a long-running dispute over what was known as the 'Cambridge capital controversy', a highly abstract debate about the measurement and role of capital in economic growth theory. In the year that Robinson was my supervisor at Cambridge, Solow was a visiting fellow, and he and Robinson were barely on speaking terms.

21 Tobin, J. (1985) 'An ebbing tide?', *The Economist*, 27 April. In this essay, Tobin suggested that governments should adopt money GDP targets for the conduct of monetary and fiscal policy, just as Meade had done earlier.

22 Hopkin, B., Miller, M. and Reddaway, B. (1982) 'An alternative economic strategy: A message of hope', *Cambridge Journal of Economics*, 6(1), 85–103.

23 Neild, R. (2014) 'The 1981 Statement by 364 Economists', in D. Needham and A. Hotson (eds) *Expansionary Fiscal Contraction: The Thatcher Government's 1981 Budget in Perspective*, Cambridge: Cambridge University Press, Chapter 1.

24 Gilmour, I. (1992) 'No thanks to the liberal revolution', *London Review of Books*, July, 14(13). For a fuller account of his critique of Thatcherism, see Gilmour, I. (1992) *Dancing with Dogma: Britain under Thatcherism*, London: Simon & Schuster.

25 Gilmour, I. (1982) 'Monetarism and history', *London Review of Books*, January, 4(1).

26 At a meeting Mrs Thatcher had with Volcker in London in February 1981, he told her that, in order to bring down inflation, it was 'better to hit hard and fast' – which, of course, is exactly what UK policy was doing. Mrs Thatcher responded that it was easier to do this in the USA because its economy was more flexible. She was right: the US economy emerged from recession more rapidly than the UK economy. (Lankester record of meeting, 11 February 1981) (www.margaretthatcher.org).

27 Wolf, M. (2019) 'The legacy and lessons of Paul Volcker', *Financial Times*, 14 December.

28 James, H. (2020) *Making a Modern Central Bank: The Bank of England 1979–2003*, Cambridge: Cambridge University Press, p 48.

29 Pepper, G. and Oliver, M. (2001) *Monetarism under Thatcher: Lessons for the Future*, Cheltenham: Edward Elgar, p 19.

Chapter 13

1 Bank of England Act, 1998, Section 11(b): www.legislation.gov.uk/ukpga/1998/11/section/11

2 King, M. (2005) 'Monetary policy: Practice ahead of theory', *Bank of England Quarterly Bulletin*, Summer.

3 Talk by Robert Lucas at a conference entitled 'The death of Keynesian economics', University of Chicago, 1979.

4 The Princeton economist Alan Blinder wrote of the rational expectations (RE) hypothesis: 'I think the weight of the evidence – both from directly observed expectation and from indirect statistical tests of rationality (usually in conjunction with some other hypothesis) – is overwhelmingly against the RE hypothesis'. See Blinder, A. (1987) 'Keynes, Lucas and scientific evidence', *The American Economic Review*, 77(2), 130–6, p 131. The crowding out argument was shown to be false at a theoretical level, except on the most extreme assumptions, by Alan Blinder and Robert Solow in their article ([1973] 'Does fiscal policy matter?', *Journal of Public Economics*, 2, 319–37). In the 2000s, a small group of economists in the USA, known as the Austerians, argued that reduced government spending could actually lead to an *increase* in output and employment – hence, the temporarily fashionable buzz phrase

'expansionary fiscal contraction'. Even the fiscally conservative International Monetary Fund (IMF) found their views too much: in a research paper in 2014, they concluded that in the advanced countries fiscal multipliers have normally been in the range of 0 to 1 (see Chapter 3, note 5). However, it has to be said that at least one British economist, the monetarist Tim Congdon, supports the Austerian view, writing: 'The evidence against "contractionary fiscal contractions" – both here and elsewhere – is so clear as to be crushing. Since the 1980s, the experience of both the USA and the UK is either that fiscal policy is ineffective or that, to the extent that it does work, the relationship is inverse and fiscal contractions are indeed expansionary' (Congdon, T. [2015] 'In praise of expansionary fiscal contraction', *Economic Affairs*, 35[1], 29).

5   Wray, L.R. (2012) *Modern Money Theory: A Primer on Macroeconomics for Sovereign Monetary Systems*, London: Palgrave Macmillan; Kelton, S. (2020) *The Deficit Myth: Modern Money Theory and How to Build a Better Economy*, London: John Murray.

6   See Lerner, A. (1943) 'Functional finance and the federal deficit', *Social Research*, 10(1), 38–57. I had the privilege of meeting Lerner in Cambridge in 1964.

7   On the intergenerational issue, see Blanchard, O.J. (2019) 'Public debt and low interest rates', *The American Economic Review*, 109(4), 1197–229. Blanchard demonstrates that higher public debt is harmful for intergenerational welfare only if the real rate of interest on public debt exceeds the rate of economic growth – which, in recent years in the UK, has not been the case.

8   Blanchard, O.J. (2021) 'The Makeya Lecture: Fiscal policy under low rates: Taking stock', *Monetary and Economic Studies*, 39, 23-34, https://econpapers. repec.org/article/imeimemes/v_3a39_3ay_3a2021_3ap_3a23-34.htm

9   For these and other estimates of debt sustainability, and for definitions, see Office for Budget Responsibility (2021) *Fiscal Risks Report*, London: The Stationery Office, p 30.

10 Reinhart, C.M. and Rogoff, K.S. (2009) *This Time Is Different: Eight Centuries of Financial Folly*, Princeton, NJ: Princeton University Press. George Osborne was wont to quote Reinhart and Rogoff's 90 per cent figure as justification for bearing down on the public debt. However, their analysis was to a considerable degree discredited after it was found to be based on faulty data and faulty methodology. See Herndon, T., Ash, M. and Pollin, R. (2014) 'Does high public debt consistently stifle economic growth?', *Cambridge Journal of Economics*, 38(2), 257–79.

11 See House of Lords Economic Affairs Committee (2021) *Quantitative Easing: A Dangerous Addiction?*, 1st Report of Session 2021–22, https://committees. parliament.uk/publications/6725/documents/71894/default

12 Allsopp, C. and Vines, D. (2015) 'Monetary and fiscal policy in the Great Moderation and the Great Recession', *Oxford Review of Economic Policy*, 31(2), 134–67.

Chapter 14

[1] Postscript: The actual rate of inflation rate for Q4 2023 turned out at 4.2 per cent, down from 10.7 per cent in Q4 2022.

[2] Dhingra, S. (2023) 'A cost of living crisis: Inflation during an unprecedented terms of trade shock', Bank of England, 8 March.

[3] Bernanke, B. and Blanchard, O.J. (2023) *What Caused the US Pandemic-Era Inflation*, Washington, DC: Brookings Institution.

[4] See Congdon, T. (2023) 'Bank of England's Covid money-printing spree "drove up inflation"', *Daily Telegraph*, 18 April.

[5] For the 4 per cent estimate, see Bank of England (2022) *Monetary Policy Report*, November, p 17.

[6] Crafts, N. and Mills, T. (2020) *Is the UK Productivity Slowdown Unprecedented?*, London: National Institute of Economic and Social Research.

[7] The most egregious example of poor public investment decision making in recent years was the decision to build the hugely expensive high-speed rail link from London to Manchester (HS2). The estimates behind the benefit-cost ratio on which the decision was taken were unrealistic from the start. In October 2023, when it had become increasingly clear that the costs had spiralled way beyond the original estimates, Prime Minister Rishi Sunak announced that the northern leg of the project – Birmingham to Manchester – was to be cancelled, but with billions of pounds already having been spent on the southern leg – London to Birmingham – construction of the latter would continue.

Chapter 15

[1] Keynes, J.M. (2018) *The General Theory of Employment, Interest and Money*, London: Palgrave Macmillan, p 340.

[2] Apart from the point about trade union reform, my list of things that the government should have done and should not have done more or less mirrors the views of Sam Brittan, an original supporter of the monetarist strategy, back in 1982. See Brittan, S. (1982) 'The "Thatcher effect" revealed, *Financial Times*, 14 January.

[3] The hydroelectric project was the infamous Pergau Dam. As accounting officer for the aid budget, I insisted on a formal direction from Foreign Secretary Douglas Hurd before releasing the funds for the project. In 1994, a judicial review in the High Court determined that the funding was unlawful. For an account of this, see Lankester, T. (2013) *The Politics and Economics of Britain's Foreign Aid: The Pergau Dam Affair*, London: Routledge.

[4] In his memoirs, Major denied that he had felt humiliated, but he admitted that the British press construed it as such. See Major, J. (2010) *The Autobiography*, London: HarperCollins.

[5] See Renwick, R. (2015) *Mission to South Africa: Diary of a Revolution*, Johannesburg and Cape Town: Jonathan Ball, pp 104–6.

Index